DISCOVERY

WRITING ABOUT YOUR WORLDS

George Eppley
Anita Dixon Eppley
Cuyahoga Community College

Holt, Rinehart and Winston, Inc.

Fort Worth   Chicago   San Francisco   Philadelphia
Montreal   Toronto   London   Sydney   Tokyo

Publisher Charlyce Jones Owen
Acquisitions Editor Michael Rosenberg
Design and Composition Publications Development Company
Production Manager Kathleen Ferguson
Cover Design Patrice Mozelewski

Library of Congress Cataloging-in-Publication Data

Eppley, George.
   Discovery : writing about your world / by George Eppley, Anita
Dixon Eppley.
      p. cm.
   Includes bibliographical references.
   ISBN 0-03-026392-1
   1. English language—Rhetoric. 2. English language—
Grammar—1950–   I. Eppley, Anita Dixon. II. Title.
PE1408.E55 1990
808'.042—dc20   89-48483
                                           CIP

Requests for permission to make copies of any part of the work should be mailed to: Copyrights and Permissions Department, Holt, Rinehart and Winston, Inc., Orlando, FL 32887

Address Editorial Correspondence to: 301 Commerce Street, Suite 3700, Fort Worth, TX 76102
                   Address Orders to: 6277 Sea Harbor Drive, Orlando, FL 32887
                           1-800-782-4479, or 1-800-433-0001 (in Florida)

Credits and permissions appear on pages 370–371.

Printed in the United States of America

0 1 2 3   039   9 8 7 6 5 4 3 2 1

Holt, Rinehart and Winston, Inc.
The Dryden Press
Saunders College Publishing

We dedicate this book to our parents
Anne and George Eppley
Edna and Craig Dixon

Contents

To the Instructor

We titled this textbook *Discovery* because we want to help students discover four things that will help them in college and later on in life: **the power of thinking, the power of writing, the power of reading, and the power of correct grammar.** New technologies will certainly bring about rapid changes in the workplace during the last decade of this century. What will not change, however, in this century and in the next, is the urgent need for people who can think, write, read, and use words effectively. Those who have such skills will always be in great demand.

In the light of these goals, this textbook has four parts:

Part I. Discovering the Power of Thinking

Part II. Discovering the Power of Writing

Part III. Discovering the Power of Reading

Part IV. Discovering the Power of Correct Grammar (Handbook)

PART I. THE POWER OF THINKING

Uniqueness a Strength

Good writing, we believe, starts with positive thinking, so in in Part I we focus on helping students realize that they are unique individuals. Each person is different from anyone who has ever lived, is living now, or will live in the future. That difference is a strength, not a weakness, although some do not see it that way.

That's because we live in a society that conditions people to think that their worth and value are measured by what they have, not by what they are. Wealth, position, social standing, credentials, and even grades become the benchmarks of one's worth to society. Students who do not have these external reference points often think of themselves as inferior and develop negative self images. *Discovery* stresses that what is inside people is what really gives them value.

The World of the Past

Discovery also tells students not to consider what might have been, but what actually is. They cannot change the past, but they can accept it. They cannot change their parents, their families, their childhoods, their past experiences, both good and bad. Nor should they even try. That past can give the students much to write about. Consider the example of Maya Angelou, who in early childhood was neglected by her parents and raised by her grandmother in the segregated town of Stamps, Arkansas. In her autobiography *I Know Why the Caged Bird Sings*, she writes movingly about what it meant to grow up as a black child in a segregated society. She could not change that past, but she could write about it. In so doing, she changed her future. *Discovery* encourages students to look into the world of their past and to write about it.

The Many Worlds in One's Universe

Discovery also encourages students to explore the many worlds that make up their present: the worlds of music, art, fashion, sports, nature, entertainment, space, history, and many other worlds. Using the techniques of brainstorming and freewriting, students find that their problem is not what to write about, but how to limit the topic about which they want to write.

Thinking Critically

We believe, however, that students should do more than just report on what's happening in the worlds that interest them. We want them to start asking questions about what is going on and write about it. For example, a student might write an essay about attending a college football game. Perhaps a more interesting essay would emerge if the process of critical thinking would lead the student to write about illegal recruiting practices caused by a win-at-all-cost mentality at the college or university. Someone might submit an essay about a fishing experience. But if he took the time to think critically about about the world of that recreation, perhaps he would write about what is happening environmentally to our rivers, lakes and streams. Or a student, fascinated by the world of medicine, might turn in an essay on how to become a doctor or a nurse. Through critical thinking, perhaps she could write a better essay on some ethical question that the medical profession faces, such as euthanasia, abortion, research on fetal tissue, the care of the elderly, and so forth. In other words, if students start asking questions about issues that are of interest to them, they may start writing papers that will be more interesting to their teachers, their peers, and even themselves.

Thinking Creatively

There's also a chapter in *Discovery* on thinking creatively. We are impressed by some of the research that shows that most of us use only the left side of the brain. We want students to use both hemispheres of the brain, especially the right side, which is the seat of creativity. We include activities to help students do whole-brain thinking.

The Need for Standards and Structure

Although the activities in Part I are unstructured, we are not telling students that anything they put down on paper is acceptable or that they can write anything they please. Rather we are urging teachers in Part I to let students be as free and creative as they possibly can be. This is, in our judgment, an essential part of the writing process. Get them to start putting things on paper without being critical and judgmental about grammatical errors and lack or organization. In Parts II, III, and IV, they will learn about structure and about standards of good writing.

PART II. THE POWER OF WRITING

Journal Writing

We encourage students to keep a daily journal to bank their thoughts, ideas, and critical judgments about what's happening in their worlds.

Topic Sentences and Paragraphs

In this section, we stress the importance of the topic sentence and show students how to build paragraphs using sentences that support the topic sentence. We provide a series of practice exercises to help them build paragraphs.

Once students see the relationship of the topic sentence to the paragraph, they are ready to consider the relationship of the thesis statement to the essay.

The Thesis Statement

In our judgment, writing a one-sentence or two-sentence thesis statement that is limited, unified, and specific is a challenging assignment. Some students never meet that challenge. As a result, they often have difficulty when a writing assignment suddenly descends upon them. We are convinced that students who learn how to write a thesis statement will find it easier to write essays, not only in composition and literature classes, but in all subjects across the curriculum. Consequently, we spend a significant amount of time explaining what a thesis is **not** and what it **is**, and we give students opportunities to practice writing thesis statements.

Outlines, Revisions, and Rough Drafts

Although some teachers may choose not to teach the use of outlines—scratch, topic, sentence—we have found them valuable in helping students structure an essay. We tell students, however, not to hesitate to depart from the outline when in the process of writing a draft they get better ideas.

A chapter on revising the manuscript is included. Many students think that the process of writing is over when they have completed a draft and made corrections. Good writers know that only after three or more drafts does the process of writing really begin.

PART III. THE POWER OF READING

Discovering the Worlds of Professional Writers

If students think about their own universe with its worlds of fashion, art, history, music, and sports, they will have much to write about. They will be able to write about so much more, however, if they enter the worlds of professional writers and see how they view their worlds and how they write about them. They will discover how authors use various modes to develop a thesis statement such as narration, description, definition, example, process, classification, comparison/contrast, and cause and effect. Chapters on each of these modes include reading selections.

Published Readings as Models of Writing and Thinking

The readings can be used as models for writing, and some teachers may want to use them that way. We prefer to use them as models for thinking and as ways by which students can enlarge their own vision of the universe. It is as if the writer of the selection is handing to students a high-powered pair of binoculars and saying to them, "Look through these and see if they can help you discover people and events in your own worlds that you can write about."

Accordingly, after each reading selection there are four activities: **warm-up, discovering new words, discovering the meaning, and discovering connections.**

Warm-up. The warm-up is a way to get students thinking and talking about the reading selection, and through the reading selection, thinking and talking about themselves. In small groups they are encouraged to express their opinions, to define them, to defend them, and to enlarge their vision. The warm-up is designed to help students discover interesting topics for their writing assignments through brainstorming and imagining, an essential part of the writing process, particularly for students who have not had much success in their writing classes in the past.

Vocabulary. The self-test after each selection is intended only as a teaser —a way to get students to focus their attention on words they might not understand. Most people enjoy doing self-tests of almost any kind. If the students enjoy the vocabulary self-tests, they just might be interested in going a step further and picking up a dictionary for a more complete definition.

Discovering the Meaning. The purpose of this activity is to help students understand the reading selection. The questions are appropriate for individual consideration or group discussion.

Discovering Connections. This section suggests writing assignments that draw on two sources: the reading selection and the student's own experiences, dreams, plans, successes, failures, remembrances. Most assignments are adaptable to either the paragraph or the essay, and they are designed to be used with the mode covered in the same chapter.

PART IV. HANDBOOK (THE POWER OF CORRECT GRAMMAR)

It is our hope that once students realize that they have something worthwhile to put in writing, they will come to understand that there are certain grammatical rules that, if observed, will make their essays more effective. We have not included all the rules, only the basic ones that we think beginning writers should know. We do not think it's good pedagogy to overwhelm students with a multitude of rules, so we have kept them to a minimum.

The Handbook section contains practice exercises for the following:

I. Basic Things to Know about Words and How They Function in a Sentence.

This section discusses nouns, pronouns, verbs, adjectives, adverbs, conjunctions, and prepositions.

II. Basic Things to Know about Writing Effective Sentences.

This part reviews what a sentence is and important elements of a sentence such as subject, verb, and subject/verb agreement. Simple, complex, and compound sentences are discussed.

III. Basic Things to Know about Punctuation

This part reviews the rules of punctuation at the end of a sentence, internal punctuation, punctuation of quoted material, and word punctuation.

In the three sections above, we discuss the common faults that student writers often make and suggest ways to avoid them. Exercises help students test themselves on the following: fragments, run-on sentences, subject/verb agreement, faulty pronoun reference, comma splices, misplaced modifiers, and nonstandard English.

To the Student

This book's for you.
It's a book about power:

- The power that comes when you think positively about yourself and your many worlds.
- The power of knowing that you are someone special, unique, unrepeatable.
- The power that comes when you think critically and creatively.
- The power that comes from writing effective sentences, paragraphs, and thesis statements.
- The power that comes from writing an essay that puts into written words the thoughts and ideas you have inside you.
- The power that comes from reading and reflecting on the thoughts and ideas of well-known writers.
- The power that comes from connecting those readings to events and persons in your own life.
- The power that comes when you hold your written words to the highest standards of excellence in grammar.
- The power that comes in knowing that good thinkers, good writers, and good readers are always in demand.
- The power that comes in knowing that you can become all three.

This book's for you.

Acknowledgments

If we tried to thank everyone who has in some way contributed to this book going back to the composition teachers we had in school, the list of names would take up many pages. Moreover, in the process we would undoubtedly forget some people whose names should be on the list. So we are taking the easy way out by simply acknowledging that there are many people who have influenced us—family members, teachers, colleagues, journalists, friends. We thank them for their friendship and support.

Some people, however, have been closely associated with us in the development of this book. Mimi Cook provided creative suggestions. Frank Cook and Laurence Mackie were always there when we needed help with the word processor or the laser printer. Ann Fletcher of the Strongsville Public Schools was extremely helpful, as was Dorothy Power of the Cleveland Public Schools. At Cuyahoga Community College, Joseph Clovesko, David Skwire, Terrance Burke, Bernice Van Tyne, Stanley Klosek, Azamul Haque, Jean Seidel, Bill Preston, and Terrance Dunford at various times gave valuable comments and advice. We are also grateful to Sister Judith Cauley, C.S.J., Colleen MacManamon, and Eileen Teare of Saint Joseph Academy for the many hours they spent critiqueing, reading and correcting the manuscript, nor should we forget Russel Faist, a retired editor, whose criticisms and comments were most helpful. We also thank our reviewers for their helpful comments and suggestions: Peter Dow Adams, Essex Community College; Shirley Ann Curtis, Polk Community College; J. L. Dillard, Northwestern State University at Louisiana; Lulie Fielder, Sumter Area Technical College; Mary Helen Halloran, The University of Wisconsin at Milwaukee; Anne M. Haselkorn, York College-CUNY; Vivian A. Thomlinson, Cameron University; Kathleen Tickner, Brevard Community College; Cheryl L. Ware, McNeese State University; Nancy Yee, Fitchburg State College.

Finally, we want to thank Kate Morgan, our former editor at Holt Rinehart and Winston. Our publisher, Charlyce Jones Owen and her staff—Tod Gross, Leslie Taggart, and Jamie Mandel—gave us wise counsel and advice throughout the project. We would also like to thank Nancy Marcus Land and the staff at Publications Development Company for their work on the design and production of our book.

G. E.

A. D. E.

Part I

Discovering the Power of Thinking

Chapter 1

Discovering
Your Uniqueness

The first step in learning how to write is to know who you are as a person. It is important for you to discover that you are a unique individual who has a story to tell. It may or may not be an outstanding story that grips the imagination and keeps the reader riveted to the chair. Either way, it is a special story, one that has not been written since the beginning of time, and one that will not be told until the end of time, unless *you* tell it—in writing.

Why in writing? Because the writing of it will cause you to think about it. You will begin to discover the connection between the writing process and the thinking process. In reflecting on those processes, we hope you will discover skills not only to help you succeed in college but also to help you successfully meet two challenges that you will face almost every day of your life: problem solving and decision making.

Start with realizing that you are unique. Step back and look at your life and all the experiences that have brought you to this time and place. Once you do that, you are in a better position to write. Your newly discovered self-identity will give power and meaning to your spoken and written words.

DISCOVERING YOURSELF THROUGH WRITING

Through the process of writing, you can discover your worth and value as a person. In writing about a fragile ego, you can strengthen it. In writing about the times you were lost or felt abandoned, you can find yourself. In writing about the stormy times of life, you can discover how to become a "rainbow splendor person," a phrase used by folk singer Joan Baez in the 1960s.

But there is much more in life to write about than just the negative things that have happened. When Mrs. Rose Kennedy wrote her autobiography, she could have spent a great deal of time dwelling on the tragedies that have dogged the Kennedy family: the death of a daughter, the loss of a son in World War II, and the assassinations of sons John F. Kennedy and Robert Kennedy. She said in the preface that she preferred to "remember the good times."

Write about the good times or the bad times, or write about both. Write about the things that shaped your life and your personality. Write about how you have felt, how you feel now, and how you would like to feel. The important thing is to *write* about you and your worlds. These are the things that you know.

Inside/Out Writing

Write from the inside/out. Start with your inner being and move out into the world. In the traditional outside/in approach you are asked to read a selection by some prominent writer and then attempt to model your own writing on that selection. While this "outside/in" approach has merit, it can intimidate beginning writers.

Several carefully chosen selections appear in this textbook. We ask you to read these selections, not necessarily to imitate the writing style of the authors, but to learn how through an experience they discovered something that contributed to their growth as persons and as writers.

For example, a barely literate black discovered in jail that his vocabulary was far too limited in light of the message that he wanted to deliver to white and black America. So he got a dictionary and every day painstakingly copied out a page of the dictionary, and memorized it. After years of doing this, he built a tremendous vocabulary and wrote a powerful message for America to hear. His name was Malcolm X.

We write this not to suggest that you model your writing on that of Malcolm X or any other author, but rather to get you to ask yourselves what sacrifices you are willing to make in order to overcome your own limitations. What price are you willing to pay to attain a goal or realize a dream? In answering those questions, you will discover something about yourself.

TECHNIQUES TO HELP YOU DISCOVER AND WRITE ABOUT YOUR UNIQUENESS

Here are four techniques you can use to help you realize that you are indeed unique and therefore have something unique to write about.

- Brainstorming
- Sharing and Comparing
- Reflecting, Questioning, Affirming
- Freewriting

Brainstorming is a prewriting exercise to help the writer warm up, much like stretching exercises help joggers warm up before running. Write down all the ideas that come to your mind about a subject no matter how crazy or off the wall they seem to be.

Now do some brainstorming about yourself. Write down all the ideas you can think of about yourself: your personality, your hopes, dreams and aspirations; your heritage, your values, your strengths and weaknesses; your joys, fears, and feelings about yourself; your successes and failures. You can add as many other topics as you please.

The following student model may give you some ideas about how to brainstorm about your inner worlds.

Just keep jotting down ideas for five or ten minutes, and remember that *no one will judge or evaluate or criticize your effort. It's against the rules.*

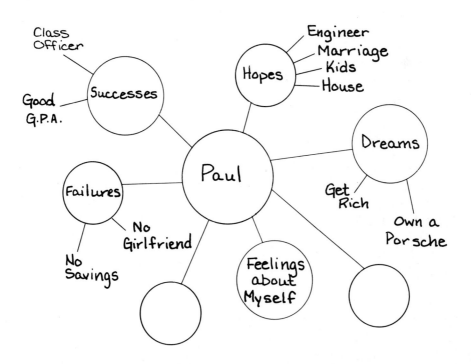

FIGURE 1.1   Student Model: Paul's Brainstorming

PRACTICE EXERCISE 1.1
Brainstorming About Yourself and Your Inner World

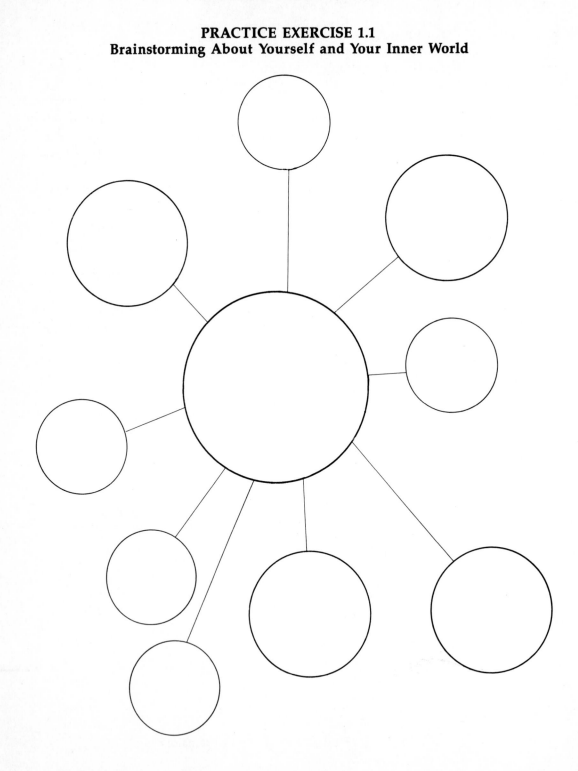

PRACTICE EXERCISE 1.2
Sharing and Comparing

DIRECTIONS: Share your brainstorming ideas with someone else—a classmate, for example, who has brainstormed about himself or herself. See how your brainstorming is alike and how it is different. You will find that your brainstorming ideas are different from those of your classmate and those of anyone else. That discovery is important because it will reinforce one of the messages of this book, namely, that you are unique.

Similarities   Differences

_____   _____

_____   _____

_____   _____

_____   _____

_____   _____

_____   _____

_____   _____

_____   _____

_____   _____

_____   _____

_____   _____

_____   _____

PRACTICE EXERCISE 1.3
Reflecting

DIRECTIONS: Think about some of those ideas you recorded in the brainstorming exercise. Then list below five or six topics that you would like to write about, along with the feedback you got from others.

PRACTICE EXERCISE 1.4
Questioning

DIRECTIONS: Ask yourself what else you could include in this picture of you and your inner world. The following questions might stimulate your thinking:

What persons had a positive effect on your life?

_____   _____

_____   _____

What persons affected you negatively?

_____   _____

_____   _____

Who were the heroes, heroines, and role models of your childhood?

_____   _____

_____   _____

Who are your heroes, heroines, and role models now?

_____   _____

_____   _____

What event had the most impact on your life?

_____

_____

What books or movies have influenced you?

_____

_____

Affirming

Student Models: We asked a class to write down ten positive statements about themselves. Here is what Lauren and Marvin wrote:

Lauren

1. I have a beautiful personality.
2. I am a good mother.
3. I am a loving wife.
4. I am a good housekeeper.
5. I am a good neighbor.
6. I am a good worker.
7. I am a good grandmother.
8. I am a good cook.
9. I am a thrifty shopper.
10. I am a good driver.

Marvin

1. I am studying to be a good surgeon's assistant.
2. I am going to be a wonderful father.
3. I plan to be prosperous in the near future.
4. I am buying my own home.
5. I am going to make some lucky lady a wonderful husband.
6. I am going to make myself proud of my accomplishments.
7. I am trying to spend more time with my family.
8. I am setting up my own limousine service.
9. I am honest with myself.
10. I am going to pass this English course.

PRACTICE EXERCISE 1.5
Affirming

DIRECTIONS: In the spaces below, write down ten positive statements about yourself.

_____

_____

_____

_____

_____

_____

_____

_____

_____

_____

_____

_____

Clustering

Clustering is the process of sorting out ideas from your brainstorming, your sharing and comparing, your reflecting, your questioning, your affirming, and later, your freewriting. You can begin to cluster your ideas now so that in your freewriting, you can focus on an idea you think you might want to explore further in an essay about yourself.

Review what you have accomplished so far in this chapter, and try to group or cluster ideas that are related. For example, you might create a cluster of thoughts and ideas you recorded about family life, another for your work life, and a third for a talent you have developed or want to develop.

PRACTICE EXERCISE 1.6
Clustering

DIRECTIONS: Use as many sheets of paper as you need to cluster your ideas. Use circles, boxes, lists—whatever works well for you.

Freewriting

Freewriting is the process of writing about a subject for five or ten minutes without stopping and without worrying about grammar, spelling, punctuation, and other elements of writing that are extremely important when you are working on an actual writing project of any kind. Freewriting is a *prewriting* activity, one that requires an unstructured approach.

Here is a sample of freewriting done by someone who was willing to share her thoughts and ramblings:

> I've been thinking about lots of ideas to write about. Keep coming back to writing about my hope to be a commercial artist. I'm not even sure what that is but whenever I see beautiful ads and colors I wish I could do that. I love color, balloons, kites, red cars racing down a country road like that TV commercial where the old lady sings the song—la la la la la la la—maybe I should be a painter—use colors all the time. I don't know what else to write about. I don't have a thought in my head. Astronauts soaring through the blue sky, seeing stars sparkle like diamonds, diamonds, floating, floating—like my thoughts—flying like a spacewoman through the sky. Hair streaming, weightless, looking down at the earth . . .

Peter Elbow, in *Writing Without Teachers*, encourages people who want to write well to freewrite often. He writes:

> The most effective way I know to improve your writing is to do freewriting exercises regularly. At least three times a week. They are sometimes called "automatic writing," "babbling," or "jabbering" exercises. The idea is simply to write for ten minutes (later on, perhaps fifteen or twenty). Don't stop for anything. Go quickly without rushing. Never stop to look back, to cross something out, to wonder how to spell something, to wonder what word or thought to use, or to think about what you are doing. If you can't think of a word or a spelling, just use a squiggle or else write, "I can't think of it." Just put down something. The easiest thing is just to put down whatever is in your mind. If you get stuck it's fine to write "I can't think what to say, I can't think what to say" as many times as you want; or repeat the last word you wrote over and over again; or anything else. The only requirement is that you *never* stop.
>
> What happens to a freewriting exercise is important. It must be a piece of writing which, even if someone reads it, doesn't send any ripples back to you. It is like writing something and putting it in a bottle in the sea. The teacherless class helps your writing by providing maximum feedback. Freewritings help you by providing no feedback at all. When I assign one, I invite the writer to let me read it. But also tell him to keep it if he prefers. I read it quickly and make no comments at all and I do not

speak with him about it. The main thing is that a freewriting must never be evaluated in any way; in fact there must be no discussion or comment at all.

For the next five or ten minutes just write about yourself without stopping. Write freely. Your exercise will not be collected or corrected. Nor will you share it with anyone else, unless you want to.

Have fun writing about yourself!

PRACTICE EXERCISE 1.7
Freewriting

_____

_____

_____

_____

_____

_____

_____

_____

_____

_____

_____

_____

_____

_____

_____

_____

_____

Chapter 2

Discovering the
Worlds in Your Universe

On August 25, 1989, the unmanned space vehicle *Voyager II,* launched in 1977, passed close to Neptune, almost three billion miles from Earth, and sent back television pictures of this planet. When it stops sending back pictures in the year 2007 A.D., *Voyager II* will have traveled nine billion miles from earth. Even at that distance, however, it still will not have reached the outer limits of the Milky Way galaxy. Since the Milky Way is just one of millions of galaxies in the universe, you can see that countless worlds remain to be discovered.

YOU AND YOUR WORLDS

Think of yourself as the center of your own personal galaxy. There are all kinds of worlds in that galaxy that you already know, but there are many more worlds waiting for you to discover and explore.

Figures 2.1 and 2.2 show models of the worlds of two students. They have left some circles unnamed, representing those worlds they have not yet discovered.

After reviewing the student models, use Figure 2.3 (p. 19) to create a visual representation of you and your universe. In the circles write the names of the worlds that are important to you either because you know them or because you would like to explore them.

Sharing and Comparing

In Practice Exercise 2.1, share your visual representation of you and your universe with at least one classmate. In the first column, list the worlds that make up your universe. In the second column list the worlds that make up the universe of your classmate.

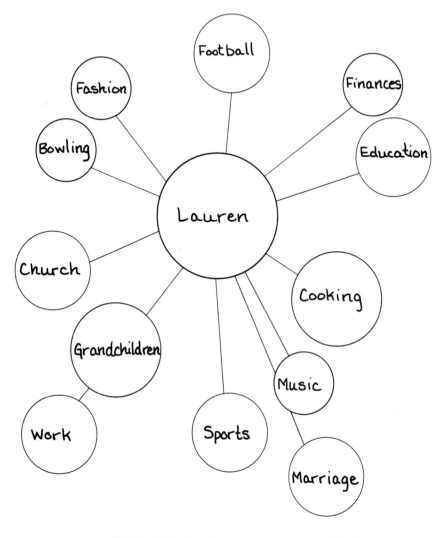

FIGURE 2.1   Student Model: Lauren's World

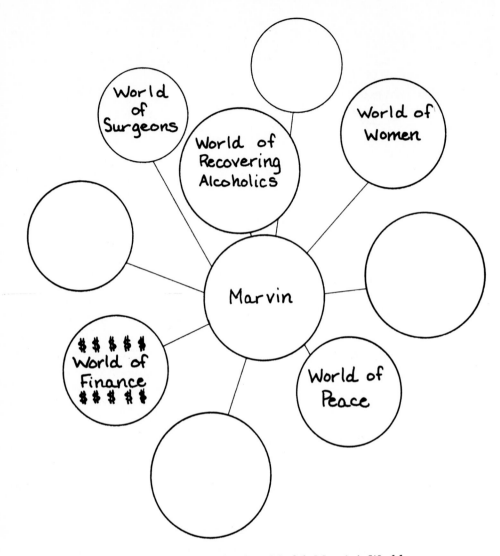

FIGURE 2.2   Student Model: Marvin's World

PRACTICE EXERCISE 2.1
Sharing and Comparing

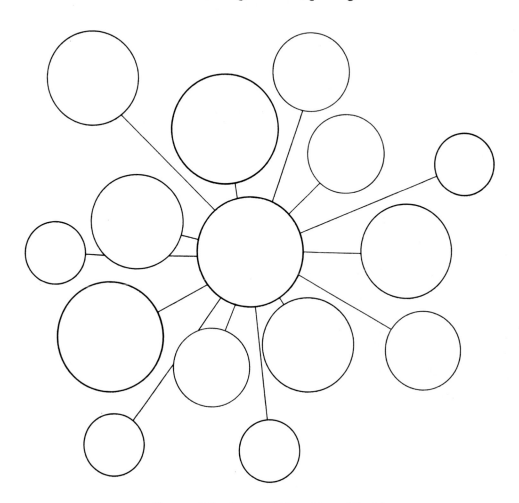

FIGURE 2.3   You and Your Many Worlds

Your Worlds   Your Classmate's Worlds

_____   _____

_____   _____

_____   _____

BRAINSTORMING ABOUT ONE OF
THE WORLDS IN YOUR GALAXY

Once you have specified some of the worlds in your galaxy, the next step is to do some brainstorming about one of those worlds that interests you more than the others you included in your drawing.

Look at Figures 2.4 and 2.5, which show how two students, Jim and Aline, brainstormed about just one of their worlds. Realize that buried in each one of your worlds are many topics about which you can write. Brainstorming alone or with others is an effective way to help dig them out.

Use Figure 2.6 to help you brainstorm for three to five minutes about one of the worlds from your personal galaxy that you recorded in *You and Your Universe* (Figure 2.3). Remember that brainstorming means putting down on paper as many ideas about the topic as you can, even if those ideas sound silly or absurd.

FIGURE 2.4   Jim's World of Sports

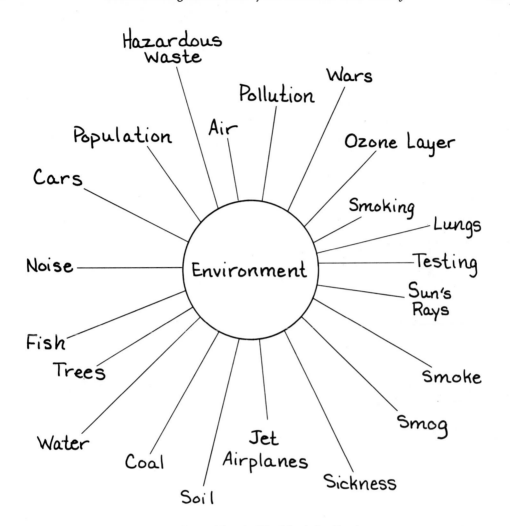

FIGURE 2.5   Aline's World of the Environment

PRACTICE EXERCISE 2.2
Sharing and Comparing

DIRECTIONS: After you have brainstormed for several minutes, share and compare your efforts with those of your classmates. Maybe one has brainstormed on politics, another on religion, another on fashion. In sharing what you wrote, you can be teaching others about a world you know something about, and by listening to others, you can learn something about other worlds you might want to discover and explore.

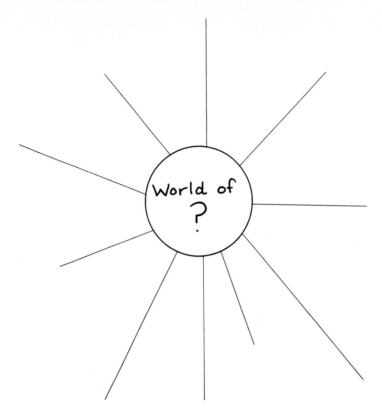

FIGURE 2.6   You and One of Your Worlds

PRACTICE EXERCISE 2.3
Reflecting and Questioning

Reflect on what you and others have brainstormed about. Ask yourself questions such as the following:

What worlds do I know something about?

The world of _____

The world of _____

The world of _____

The world of _____

What worlds do I need to explore more?

The world of _____

The world of _____

The world of _____

What are some unknown worlds that I would like to discover?

The world of _____

The world of _____

The world of _____

How would I begin the process of discovering more about a world I want to explore?

_____

_____

_____

_____

A Message About Your Worlds to the Universe

We began this chapter by telling you about the incredible journey of *Voyager II* across the Milky Way galaxy.

Voyager II not only carries television cameras; it carries radios and recordings that broadcast the sounds of earth and messages in sixty different languages. Imagine that scientists at the National Aeronautics and Space Administration (NASA) have asked you to make a recording that will be broadcast in space by an unmanned spacecraft soon to be launched. Start freewriting about what you would include in your statement to people on earth and to people who might be listening on other planets.

Note: In freewriting you don't worry about grammar, spelling, punctuation, and other important elements of good writing. Freewriting is a totally unstructured process that can help you release ideas that are buried deep inside of you. Let yourself go. Just start writing, and keep writing continuously for five to ten minutes. Save what you have written. You may want to refer to it in a future essay.

PRACTICE EXERCISE 2.4
A Message About Your Worlds to the Universe

Chapter 3

How to Zoom in on
One of Your Worlds

In Chapter 2, you discovered through brainstorming and freewriting that there are many worlds in your universe and that you know something about these worlds—more perhaps than you realized. If you completed the exercises in Chapters 1 and 2, you now know that you have too much to write about. That happens once you begin to reflect on your worlds.

Figures 3.1 and 3.2 show two examples of brainstorming. One person chose the world of fashion, and the other selected the world of business.

Notice that not all of the circles are connected to the main circle in the middle of the diagrams. Some of the circles seem to sprout from other circles that represent similar ideas. Both people were using "clustering" to group their ideas.

As the brainstorming progressed, the students became aware that they had an overload of information. There was simply too much to write about, so in their freewriting exercises they narrow their topics considerably.

The person who brainstormed about the world of fashion freewrites about swimsuits. The student who brainstormed about the world of business freewrites about word processors.

Although both writers have begun to narrow the topics on which they are going to write, they still have not narrowed those topics enough. They need to bring their topics into even sharper focus.

Model 1: Freewriting About the World of Fashion

I wish I had a lots of money to buy all the clothes I want. I love to read fashion magazines. Like to watch the skinny models on TV—strutting across the stage—I would like to travel to Paris or Hong Kong to buy the latest fashions for a women's clothing store. Catalogs, patterns, advertising, sportswear. Jeans, jackets, tennis outfits, t-shirts, swimwear. Bikinis,

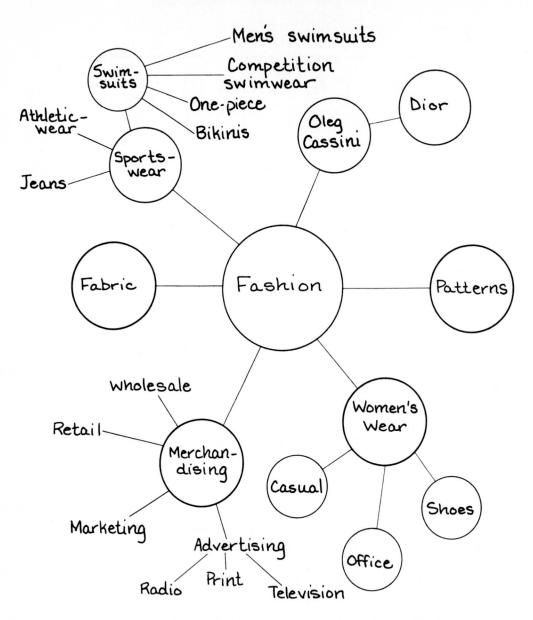

Figure 3.1 Student Model: Brainstorming About the World of Fashion

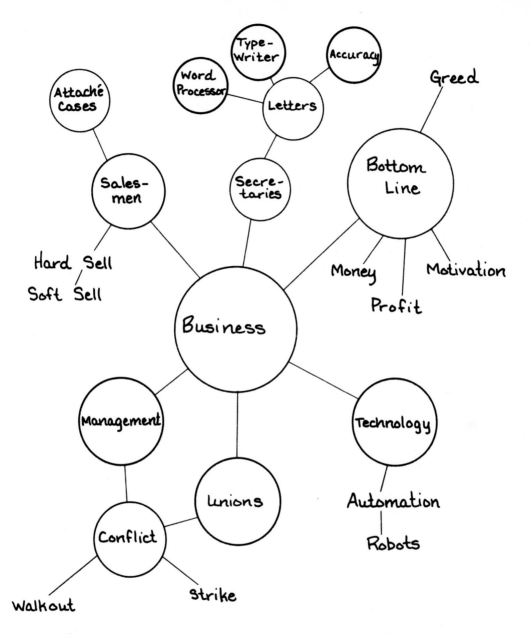

FIGURE 3.2   Student Model: Brainstorming About the World of Business

swimsuits for Olympic swimmers. One-piece swim suits. Men's bathing suits—I don't like men's bikinis. Don't like women's either because they only look good on beautiful thin girls.

Model 2: Freewriting About the World of Business

Here I am in the world of business. Lots of guys in three piece suits. This is a male dominated company. Men at top. High wages. Women at the bottom. Lower wages. No career ladder for women. Exec secretary is the end of the line. A couple of women in middle management. Relatives of CEO. One's boyfriend is a VP. Life as a secretary. Not easy. Typewriter always in need of repair. Bottom line company? That's a laugh. Repairman here at least once a week. The guy is cute so I don't mind.

Zooming in on the Topic

Visually we can show how the topics are being narrowed in the following chart:

General	*Focused*	*More focused*
fashion	swimwear	_____
business	typewriters	_____

Note that the third column—*More Focused*—is blank. That's because in each case the topic can be narrowed further. The writer who begins to write an essay on swimwear must decide whether to write about swim fashions for men or for women or for children. The person who writes about word processors must decide whether to write about hardware or software.

One device you can use to bring the subject into sharper focus is double loop writing, a phrase and concept advanced by author Peter Elbow. Double loop writing is really a continuation of freewriting. After freewriting on a topic for five or ten minutes, pause and reflect. A particular word or phrase or sentence may attract you more than others in that freewriting exercise. Use that word or phrase or sentence as a springboard to do more freewriting. This process is an effective way to further narrow the subject.

Take a look at the models.

Model 1: Double Loop Writing About Swimwear

Serious swimmers wear plain styles in swim suits. Some designers think everyone has a perfect shape. Young skinny girls look great in anything. How can you swim in something you're afraid you will lose in the water. Wish I could wear a bikini and look like a model. I guess that's why I hate bikinis. I have to go on a diet or just give up on bikinis. Why don't they make swimsuits that look good on heavier girls. Some designer should specialize in swimwear for ordinary shaped women—things that make them look thinner. Swimsuits should be colorful, easy to dry, strong fabric. Think I'll write about swim fashions for women who don't look good in bikinis.

Model 2: Double Loop Writing About Word Processors

I was writing about typewriters in this company where I work. How can we be efficient and productive if the damn things are always under repair. This company needs word processors to replace the typewriters. Keep a few typewriters but buy a lot of word processors. They are fast, easy to operate, easy to correct mistakes. If you have a good printer, the correspondence quality is terrific. My boss is afraid of new technology. Afraid of computers. Afraid of word processors. Big mystery to him. So maybe I should write a paper on why word processors would improve productivity and increase profit. He's a bottom line guy. I have to tie in word processors with the bottom line.

Getting More Specific

Both writers are getting more specific. The writer who started out with the world of fashion is directing her anger at swimsuit designers who apparently don't realize that bikinis are not for everyone. The writer who started with the world of business is stating a preference for word processors over typewriters.

The graphic now looks like this:

General	*Focused*	*More focused*
fashion	swimwear	swimwear for average shaped women
business	word processors	better than typewriter

You can easily see that the topics have been narrowed considerably. This is not to say that the topics could not be narrowed more. More freewriting and double loop writing could bring that about.

Brainstorming, Freewriting, and Double Loop Writing

Topics in the list that follows are rather general and vague. Through brainstorming, freewriting, and double loop writing (Practice Exercises 3.1, 3.2, and 3.3), try to narrow them to specific and limited topics that you could use as the subject of an essay. *Don't shortcut this process.*

birds	plants	politics
fish	students	food
animals	travel	careers

PRACTICE EXERCISE 3.1
Brainstorming About a Focused Topic

PRACTICE EXERCISE 3.2
Freewriting

PRACTICE EXERCISE 3.3
Double Loop Writing

_____

_____

_____

_____

_____

_____

_____

_____

_____

_____

_____

_____

_____

_____

_____

_____

_____

PRACTICE EXERCISE 3.4
Sharing and Comparing

DIRECTIONS: Team up with one or two other people and share what you have written. After consulting with them, record your process of focusing in columns 2 and 3. The topics in column 3 should be much more focused than the topics you started with in Exercise 3.1.

General	More focused	Much more focused
birds	_____	_____
fish	_____	_____
animals	_____	_____
plants	_____	_____
students	_____	_____
travel	_____	_____
politics	_____	_____
food	_____	_____
careers	_____	_____

Although the process of narrowing topics requires time, you will find that it shortens your writing time considerably. If you begin to write without going through the process, you will probably spend far more time revising your paragraph or essay than you would have spent narrowing the topic.

Chapter 4

The World of Words

The way we speak influences the way we write. If we constantly use slang, trite expressions, and nonstandard English when we speak, the chances are good that we will use them when we write. The following sentences may make sense in some special instances, but they are not acceptable in writing, unless you are writing to show specific language use in dialogue.

He outside.

Don't jive me!

Hanging out is cool.

The used car salesman tried to rip me off.

The couple has two kids.

Albert be good for the job.

The music's groovy.

Maya Angelou, the gifted poet, writer, and artist, makes this point well in Chapter 29 of her autobiography *I Know Why the Caged Bird Sings*. She contrasts her education in a San Francisco public school with that of some of her white counterparts.

"We were alert," she writes, "to the gap separating the written word from the colloquial. We learned to slide out of one language and into another without being conscious of the effort. At school, in a given situation, we might respond with, 'That's not unusual.' But in the street, meeting the same situation, we easily said, 'It be's like that sometimes.'"

KNOWING WHEN TO SLIDE

The most important sentence in the quotation from Angelou is the one in which she says that she and her classmates could slide from one language into the other without being conscious of the effort. Eric Fitch, a student at Cuyahoga Community College, paraphrased that sentence in his journal: "Being educated means knowing when to slide."

Eric has it exactly right. There are times when formal or standard English is appropriate. We expect the president of the United States to use formal language when he gives his State of the Union address. We expect the same when we listen to a minister, priest, or rabbi giving a sermon. At a college convocation, faculty and students expect the college president to use formal English in addressing them. At a parent-teacher meeting, parents want the superintendent and the principal to use standard or formal English in public remarks. Chief executive officers of corporations want employees to use standard or formal English when communicating with the company's stockholders or customers. The secretary who asks a waiting client, "Can I get youse a cup of coffee?" will soon be transferred to a position that does not require dealing with the public.

If you are thinking of entering the world of business, or the world of law or medicine, or the world of the classroom, you will be wise to use standard English.

There are times, of course, that nonstandard English is appropriate. A school counselor who wants to relate to students who are tough and street smart will get nowhere by insisting that the students use standard English in counseling sessions. A football coach is expected to use standard English when he is representing the school at a program or a football banquet. However, when he is talking to his players in the locker room or on the field, he may use informal or nonstandard English. In other words, he will know when to slide out of one language and into another.

The following guidelines will help you choose the appropriate style:

1. *In formal speech and in formal writing, avoid the use of slang phrases and expressions.*

The worlds of music, entertainment, and sports have generated a rich and colorful vocabulary of slang terms and expressions. That's because English is a living language, not a dead one like Latin or Greek. Some of these words and expressions may eventually be accepted as standard English. The word "jazz," for example, was originally a slang word, but now it is accepted as a standard English word. The truth of the matter is, however, that most slang expressions do not endure. After a few years, they lose their power and people who continue to use outdated expressions, such as "jive," "groovy", and "neato," date themselves. This is not to say that you should not be aware of slang expressions and even use them occasionally. What you must do is make sure that you do not mistake slang expressions for standard English.

2. *Be sure to add endings to the past tense of verbs.*

Frequently, the endings of the past tense of verbs are dropped in nonstandard English. It takes practice to revise some of these expressions, such as the following:

> My mother call me. (faulty)
> My mother *called* me. (revised)

> He help put out the fire. (faulty)
> He *helped* put out the fire. (revised)

> The minister preach a good sermon. (faulty)
> The minister *preached* a good sermon. (revised)

> The hunter fire the rifle. (faulty)
> The hunter *fired* the rifle. (revised)

3. *Do not drop -s endings from verbs.*

> Shirle save money every paycheck. (faulty)
> Shirle *saves* money every paycheck. (revised)

> Marylee enjoy dancing at the disco. (faulty)
> Marylee *enjoys* dancing at the disco. (revised)

> Eric type sixty words a minute. (faulty)
> Eric *types* sixty words a minute. (revised)

> Gene like to play racquetball with Chris. (faulty)
> Gene *likes* to play racquetball with Chris. (revised)

4. *Do not omit verbs that are needed.*

We certainly understand the meaning of the following sentences when we hear them spoken:

> I been working.

> Terry been swimming.

> Joe's boss mad at him.

> The car not running.

This is the way some people speak among themselves, and their listeners usually understand what they mean. Such expressions, however, are not acceptable in formal writing. Using standard English, one could revise the sentences in this way:

I have been working.

Terry has been swimming.

Joe's boss is mad at him.

The car is not running.

5. *Avoid double negatives.*
Two negatives cancel each other out; therefore, do not use them.

The chief said he *don't* know *nothing* about the drug raid. (The double negative implies that the chief did know something about the raid.)

The mechanic said he was *not* going to do *nothing.* (The use of two negatives means that the mechanic will do something.)

Note: The word *hardly* cancels out part of the effect of the word *not*; do not use it in a sentence with *not.*

Sharon's car has such mechanical problems that she could not hardly start it. (Implies she could start it a little bit.)

The child was so frightened by the roller coaster ride that he could not hardly speak. (Implies the child could speak a little bit.)

To revise both sentences, simply omit the word *not*.

6. *Avoid using nonstandard language in formal writing.*
Expressions such as the following should not appear in your formal writing:

Them grits were good.

I'll never shop again in that there store.

What's wrong with this here car?

Henry told me hisself.

Me and her are engaged.

The manager could of told us the concert was sold out.

How did youse girls know we ain't college boys?

HAVING A WAY WITH WORDS

Whatever your age, status, or job, you will find life more interesting, more exciting, and more rewarding if you discover the world of words, and if you discover persons who can teach the power and beauty of words.

Who are these people? They are poets, essayists, novelists, critics, letter writers, playwrights, journalists, biographers, and others whose words challenge us to think, reflect, laugh, mourn, remember. They often call us to leave the dark shadows of human nature and move out into the light of truth and beauty where we can become our best possible selves.

In Part III, you will meet some men and women who know how to use words. These wordsmiths can help to make your life more interesting, more exciting, and more rewarding. They can teach you the power and beauty of words.

Keep in mind examples such as Abraham Lincoln, Winston Churchill, and Martin Luther King, Jr., Malcolm X, and Emily Dickinson, who rose to prominence because they knew how to use words.

Abraham Lincoln.   The principal speaker at the dedication of the National Cemetery at Gettysburg, Pennsylvania, was not Abraham Lincoln but Edward Everett, who spoke for two hours. Lincoln followed him to the podium and spoke only 269 words, but those words will be remembered as long as this nation lives.

Winston Churchill.   As a young student at Harrow in England, Winston Churchill was not smart enough to get into the classes where brighter students learned Latin and Greek. "We were considered such dunces," he writes, "that we could learn only English." So Churchill studied English. "I learned it thoroughly. Thus I got into my bones the essential structure of the ordinary British sentence—which is a noble thing. And when in after years my schoolfellows who had won prizes and distinction for writing such beautiful Latin poetry and pithy Greek epigrams had to come down again to common English, to earn their living or make their way, I did not feel myself at any disadvantage."

Indeed, he was not. Churchill went on to become one of the most outstanding statesmen and writers of the twentieth century.

Rev. Martin Luther King, Jr.   The Rev. Martin Luther King, Jr. was a leader of the civil rights movement who knew the power of words, both spoken and written. His "I Have a Dream" speech, delivered on August 28, 1963, before a gathering of 250,000 people in Washington, D.C., and a television audience of millions, stirred the conscience of the nation and catapulted King into national prominence.

Malcolm X.   In his autobiography, Malcolm X remarks that many people who heard him on radio or television or read his works thought that he went far beyond his eighth grade education, but the truth is that he educated himself in prison. He asked for and received a dictionary. Every day he would painstakingly copy all the words and definitions on a page in the dictionary and memorize them. He writes:

    "I suppose it was inevitable that as my word base broadened, I could for the first time pick up a book and now begin to understand what the book was saying. Anyone who has read a great deal can imagine the new world that opened. Let me tell you something: from then on until I left that prison, in every free moment I had, if I was not reading in the library, I was reading on my bunk. You couldn't have gotten me out of books with a wedge. . . ."

Emily Dickinson.   The American poet, Emily Dickinson, died over a hundred years ago, yet her poetry lives today. In her lifetime, only two of her two thousand poems were published. Today her poems are enjoyed not only by scholars and students at colleges and universities but lovers of words everywhere. She teaches us how simple words can be used to convey great thoughts, as the following poem illustrates:

> A word is dead
> When it is said
> Some say.
> I say it just
> Begins to live
> that day.

    No one can deny the power and beauty of the spoken word. We believe, however, that those who can write well have an advantage over those who can only speak well. Robert Maynard, publisher and editor of *The Tribune* (Oakland, California), makes that point in an essay he wrote about teaching writing. Part of it is reprinted here.

Lions Who Learned to Write

Robert C. Maynard

The fable goes this way: An African child came home from school one day and told his mother of a story his teacher had read to him. It was about a man in the jungle named Tarzan and he was mightier than even the lion, whom the child had always thought to be the king of the jungle.

When his mother heard the child's expressions of dismay, she replied: "Always will it be that way, my son, until the lions learn to write."

My parents, often using that fable for fuel, drove us to write from our earliest days. They held up examples of good writing for our attention even before we could read or write. Mostly, they used the Bible, but often they turned to Shakespeare and the classics.

In 1983, the Carnegie Commission study of secondary education urged the schools of the nation to place greater emphasis on writing in their curricula. The commission said the inability to write effectively is proving to be a material deficit in the lives of American students.

It is not just students. All too many adults in responsible jobs achieved those jobs without learning how to write a clear and concise exposition of a problem or a position.

More than that, I have known people who claimed writing made them ill. One colleague in school many years ago doubled over with cramps the closer a writing deadline approached. Another professional person I know was so terrified of ever having to write anything strangers might read that he literally shook and perspired when an unavoidable writing obligation descended upon him.

Those may be extreme cases, but there are too many of those and the more common case of the citizen who simply never learned even a minimal amount about putting thoughts on paper.

Such people are, in my opinion, deprived. They are deprived because written expression can help advance almost any goal, particularly career goals.

Regardless of their discipline, people who can sell their ideas on paper are ahead of those who can only describe their intentions orally.

There is nothing wrong with oral skill, but being able to back it up on paper can make all the difference.

My dad had a wonderful way of making that point. He used to play a game in which he would ask one of us how many followers Jesus had. We would say we didn't know; but it was in the thousands. Then he would ask us how many we could name. When we named the apostles, he would always remind us that we remembered best those who had written down their accounts of what they had witnessed.

"Those were not necessarily the best servants. They were just the best writers who were servants," he would say. Or, to put it another way, they were lions who had learned to write. . . .

Chapter 5

Discovering Connections

The ears of an elephant and the ears of a nurse have, on the face of it, no connection; but a speaker at a baccalaureate exercise for nurses made a connection.

The exercise took place in the chapel of a hospital. That day someone had placed at the chapel entrance a small table on which there stood a beautiful hand-carved statue of an elephant, perhaps eighteen inches in height. As guests and graduates entered the chapel, they had to pass the statue.

A priest began the ceremony with a short but effective speech to the graduates. He said that he was the one who placed the table and the statue of the elephant at the entrance of the chapel so that everyone would be certain to see it. The elephant, he said, was an African elephant, a type that has the largest ears of all species of elephants. With those ears, the African elephant can hear sounds from many miles away. Really good nurses, he said, must have sensitive ears so that they can more effectively tend to the needs of patients. His speech contained many examples of how the graduates could be nurses with truly sensitive ears.

A friend attended that service more than fifteen years ago, but he still recalls that story. Obviously, the speaker made the right connection.

HOW TO MAKE CONNECTIONS

Through a number of techniques, a writer can learn how to make connections that will make an essay or a story come to life. Some of the following techniques are helpful.

Seeing Similarities in Things That Are Different

The little story at the beginning of this chapter illustrates this point: making the connection between things as dissimilar as elephants and nurses can be attention catching.

Seeing Differences in Things That Are Similar

Another way to make connections is to look for differences in things that are similar. One evening I was switching channels as television viewers often do. One channel was showing starving people in Ethiopia running for food, water, and life. At the same time, another channel was showing superbly conditioned black athletes running in the Olympics for gold, bronze, and silver at the summer Olympics in Los Angeles. After thinking about the two programs, I made a connection between the seemingly dissimilar events and then wrote an essay published in a Cleveland newspaper, *The Plain Dealer,* and titled "The World's Starving Must Hold Center Stage."

Being a Good Listener

Listen to the sounds around you. Listen to what people are saying on the bus or at work. Insignificant remarks can sometimes be the subject of an essay. For example, some years ago, my wife and I were seated on the top deck of a bus in London, England. A young lady seated near us was complaining to her friend that her college education was useless because she had never been taught the meaning of the word "mezzanine." On her first job after graduation, her boss told her to get something on the mezzanine. She was embarrassed that she did not know what he meant. After we returned from that trip, I used that incident in an essay published by *The Plain Dealer* and titled, "An absolutely peerless graduation speech." The essay was a humorous graduation speech in which I defined a mezzanine as a small floor sandwiched between two larger floors. I told the graduates they were now on life's mezzanine floor but not to get stuck there. Each year they should continue their education. I concluded with this: "The view of a city and indeed, the world, is vastly different depending on where you're standing—the mezzanine or the 85th floor. Be glad that you have reached the mezzanine of education, but do not be content to remain there."

Being a Good Observer

Keep your eyes and ears open. Read the newspapers, watch television that informs. Watch people at sports events, church services, shopping malls, neighborhood taverns—wherever people gather.

Being a Good Recorder

Keep a journal or a day book. Each day try to record things you have read, seen, or heard. Clip out newspaper and magazine articles that you like and paste them in your journal. Just as you put money in your savings account at the bank for a rainy day, so you can put ideas into your think bank. You can draw out those ideas at a future time.

Being a Good Questioner

It is important to ask questions such as what is happening, what was happening, what could have happened, what should have happened? Ask "what if" questions.

One day after a terrorist attack on U.S. citizens, I began wondering: What if there were no terrorist nations like Libya? What if there were no wars anywhere in the world? What if there were no markets for weapons and guns? After answering those questions, I made some connections and wrote an article, "What If Peace Stormed the Earth," reprinted from *The Plain Dealer* in Chapter 17.

When you are looking for a topic for your writing assignments, try the technique of making connections. Let's say that in Chapter 1, you brainstormed about famous baseball players, and others brainstormed about movie stars or musicians or politicians or scientists or artists. What connections could you make between your brainstorming and someone else's brainstorming? Be as imaginative and creative as you can be. There are no right or wrong responses.

PRACTICE EXERCISE 5.1
Exploring Connections

DIRECTIONS: List some things that could connect professional baseball players and movie actors.

_____

_____

_____

_____

List some things that could connect artists and scientists.

_____

_____

_____

_____

List some things that could connect teachers and deep sea divers.

_____

_____

_____

_____

List some things that could connect truck drivers and ballet dancers.

_____

_____

_____

_____

Exploring Connections Between the
Present and the Past

It's fun to try to connect people from the visible side of a world to those who are on the invisible or underside of that world. For example, the visible side of a world are the people who at this time are prominent in the worlds of entertainment, politics, religion, music, sports, literature, art, business, and so on. The underside could be people who are no longer prominent because they have retired or because they have died.

PRACTICE EXERCISE 5.2
Making Connections

DIRECTIONS: Let the circle in Figure 5.1 represent a world that you know something about. In the left half of the circle, write down the names of people who at one time were celebrities in that world. In the right half of that circle, write down all the people who are celebrities in that world today.

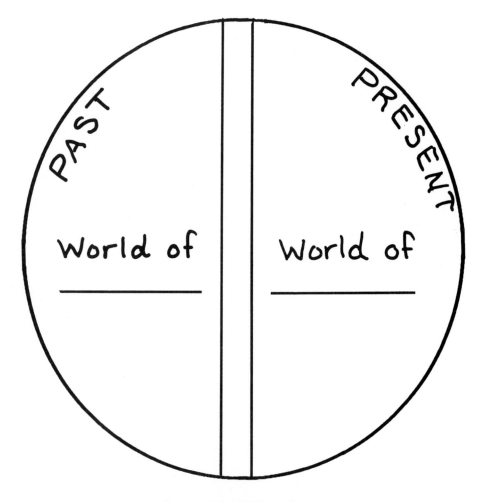

FIGURE 5.1   Making Connections

PRACTICE EXERCISE 5.3
A Fantasy

DIRECTIONS: Give an imaginary dinner party for four guests: two from the world of the past and two from the world of the present. What seating arrangement would you use? What would you serve at this dinner? What would be the topics of discussion that evening?

_____

_____

_____

_____

_____

_____

_____

_____

_____

_____

_____

_____

_____

_____

_____

_____

The Process: From Making
Connections to Writing the Essay

It is one thing to write theory; it is quite another to put that theory into practice. What follows here are some articles I published after going through the process of making connections. Perhaps these articles can help you make connections that will suggest topics for your essay writing.

Example 1   "Looking Back at Immigrant Parents"
This essay was published in *The Plain Dealer* shortly before the Fourth of July, 1986. That year was the 100th anniversary of the Statue of Liberty. All sorts of stories appeared in the media about the immigrants who passed that statue on their way to Ellis Island and eventual citizenship in America. A series of questions helped make the connections.

June 1986: What is happening?
Statue of Liberty refurbished
Boats, ships, whistles
Fireworks
Speeches by President, Governor, etc.
Tourists—millions of them
Television crews everywhere
Beautiful long ships in harbor
Festive mood
Great American picnic
Stories about immigrant parents
Recall my immigrant grandparents and recall that they came to America almost 100 years ago

June 1889 in Hamburg, Germany: What was happening?
My grandparents are getting ready to come to America
They are young; he 21, she 19
They have two infants
They are poor—they are afraid
Why are they leaving? Economy? Persecution? Better future?
Don't know
They make voyage
Recall seeing movie about immigrants—voyage takes three months—hundreds die without reaching America
Hardships of trips in steerage
See Statue of Liberty
Arrive Ellis Island. Frightened. Happy. Anxious.
Can't speak language
Took a lot of guts to come to America

What happened when they came to Cleveland?
Lived in German section of city
He worked as a laborer—unloaded ore boats on Cuyahoga River
Worked six days a week—10 hours a day
Walked two miles to and from work each day
Lived frugally
Loved America—Displayed American flag proudly
Glad to be U.S. citizens
She was homemaker
She raised family—had nine kids
Cooked, baked, sewed, cleaned
Great house—always clean—everything in place
Was gentle and tough
Had to be tough raising all those kids
Both died in 1944—both in the eighties

What if they had stayed in Germany?
My parents would never have met
Would not have been born in America
Could have been born in Germany
Could have lived through the Nazi era
Could have been drafted in the German army
Could have killed Americans in battle
Could have been killed
Could have survived and married
Remained in Germany and worked there
Never see America
Thankful that they left—maybe not thankful enough
What guts it must have taken to leave family and homeland

July 1986: What should happen?
I should go to New York City
I should see the Statue
I should be there waving flag
Should go to Ellis Island
Should be part of the crowd
Decide not to go
Better view from living room, watching television
Should not forget grandparents
Buried in St. Mary Cemetery
Visit their grave, say a prayer
Say "danke shön" and "aufwiedersehen"
Place an American flag on grave

Product.   After going through that process, I was able to make some connections and, finally, to write the essay which follows.

Looking Back at Immigrant Parents

George Eppley

Some 15 years ago I viewed "The Emigrants," a remarkable film with Liv Ullman and Max von Sydow in leading roles. It told the story of a group of people from Sweden who emigrated to America in the mid-19th century because of the repressive policies of their government. In graphic fashion the movie showed the emigrants' long brutal voyage across the Atlantic. Most of them were ill with dysentery. Many of them died and were buried at sea.

That film had a profound effect on me. It caused me to think about my maternal grandparents who emigrated from Germany almost a century ago. Until I saw "The Emigrants" I viewed my grandparents as two old people who had come from the "Old Country." I had never thought of them as a young married couple in their early 20s—who must have agonized long and hard over a decision to leave their parents, their friends and their homeland to begin life anew in a new land.

What prompted them to leave? Was it high unemployment? Did they leave because of the repressive policies of the Bismarck government toward German Catholics? Was it because friends and relatives in America were telling them about opportunities in America? Unfortunately, I don't know. Perhaps it was a combination of all these things.

What I do know is that they did leave and that they made a long, tough journey across the Atlantic, with their two infants. Seven more children would be born in America. Like most of the immigrants who came to America in the 19th century, they were poor.

On the Fourth of July the nation will be awash in nostalgia and patriotism as it celebrates the 100th anniversary of the Statue of Liberty. Orators will quote those famous words on the base of the statue—"Give me your tired, your poor, your huddled masses yearning to breathe free. . . ." With the celebration comes the temptation to make our immigrant ancestors larger than life.

My grandparents—John and Dorothea Kindel—were simple people who came to Cleveland to live in the Clark Ave.-Scranton Rd. Area. He was a laborer who walked to his job in the Flats each day to help unload the ore boats. She was a housewife and mother who ruled their nine children with a firm hand while he was at work sometimes 12 or 14 hours a day.

Like so many others who formed the ethnic pockets of this city, their lives centered around their families, churches, schools and neighborhoods.

Like so many others they taught a value system which had formed them. They were honest, humble and hard-working.

And like so many others they became American citizens who loved this land which had made them free. I can never recall my grandparents yearning to return to the old country. I do recall, however, that on Memorial Day, Flag Day and the Fourth of July my grandfather's yard was filled with small American flags. I also recall that he was buried in St. Mary Cemetery on July 4, 1944.

My favorite picture of my grandparents is a portrait taken with their children in 1912 on their 25th wedding anniversary. It shows better than anything else that they considered themselves rich, although economically they were never that. All the people in that picture are dead, but numerous descendants live on enjoying freedom and a standard of living that my grandparents never could have imagined when they first set foot on this land.

It would be nice to go to New York this Fourth of July and recall the day my grandparents first saw Miss Liberty when she was only 4 years old. Instead I will go to St. Mary Cemetery on Clark Ave. and place a small American flag on their grave. I would like to be able to thank them personally for the decision they made to come to America almost a century ago. Until I see them in eternity, however, a simple *danke shön* and *aufwiedersehen* will have to do.

Example 2 "The Struggle Across the Beaches"

This essay was published in *The Plain Dealer* on March 31, 1988. Three unconnected events were in progress: (1) the spring quarter was about to begin and I would be facing 25 English 099 students; (2) the final four basketball teams were getting ready to compete in Kansas City for the NCAA title; and (3) giant female sea turtles were swimming toward the coast of South Carolina to lay their eggs near the sandy beaches. Using the process listed next, certain connections about those events became apparent.

March 1988: What is happening in the world of nature?
On the coast of South Carolina:
Giant female sea turtles swim towards coast of S. Carolina. Reach land.
Walk over sandy beaches. Find bushes or undergrowth.
Lay their eggs. Shed tears as they lay eggs.
Eggs hatch after a few weeks.
Baby sea turtles leave shell and crawl towards water.
Painstakingly slow. Dangerous. Birds and predators eat them.
Tourists watch in great numbers. Tempted to carry baby turtles to water.
Wrong to do so.
Baby turtles need to struggle themselves. Build up lung power.
Can swim in ocean when they reach the water. Will drown unless they struggle across the beach by themselves.

March 1988: What's happening in the worlds of sports?
In the city of Kansas City:
National Collegiate Athletic Association about to begin basketball tournament. Four top teams in country will compete.
Winner will be national champion.
Outstanding basketball players. Can shoot, run, dribble, slam dunk. Superbly conditioned. Have practiced for hours each day of year. Punished their bodies. Made sacrifices. Did it to excel. To win. To be No. 1.
Some will make pros and earn six figure salaries.
Most will not make the pros. Too few places in the pro ranks. Competition for pros intense. Hope someone taught them in college reading writing and thinking skills.
They'll need those skills to survive in the world of work.

March 1988: What's happening in the world of college?
In Cleveland, Ohio's Metropolitan Campus of Cuyahoga Community College:
Students about to begin class for spring quarter.
Must pass developmental English class.
Tell them about the writing, speaking, reading, and thinking skills they need to survive in the world of work. Important.
No one can read or think or write for them. Have to do these things themselves. Like baby turtle who has to struggle across the beach. Like basketball players. No one can run, shoot, dribble, pass for them.
Tell them about presidential candidate who had to drop out of race because of plagiarism in law school and in politics.
Did not learn the lesson of the baby turtle.
Tell them about the thousands of companies listed each day on the financial pages. All need people who can read, write, speak, think. Makes good sense to practice these skills.
Makes good sense to learn the lesson of the sea turtles.

Product: That was a lengthy process, but in the essay that follows you can see the various connections.

The Struggle Across the Beaches

George Eppley

On the face of it, there is no connection between the sea turtles who swim to the beaches of South Carolina and the final four college basketball teams in the NCAA tournament. But this quarter as I start teaching another class in freshman college composition, I will show my students the connection.

In early spring giant female sea turtles swim toward the coast of South Carolina. On reaching land, they slowly make their way across the sandy beaches until they find some bushes or undergrowth where they can deposit their eggs. As they lay their eggs, these mother turtles shed tears.

A few years ago a CBS camera crew captured on film the turtles in the act of laying their eggs and shedding tears. A few weeks later the crew returned to film the hatching of the eggs. As soon as the baby turtles—no larger than the palm of one's hand—break free of the shell, they make their way across the beach to the ocean.

Many never make it. The short journey is in peril because birds and other predators attack them and eat them before they reach the water's edge. Other turtles just give up and die on the beach. For them the struggle to reach the sea is too painful.

A friend who with thousands of other tourists once watched the tiny sea turtles struggling to reach the sea told me that he felt a compulsion to pick them up and carry them to the ocean. One would think that gesture would be an act of kindness. On the contrary, he said, it would be an act of cruelty. In struggling by themselves to reach the sea, the baby turtles build up their lung power and capacity to live in the sea. When deprived of that difficult and painful exercise, the turtles soon drown.

After telling my students the saga of the baby sea turtles, I try to point out some lessons. I try to show them that the thinking and reading and writing exercises we will be doing in the 11 weeks of the quarter are not without difficulty and pain . . . that they will be tempted to give up and drop out . . . that well-meaning friends will try to convince them that the struggle to succeed in writing is not really worthwhile.

I tell them, they will be tempted to listen to and heed those siren voices telling them that an easier way is to get someone else to do the writing for them. That, I point out, will lead to disaster.

This quarter I will tell my students about a presidential candidate who dropped out of the race because it was discovered that he was too lazy in law school to write his own briefs. He thought that writings and opinions of others, cleverly disguised, could carry him along. In debates with his Democratic rivals he thought he could use the speeches of a British politician to score points.

Undoubtedly, that senator has many fine qualities. He might have made an excellent president. Unfortunately, history will remember him for his plagiarism. And English teachers like me will remember him as a little sea turtle who all through life was carried along by the thoughts and ideas of others until one day he drowned in the sea of presidential politics.

But what has all this to do with the final four college teams competing this weekend for the national collegiate basketball crown? Simply this. The members of those teams got there by discipline, practice and hard work. Every day in season and out of season, these superbly conditioned athletes practiced running, shooting, dribbling and passing for endless hours. No one could do those things for them. They teach the same lessons as do the sea turtles.

Some of them will go on to the pros and eventually earn six-figure salaries. Those who don't become pros will have to enter the world of work, where they will have to read, write and think to survive. Let's hope that they have learned academic skills in their four years of college. Let's hope they haven't been carried along. If they have, they will meet the same fate as sea turtles carried over the beach and deprived of the opportunity to develop their powers.

Very few students who play basketball make it to the pros. To make this point, I show students that the National Basketball Association has 23 teams. If each team has 12 players on its roster, only 276 positions are available.

The New York Stock Exchange and the American Stock Exchange list on the financial pages thousands of companies. So it makes eminently good sense for students to struggle to reach the large ocean of business rather than the small sea of professional sports.

Even if my students can run, pass, dribble, shoot and slam-dunk, I can't guarantee they will make it to the pros. But I can guarantee them that if they excel in reading, writing and thinking they will be able to command a good salary and a good job long after most of the flashy basketball players from the final four are gone and forgotten.

PRACTICE EXERCISE 5.4
Making Connections in Your Worlds

Here are some questions that may help you make connections about two different worlds:

What is happening in the world of _____ on _____?
(Supply the name of the world and the date.)

What is happening in the world of _____ on _____?
(Supply the name of the world and the date.)

Do these two separate worlds have anything in common? If so, what? Are there great differences?

If people from those separate worlds ever met, how would they begin a conversation? List the topics they might discuss.

Would they have any values in common? Children? Family? Freedom? Money? Education? Religious beliefs? Political beliefs?

Could they function in one another's world? Why or why not?

If these two worlds would disappear, what would these people do?

List the connections between the two worlds no matter how wild and absurd they may seem.

Chapter 6

Thinking Critically

It has been said that confession is good for the soul. All of us have made some bad decisions in our lives. As we analyze those decisions, we realize that our decisions were poor because our thinking was poor. We didn't ask enough questions, we did not have all the information we needed, we did not carefully weigh the pros and cons, and we did not adequately consider the long-term consequences of the decisions. In other words, we were not thinking *critically*.

Critical here does not mean focusing on someone's shortcomings. We are aware that the word *critical* means different things to different people. High school students sometimes think that *critical* means bad-mouthing others such as teachers for the way they teach, classmates for the way they behave, and so on. It's not unusual for a father to become upset with his son because the son doesn't cut the grass, wash the car, keep his room clean. No doubt the son would say that his father is being too critical.

THINKING THINGS THROUGH

When we write about critical thinking, we mean taking the time to think things through; considering the pros and cons of an issue or a decision.

If we are to survive and grow in the world in which we live, we must try to become critical thinkers. Failure to become critical thinkers puts us at risk and makes us vulnerable to those who exploit poor thinkers for their own selfish purposes. In failing to become critical thinkers, we surrender power to others. Failure to become critical thinkers causes us to spend time correcting our mistakes when we should be moving on to new discoveries and new opportunities.

EXAMPLES OF POOR THINKING

Examples of poor thinking are numerous. Finance companies in many cities have parking lots filled with repossessed cars of buyers who defaulted on meeting their scheduled car payments. Many of these former "owners" let their hearts rule their heads at the time of purchase. A Porsche looks terrific in the driveway and may impress friends, but a luxury car doesn't fit everyone's budget. Wanting and wishing and hoping are not substitutes for thinking critically. Critical thinking is important in most decisions, certainly those involving the purchase of large-ticket items such as a car or a home or a boat.

Consider another example, that of becoming engaged, a natural and wonderful and important event in the life of a couple. Often prospective brides and grooms fail to ask critical questions about their partners: questions about personality, lifestyle, finances, behavior patterns, religion, education, family background, physical and mental health. Failure to ask those questions before marriage often leads to some painful consequences after marriage for the couple and their children. Wanting and wishing and hoping are not substitutes for critical thinking.

Changing jobs is another example. Sometimes a person leaves a job because someone or some duty at work makes the job a drudgery. Perhaps changing jobs is a good decision for that person, but only after doing some critical thinking. And only after making sure he or she has another job.

Some people leave jobs because they were passed over for a promotion. Or they resign because they were reprimanded by a superior. They leave because they perceive that they are the victims of sexism, or racism or ageism. Maybe they are. Before they decide to resign, however, they should carefully think through how those wrongs might be redressed.

Perhaps one gets a measure of satisfaction from telling off a boss, slamming the door, and leaving the company. That might make for good conversation with friends; but that small measure of satisfaction will not pay bills, nor will it help get another job. In fact, the display of temper might make it more difficult for a person to get another job, because in response to reference checks the company may label that person a disgruntled employee.

There are right ways and wrong ways to leave a job, and these ways have much to do with whether a person is a good thinker or a poor one.

Before you read on, just spend a few minutes thinking about a time in your own life when you acted before you thought of all the angles. Make a list of the questions you should have asked, but didn't.

TRAITS OF POOR THINKERS

The reason we can write about this section with conviction is that many times we have been guilty of poor thinking. Experience has taught us something about the consequences of poor thinking. In fact, most adults can recall times in their lives when their thought processes were not the best.

Poor thinkers act on impulse. Poor thinkers don't look at consequences and don't consider alternatives. Nor do they devise strategies that could help them cope with seemingly hopeless situations. Poor thinkers look for immediate results. Poor thinkers act on emotion rather than reason and do not consider all sides of an issue. Poor thinkers are easily conned because they mistake style for substance. Rarely do they share their thinking with friends and associates before they make important decisions. They avoid seeking advice, especially from those they fear will disagree with them. They do not ask the hard questions because they are afraid of the answers.

TRAITS OF GOOD THINKERS

Critical thinkers, on the other hand, act logically. They consider consequences of their actions, and they try to look at various alternatives. Critical thinkers try to devise strategies to cope with seemingly hopeless situations. They are governed more by reason than by emotion. They try to look at all sides of an issue. Consequently, they are not easily fooled by those who try to sell style for substance. They are not afraid to ask the hard questions, because they can accept the answers even though acceptance will cause them great difficulty. Because of that, they share their thinking with friends and associates before making important decisions.

THINKING ABOUT THINKING

One becomes a good tennis player, a good place kicker, a good figure skater, a good long distance runner, a good dancer, a good jazz pianist, a good anything, by practice. So how does one become a critical thinker? By practice over a period of a lifetime. Let's run through some practice exercises on critical thinking.

PRACTICE EXERCISE 6.1
Critical Thinking

Scenario. Debbie, a twenty-year-old honor student completing her sophomore year at a local community college, has been accepted in the business administration program at an out-of-state university, where her boyfriend is now a senior in pre-med. Her parents had promised her that they would pay her tuition and board at the college of her choice if she did well in her freshman and sophomore years. Her father, however, recently lost his executive position with a tire company that was taken over by a larger company. At age fifty-eight, he is fearful that he will not find another job at his former salary level. Consequently, he and Debbie's mother have told her that they can pay only her tuition, but not room and board. They have suggested that (1) she stay at home and attend a local college that has an excellent business program; or (2) work full-time for one or two years, then go to the out-of-state college; or (3) earn enough to pay for her room and board out of state by getting a full-time summer job and part-time work during the school year.

Although Debbie understands why her parents cannot keep their promise, she is bitterly disappointed. She has decided that no matter how difficult it is, she will go to the out-of-state college. She doesn't want to miss all the parties, dances and fun she could attend with her boyfriend. Besides, she is worried that he will meet someone else if she is not there.

She has a summer job lined up, but she won't earn enough to pay her room and board, travel, and all the other expenses she knows she will have. Her boyfriend says, "Don't worry. You'll find a job when you get here. I'll help you out if you get in a pinch." Friends who attend the out-of-state college have told her that jobs are scarce in the area. They have also hinted that her boyfriend is somewhat of a playboy.

Discussion: In groups of 2 to 5, discuss Debbie's case. Do not try to come up with a solution. Rather try to think of some critical questions you would ask yourself if you found yourself in a similar situation.

PRACTICE EXERCISE 6.2
Critical Thinking

Creating your own scenario. In groups, with two to five in each group, write an imaginary case based on one of the topics listed below or some other topic agreed upon by the group. Exchange case studies with another group.

After carefully reading the other group's case study, write a series of questions that should be considered before making a decision about the problem. In a joint session with the two groups, discuss the results of your critical thinking about the two case studies.

Suggested Topics:

Starting one's own business

Going back to school

Aborting, allowing adoption, or keeping a child after an unwanted pregnancy

Joining a political party

Deciding whether to live on one's own

Informing on a crooked coworker

Accepting help from in-laws

Sharing a home with in-laws

Loaning a large sum of money to help a good friend start a business

Sharing an apartment with a friend

Getting a credit card

Buying a car

Choosing a career

Deciding whether or not to file for divorce

The Importance of Critical Thinking

Thinking critically means thinking sensibly and rationally, considering the whole problem rather than just thinking about one aspect of the problem, and thinking about long-range effects about possible solutions to the problem.

Consider, for example, the inflated salaries of professional athletes. It's easy to jump to the conclusion that they are overpaid. Looking at both sides of the issue, however, may lead some to conclude they are not paid enough.

Think about the issue of drug abuse. Should the millions of dollars required to wage war against drugs be used to stop the drug flow into our country at the borders or should we spend the money in rehabilitating drug users? What factors do we need to consider before we can make an informed decision?

We live in an age of hype and media blitzes. When elections roll around, candidates use advertising agencies to bombard us with radio spots and thirty-second and sixty-second television spots to capture our votes. People who think critically are swayed little by political advertising. They look for articles, talk shows, and other information that can inform them what the candidate believes, what the candidate has said under tough questioning, and how the candidate has performed in the past.

Before Christmas, mailboxes are stuffed with colorful catalogs urging us to buy, buy, buy. Critical thinkers carefully weigh price, convenience, quality—and their budget—before they make purchases. They consider whether the purchase is motivated by need or want.

Poor thinkers simply buy. In January and February, when mailboxes are stuffed with credit card statements instead of catalogs, poor thinkers are trying to figure out why they never have enough money for the things they need.

Critical Thinking Is for Everyone

There is no magic formula for becoming a critical thinker. Nor is critical thinking something mysterious and out of the reach of most people. If one takes the time to reflect and analyze, one can become a critical thinker.

In fact, some people spend a great deal of time each day thinking critically or listening to people who could qualify as critical thinkers. Many radio stations run sports talk shows that invite listeners to call in and discuss topics related to sports. Often callers find it difficult to get through to the talk show host because so many listeners want to air their comments, opinions, and gripes about the team ownership, the head coach, the players, the fans.

When our city's pro football team loses a Sunday afternoon game, fans spend the following several hours discussing the team's poor play selections, the mediocre performance of the quarterback, the sanity of the head coach, the weak pass rush, the poor defense. Some of the callers are so emotionally charged with rage that they remind one that the word *fan* is derived from *fanatic*. These people do not qualify as critical thinkers because they are too emotional. Many callers, however, are rational, objective, and sensible as they critique the game. They frequently offer creative suggestions for the improvement of the team. They are the critical thinkers.

This example illustrates that critical thinking is not something that only brilliant people can do about an intellectual subject. It is something that can be done by young and old alike, by men and women, by blue collar workers, and by lawyers and brokers in three-piece suits.

BEFORE YOU WRITE—THINK

When given an assignment to write a paragraph or an essay, what is the first thing you do? For most people, just the thought of selecting a topic is as much fun as entering a torture chamber. The typical reaction is to choose the least threatening item on a list of suggested topics and begin writing. "Let's get this over with as soon as possible!" Actually, those who take that route are taking the longest route possible to producing a good—or even mediocre—paper.

Before you pick up a pen, THINK!

If you spend the first five minutes thinking—without a pen in your hand—you will probably save yourself a lot of time later.

Then, taking pen in hand, or computer, spend another twenty minutes or so jotting down your ideas as you do some critical thinking. You may get so caught up in thinking, especially if you choose a problem or issue that is actually a part of one of your worlds, that you will lose all track of time.

The payoff, however, is the relative ease you will experience when you begin to write the paragraph or essay. We guarantee that if you take time to go through the following steps, you will not only take hours off your writing time, but you will end up with a piece of writing you are proud to claim as your work.

TEN STEPS TO CRITICAL THINKING

Here are ten steps that you will find helpful whether you are writing a paragraph, an essay, a response to a question on an essay test, a business letter, a memo, or any other kind of writing or thinking about complex issues. The order in which they are listed is not crucial to the process. Clustering, for example, can be done at several steps: during or after brainstorming, freewriting, weighing evidence, or gathering information.

Step 1. Brainstorming About an Issue or a Problem

Step 2. Clustering

Step 3. Freewriting

Step 4. Narrowing the Topic to a Critical Issue

Step 5. Writing a First-Draft Thesis Statement

Step 6. Raising Critical Questions About the Issue

Step 7. Sharing and Comparing

Step 8. Gathering More Information

Step 9. Weighing the Evidence and Making the Decision

Step 10. Rewriting the Thesis Statement

USING THE TEN STEPS TO CRITICAL THINKING

A thirty-six-year-old executive secretary for a growing corporation is thinking about going back to school. She is divorced and has three children, one a freshman in high school, the other two in middle school. Observe how she uses the ten steps to arrive at a decision and to develop a thesis for an essay.

Step 1.   Brainstorming About an Issue or a Problem
We discussed brainstorming in Chapter 1. Briefly it means putting down on paper all your thoughts and ideas about a certain subject without making any judgments about those ideas.

Step 2.   Clustering
After the prospective student brainstormed, she then put into clusters her ideas and thoughts that seem to belong together:

Goals for family:
Money for college education for three children
Good example for children to get a college degree
Need bigger house

Family Sharing:
Laundry, cleaning, cooking
Family is supportive

Finances:
Money will be tight
Company will reimburse for courses

Course of Study:
Business or marketing? Art?

Present Job:
Understanding boss
No time to study on the job
Possibility for promotion? Benefits

Personal goals:
More responsibility, better salary, more security
Show ex I can make it
Help my children

Step 3.   Freewriting

In Chapters 1 and 2 we discussed freewriting. One just starts writing about a topic suggested by the brainstorming and clustering exercises. At this point, the freewriter does not worry about spelling and grammar and is not too concerned about how the paper will look or how the words will sound.

Here is the executive secretary's freewriting:

> My personal goals in returning to school—Help my children complete high school and if they wish, go to college. I have to show them I can be independent and that hard work produces good results. I know I am smart enough and that there are opportunities for advancements with my company. Maybe my boss will recommend me for a promotion when he sees what I am willing to do to get an education. He has a lot of confidence in me. I'm making a pretty good salary, but I know I can take on more responsibility. Need a college degree. Want to do something with my art. I like to paint, to draw, and I'm good at it. Think if I talk to a counselor, I can find the right courses. Business is where the jobs are right now. I don't have a heck of a lot of time—I'm 36 already. Not going to let that bother me. If I study for 10 years, I'll be 46 when I'm finished. So what, I'll be 46 in ten years even if I don't study. I can see it now—a sign on my door: Executive Vice President. Pretty funny? Maybe, but maybe not. Marketing, advertising. Use business skills and art skills. I want to be secure financially, want my children to have financial security and a chance to go to college, to succeed at whatever they try. I want to have more responsibility in my company, to do things I enjoy. There are several people in our company in middle management who are not as intelligent as I am. I think with an education I could be much more effective—certainly easier to work for—than

they are. But they have the degree, and I do not. I'm determined to get a degree so that I can use my abilities in something I enjoy, earn more money, have more financial security, help my children.

Step 4. Narrowing the Topic or Finding a Critical Issue

What critical issues are involved in my decision?

A college degree will help me get a promotion—a more interesting job.

A college degree will help me earn more money.

I need a college degree to compete with others in the company.

If I earn more money, I can help my children more when they are in college.

Step 5. Writing a First-Draft Thesis Statement

Going back to school is a good decision for me because I can get reimbursed for courses and a degree will help me compete with others in the company for promotions so that I can get a better job with more pay and more responsibility and help my children more.

Step 6. Raising Critical Questions About the Issue

What are the pluses in returning to school for a degree?

What are the minuses?

What things in my first-draft thesis statement are interesting but perhaps irrelevant?

Pluses:
Company likes to promote from within.
I have the ability to earn a degree.
Company offers tuition reimbursement if you earn a C.
My children are supportive. They will have to help with household chores, take more responsibility.
My boss will be supportive.
My secretarial background will help with taking notes, typing reports.
I will earn more money with a degree.
Even though it will be hard on my children now, I can do much more for them later.

Minuses:
Working and going to college will be difficult.
Can't study on the job. Too busy.

Younger children might feel neglected. Might have problems.
I'll be older than most students.
Going part-time will take several years.
Going to school will be expensive.

Interesting but irrelevant to the issue:
The fact that the company will reimburse me for money spent on college is important to me, but not relevant to the ultimate reasons I want to return to school.

More questions:
Why is this an issue?
How will it affect me?
How will it affect others?
What are the facts and what are the opinions?
What are the biases and prejudices about those issues?
Can I deal with those biases and prejudices?

As a divorced mother, I have responsibilities to my children. Am I selfish in thinking about improving myself through education?

How will my return to school affect my children? The two younger boys might get into trouble. How can I be at work, at school, and at home all at the same time? We'll have to work out our plans as a family.

Is it a fact that I will be promoted if I get a degree? Will men with similar training and education be chosen over me when promotions are available? I had better talk this over with my boss. Maybe he can work out a career plan with me if he knows what my goals are. If I don't end up with a better job and more money, is it worth all the time and effort to earn a degree?

Will my age cause me to be without friends on campus? Will younger students feel uncomfortable around me?

Step 7. Sharing and Comparing
At this point, the secretary discussed the issue with her boss and the company's personnel department, with her children, and with close friends and confidantes.

In discussing with her children her desire to get a college degree, she found them excited and supportive. Together they worked out a plan for sharing household responsibilities. Her boss was pleased that she wanted to stay with the company and assured her that he would recommend her for advancement at the appropriate time. He even offered to request that she be given some released time to complete her degree if necessary. The personnel department gave her published information about the company's policy for reimbursing education expenses. Some of her friends were encouraging, but some told her it would be too hard and take too much time.

Step 8. Gathering More Information

While the executive secretary felt that she had done sufficient questioning and thinking to make her decision, she decided to do some additional research on the subject. With the help of a librarian, she discovered some current magazine and newspaper articles about the relationship between earning potential and education. She also made an appointment with a college counselor, who pointed out curriculum choices and offered her enthusiastic support.

In this step, our executive secretary learned that gathering more information through reading and seeking expert opinion can be invaluable in the decision making process.

Step 9. Weighing the Evidence and Making the Decision

By this time, the secretary in our scenario was ready to make one of three decisions: (1) go back to school immediately; (2) go back to school when the children are a little older; (3) forget about earning a college degree.

As you probably have guessed, she decided to go back to school immediately and enrolled in the evening program of a local community college.

Step 10. Rewriting the Thesis Statement

One of the requirements of admission to the evening program was an essay stating one's reasons for seeking a degree. This is our executive secretary's revised thesis statement:

> I am going to earn a college degree because it will help me advance to a more responsible position in my company, give me the opportunity to develop my talents, and give me the potential to earn enough money to help my children.

PRACTICE EXERCISE 6.3
Doing Your Own Critical Thinking

You have walked through the various steps of critical thinking. Now it's time to do some critical thinking of your own. Think about some problem you or someone close to you may be having at home, at school, or at work.

To get you started, here are some problems and issues you may want to consider (your instructor may suggest other topics):

Personal problems:
Changing majors
Changing jobs
Getting married
Breaking off a relationship
Placing an elderly grandparent or parent in a nursing home
Buying a car
Joining the military service
Moving to another part of the country

Issues:
Should the federal government's war against drug abuse be directed against suppliers or users?
Gun control
Providing day care for the children of working parents: whose responsibility?
Should teachers be required to take competency tests?
Should the Nazi party be allowed to function in the United States?
In police department promotions, should filling minority quotas have priority over placement on qualifying examinations?
Should religious organizations be required to pay taxes?
Lack of affordable housing for the poor
Care for the mentally ill

DIRECTIONS: Go through the steps of critical thinking and try to resolve a problem or take a stand on a controversial issue. Start each step of the process on a separate sheet of paper with one of the following labels:

Step 1.   Brainstorming About an Issue or a Problem

Step 2.   Clustering

Step 3.   Freewriting

Step 4.   Narrowing the Topic to a Critical Issue

Step 5.   Writing a First-Draft Thesis Statement

Step 6. Raising Critical Questions About the Issue

Step 7. Sharing and Comparing

Step 8. Gathering More Information

Step 9. Weighing the Evidence and Making the Decision

Step 10. Rewriting the Thesis Statement

Chapter 7

Thinking Creatively

The CBS program *Sunday Morning* is an example of television at its very best. Hosted by Charles Kuralt, the program consistently is of high quality. Kuralt and his staff often examine the lives of the rich and famous; at other times, however, they call our attention to little known and unknown people whose creativity and imagination improve the quality of life of those around them.

One Sunday, *Sunday Morning* highlighted the paintings of two black folk artists—Clementine Hunter and Nellie May Rowe—whose works were being exhibited that week at the University of Miami in Oxford, Ohio.

Hunter and Rowe never knew one another, but their lives have striking similarities. Both grew up in extreme poverty in the South. Neither of them had studied art at a college or art institute. The most striking similarity, however, is that both Hunter and Rowe began to paint when they were in their sixties. Nellie Rowe died in the early 1980s at the age of eighty-two. At the time of the CBS program, Clementine Hunter was more than one hundred years old and still painting.

An art critic on the show that morning pointed out that both artists had experiences that colored their imaginations. He said that when Hunter and Rowe were children, they did not have the toys and dolls of childhood. So their painting in later life is like a second childhood in the best sense of that term. According to the art critic, folk artists are rarely young. In the world of folk art, old age seems almost to be a necessity for those who want to produce high quality works like those of Hunter and Rowe.

Before Clementine Hunter began to paint, she worked as a maid in an artists' colony. One day she told an artist that she thought she could produce paintings that would be just as good as those she had seen. So the artist gave her a brush, an old window shade, a can of paint, and a can of turpentine and told her to start painting. The world of art would have been diminished if she had not had the courage to try.

We know Hunter and Rowe only by their folk art paintings. However, we would be willing to bet that both of them are right-brain rather than left-brain people. We say that because they are such creative, imaginative people, as their folk art reveals.

If we are not as creative or imaginative as we would like to be, perhaps it is because the left brain rather than the right brain is dominant in us. But you won't know if you don't experiment to find out. Also, let's see if there are some things we can do to make us more creative, imaginative people.

RIGHT-BRAIN OR LEFT-BRAIN? WHICH ARE YOU?

When we talk about the world in which we live, we use the term "hemisphere," which means half of a ball-shaped object called a sphere. The earth is divided into a northern hemisphere and a southern hemisphere by an imaginary line we call the equator. We use another imaginary line, a meridian, to divide the earth into eastern and western hemispheres.

Think of your brain as a somewhat round object with two hemispheres, the right brain and the left brain. Scientists once thought that the right and left hemispheres of the brain were similar and functioned in the same ways. Recent research on the brain, however, has convinced many that the two hemispheres are not alike in their functions.

The right brain controls the left side of our body; the left brain controls the right side. One side, usually the left brain, is dominant in most people. While all of us use both our right brain and our left brain, most of us are left-brain people, that is, we function mainly out of the left hemisphere of the brain.

Characteristics of Left-Brain People

Left-brain people are usually reflective, analytical, logical, and verbal people. They are interested in order, reason, schedules, time frames, results. In most successful corporations and institutions, it appears that left-brain people are in charge.

Characteristics of Right-Brain People

Right-brain people are creative and imaginative. They are more visual than verbal. Most artists, musicians, and playwrights are right-brain, but mathematicians, journalists, and athletes can be right-brain as well.

Right-brain persons frequently ask "why" questions and "what if" questions: "Why do we have to do it this way?" "What if we did it another way?" "What if we tried this?"

Most of us neglect the right brain, and that is to our disadvantage. Schools and companies tend to encourage left-brain development and in many ways discourage and even frown on right-brain activity. Perhaps that is because as a society we seem to place too much emphasis on order, often at the expense of creative and imaginative thinking and learning.

An artist friend whose five-year-old son shows remarkable potential in painting is often urged to send him to art school. She hesitates to do that, she says, because she is afraid that left-brain teachers will cause him to lose his magnificent spontaneity and uniqueness.

The Care and Nurture of Your Right Brain

Here are some things you can do to foster right-brain activity:

1. Try drawing cartoons of things that happened to you during the past day.
2. Doodle. Get a sheet of paper and just doodle for five or ten minutes.
3. Fantasize. Try to write a dialogue between people from two different worlds. Examples: a baseball player and a scientist; a wrestler and a librarian; a pilot and a first-grade teacher; a jazz musician and a writer; a deep sea diver and a chef.
4. Keep a dream journal next to your bed. When you awake from a dream, jot the dream down and try to analyze what your right brain may be trying to say to you.
5. Try free association. Think of a topic and then write down all the words you can associate with that topic. In her book *The Right-Brain Experience*, Marilee Zdenek relates that she asked comedian Steve Allen whether he has ever consciously used free association to trigger right hemisphere activity. He explained how he used this technique.

ALLEN: Yeah, especially when I was new in the joke business. I would get a yellow legal pad and write down all the words that occurred to me about the slice of society I was dealing with. If it was a cowboy sketch, I would write, "bunkhouse, OK Coral, sagebrush, ornery sidewinder, gunfight, sheriff, posse." Whatever would occur to me. Something about just making a list of about forty-two such words and phrases would suddenly get the wheels clicking in the part of my brain that apparently has some gift for the making of jokes.

Most of my comedy writing comes about very quickly in response to some little silly thought. In fact, I wrote a comedy sketch just before I came into the building about forty minutes ago. I was listening to the radio and somebody used the phrase "star spangled celebration." So for some reason or other my attention centered on the word spangled. Ever since I was a child, words have sounded different to me than I think they do to most people. Certain of us in the joke business are either addicted or gifted, as the case may be, with that way of looking at words. Groucho Marx did that—whatever you said, he would take the word and twist it around and make some silly answer to it. I do that. Anyway, it occurred to me that if something is spangled there must be a verb "to spangle," and of course there is. And I wrote this silly interview sketch about a member of the Spanglers Union: If you want some star spangled on your banner or anywhere, on the wall or the ceiling—whatever—you have to call a professional spangler. He will come in and spangle all these . . . And then it went from there to: The reporter says, "Well now, if you're a stickler for accuracy . . ." And he says, "No, for that you call the Sticklers Union, and they will come in and stickle for you." It's just playing a silly way with these verbs. And the reporter says, "Well, I noticed that you're a good family man. I saw you dandling your child . . ." And he says, "For dandling, it's a whole other thing."

6. Ask a series of what if questions, such as

What if no one ever died?

What if men had babies?

What if paper had never been invented?

What if there were no laws?

What if there were no sun?

What if there were no laughter?

What if people showed no signs of aging?

What if we had no telephones?

7. Write down a series of questions. Then write the answers with your opposite hand, the hand you do not ordinarily use for writing.
8. Listen to your favorite record or disk. Imagine colors accompanying the sound. What color is the male voice, the trumpet, the drums?
9. Turn off the sound on the television and interpret the body language of the people on the program.

10. Compose a short song. If you know how to write the notes, fine, but it's not necessary.

Some Suggestions from a Pro

Dr. Joseph Clovesko, a professor of biology at Cuyahoga Community College, has for many years done extensive research on the two hemispheres of the brain. He conducts workshops for teachers, parents, and business executives to help them realize their full potential by developing both right-brain and left-brain power.

Here are some of his suggestions for people who are more *left hemispheric* and are trying to practice using the right side of the brain:

1. Learn to have fun without questioning what it leads to or if it will last.
2. Don't analyze everyone's behavior or motives. (If someone flirts with you, just flirt back.)
3. Relax more. Learn to daydream and meditate. Learn to float. Try to develop more visual pictures and scenes. Drift. Try it at least once a day for ten minutes or so.
4. Try to break your routine. Don't do things the same each day. Walk, shop, drive in different areas; eat at different restaurants. Try new ways of doing things, such as eating with chopsticks or writing with your left hand.
5. Try expressing what you wish to convey by drawing pictures rather than by writing. In class, after taking notes make visual notes on the opposite page as a summary study guide.
6. Take up painting, guitar, or another creative activity.
7. Keep a dream diary or a fantasy diary.
8. Try following your intuition, your hunches and feelings. Respond to your first impressions at times, such as when answering test questions or buying a new sweater.
9. Try to develop your ability to tell jokes and stories, especially those that have twists to them.
10. Try singing your notes when studying.
11. Play pantomime games.
12. Become involved in creative organizations such as a local theater group.

Here are some of Dr. Joseph Clovesko's suggestions for people who are more *right hemispheric* and are trying to work the left side of the brain.

1. When you have a strong feeling, try making a list of how you feel. Use words to express those feelings and their sequence.
2. Don't allow things to pile up on you. Become more systematic in approaching your problems. Don't just dive into them; try to develop a plan.
3. Try planning your day's activities, including things you don't particularly like to do as well as the enjoyable activities.
4. Try new activities, especially those involving new skills which require you to follow directions: gardening, fixing a bike, knitting. Make sure some of these activities include a waiting period before completing the project or evaluating its success.
5. Make a point to be on time. Leave earlier, show up at scheduled meetings, parties, and other appointments.
6. When asked questions or given criticism, try not to take it personally.
7. Don't jump to conclusions easily. Don't make snap judgments; find out more about a situation or individuals before making a judgment.
8. Learn some new games that have rules and guidelines which must be learned and followed. This kind of game (bridge, for example) requires that you train yourself to follow set procedures rather than "hunch" your way through or just let things happen.
9. Join a group sport team (volleyball, basketball, softball) which requires that you follow some managerial direction.
10. Develop new acquaintances and new skills. Learn more about investing money or accounting. If you share a check book, try managing it for a while. Attend seminars.
11. Try writing a story or a poem in which you describe something as accurately as possible. Write out your favorite meals as recipes.
12. Make out lists: shopping lists, things to be done for the day, and so forth.

USING YOUR RIGHT BRAIN TO BECOME A BETTER WRITER

Your right brain helps you to *see* things in new ways. Developing your right brain power will unlock your creativity, give you confidence to explore your worlds, and give you courage to try new ways of expressing your experiences in your worlds.

It doesn't matter whether you are a left-brain or a right-brain person. What does matter is that you try to develop the full potential of both hemispheres of your brain.

Research shows that it is possible to improve both right-brain and left-brain functions through practice. Just as you can develop your muscle power through physical exercise such as walking, jogging, and lifting weights, so you can improve your brain power by consciously exercising both sides of your brain. Try it! You'll never know what you are capable of achieving unless you stretch to the limit.

Do not be threatened and intimidated by what others have written. At age sixty Clementine Hunter was not intimidated by the art of others. She thought to herself, I can do just as well, if not better. So she picked up her paint brush and colored her experiences with the brush of imagination.

Pick up your pen and paper and start to write. Write about what you have experienced in your worlds. Be courageous, imaginative, and creative. Go for it. You have nothing to lose.

Part II

Discovering the
Power of Writing

Chapter 8

Using a Journal to Record Your Observations

Undoubtedly you have met people with phenomenal memories. Go to a class reunion and invariably you will find a classmate who can remember to the smallest detail some incident that happened many years earlier. At a family reunion, you will find a relative who, without being asked, will recall some event in the family history that happened almost a half century ago.

Most of us are not like that. We are not blessed with photographic memories. We can recall things that have happened, but the more we distance ourselves from an event, the more the details fade. We cannot recall all the persons who were there. We forget the date. We cannot remember who said what and to whom.

To be sure, there are exceptions. Ask most people what they were doing when the news came that the space shuttle *Challenger* exploded on January 28, 1986, killing all seven astronauts. They will tell you because the day was so significant. Ask them what they were doing on January 28, 1985, and they probably will not be able to tell you—unless, they kept a diary or a journal.

THE IMPORTANCE OF KEEPING A JOURNAL

In this chapter, we stress the importance of keeping a journal. A journal can mean many things to many people. For some, a journal is an old-fashioned diary. We don't think it is for reasons that we will soon explain. For other people, a journal can be a daybook, or scrapbook, a bank for ideas, or a combination of all of these. We don't care what you call it as long as you are faithful to writing in it every day. Let's consider these points in greater detail.

A Journal Is Not a Diary.   A diary is a personal record of your thoughts and feelings about close relationships with other people. Some young people keep diaries that record their moods and attitudes and their feelings about parents, brothers and sisters, teachers, boyfriends and girlfriends, school, classmates, neighbors, pets, and so on. It's for their eyes only; that's why they keep their diaries hidden. Anyone reading a diary without permission is the equivalent of a "peeping Tom."

The Journal Is Concerned with the Many Worlds of the Writer.   Unlike the diary, the journal does not concern itself with close personal relationships. While the diary revolves around the world of self, the journal is concerned with many more worlds and how they impact the writer.

In a journal, the writer records observations about what's happening in the world of politics, fashion, sports, entertainment, and religion. The journal writer records things that he or she has read or seen. Suppose, for example, the journal writer reads a story in the morning newspaper about an elderly woman who froze to death after the utility company had turned off the heat because she did not pay her bill. That article could serve as a starting point for the writer's observation on how American society treats its elderly. Or the sports pages may have a story about a fight that involved two college basketball teams. That article could serve as a takeoff point for some comments about violence in sports, competition, and the desire to win at all costs.

A Journal Is a Daybook.   It's a companion that you keep close to you so that you can record what you are thinking about. Suppose you have to write a term paper. Use the daybook to start jotting down your thoughts and ideas about the topic.

Or let's say that you are on a bus some morning. An elderly woman boards the bus with her small grandchild. No one in the bus offers her a seat. In fact, most people look away and pretend that the woman and child are not there. Record that incident, because some time you might want to use it as the subject of an essay.

A Journal Is a Scrapbook.   When you have a journal, you can clip articles from newspapers, magazines, and other publications, and paste them in your journal along with your comments.

Suppose you have gone to a movie or a play that you thought was great entertainment. The next morning you read in your newspaper a rather negative review of the event. The event did not impress the reviewer. In fact, he suggests that people stay home and save their money. You strongly disagree. What can you do?

First, resist the urge to call the critic to heap verbal abuse upon him for his negative reporting. Such highly emotional conversations usually go nowhere. Remember that the critic is a professional who has been educated for his job. For every movie you have seen, he has probably seen at least ten or fifteen. That does not mean that he's right about the movie and you are wrong. It only means that the critic probably has some basis for his opinion. He's not just blowing smoke.

A better action would be to start writing in your journal. List all of the critic's points, and try to refute them, one by one. For every point he makes, try to have a counterpoint. At the end of this exercise, one of two things will happen. You will be more firmly convinced of the validity of your position, or you may come to the conclusion that perhaps the critic's position is stronger than yours.

Wait for a day and then call or write to the critic to express your opinion. Critics like to receive calls and letters even from people who disagree with them, especially when they give rational rather than emotional arguments for their positions.

A Journal Is a Bank for Your Ideas.   Most people who think about the future try to build up a savings account. Every payday they pay themselves first by depositing some money, however small, into their savings account. Gradually that account grows and earns interest. They dip into their savings only when absolutely necessary or when they find a way to get a better return on their money. People like that are indeed wise.

Think of your journal in somewhat the same way. It's a place where you can store, not money, but ideas. When you have a good idea that you can't use in your writing at the time, put it in that bank. Just as you look over your bank statements periodically, page through your journal from time to time to review your ideas. One day, you will find a way to use those ideas and quotes in an essay. Just as you withdraw bank savings when you need money, so you can withdraw ideas and concepts from your journal when you need them.

A Journal Is a Place to Fail.   That's not an original idea. It's something that writer Dorothy Lambert said. We like it. She means that the journal is a place where students can experiment with words and ideas without fear of getting a low grade or inviting ridicule and derision. We don't like the word *failure.* In fact, we believe, along with psychologist Arthur Combs, that we need a word that means "I tried something and it didn't work." Maybe the word *journal* will do until a better word comes along.

SOME TIPS FOR JOURNAL WRITERS

There are no rules for journal writing. Journal writing is a discipline, and it is also a matter of using your common sense. Here are some tips that have helped us. Maybe they can help you.

1. Write in a notebook that has a spiral binder. When you write in a loose-leaf notebook, there's always the danger that your pages will go flying in case you drop it.
2. Use ink or ball point instead of a pencil.
3. Write only on one side of the paper.
4. Write neatly and use every other line. This will make it easier for you to read your journal and to pen in any afterthoughts you might have about what you wrote.
5. Try to have a set time each day for journal writing. We find the morning is the best time for us to do journal writing. That's because we are morning persons. We don't function well late at night. Night persons should do journal writing late at night. There's no right time or wrong time for journal writing. Whatever is best for you is the right time.
6. Avoid burnout. Don't try to write too much in your journal. It's better to write just one page a day for thirty days than to write thirty pages the first day. If you take that route, you will probably burn out in a few days and will give up journal writing because it's too tedious.

Keep it brief, keep it simple, and keep it interesting. That's a good formula for good journal writing.

Some Journal Exercises

These exercises are designed to help you sharpen your powers of observation and develop the habit of writing in your journal every day. Think about the brainstorming exercise you did about the many worlds that make up your universe. Watch for anything that relates to those worlds, and record your observations in your journal.

First Day. This is an exercise in narration. In your journal write down something that is happening. Maybe you went to a baseball game or a rock concert. Or maybe your car or bus was involved in an accident on the way to college. Simply tell what happened.

Second Day. In this exercise, describe some person or some scene that has impressed you—your sister or brother baking a birthday cake, your father leaving the house each morning for work, an elderly person, a street person, a sunrise or sunset.

Third Day. Try to define something from one of those worlds such as a new word that you discover in a book. Some examples of words you could record and define are *parenting, politicking, detente, boycott, apartheid, assertiveness, designated hitter, infield fly rule.*

Fourth Day. Give examples of people who are outstanding in one of your worlds: entertainment, school, politics, fashion, sports, comedy, racing, etc. After each name, write a few sentences explaining why you picked that person.

Fifth Day. On a page in your diary, write about some process. The following will give you some ideas: How to get a job. How to prepare for a job interview. How to raise a child. How to study for a test. How to buy a car. How to sell something. How to change a tire. How to become a wise shopper. How bees make honey. How a flower is pollinated. How a pearl is formed. How to get along with a difficult person.

Sixth Day. On this day try to classify persons, events, or things or put them into various categories. You could, for example, classify TV sitcoms as excellent, mediocre, or poor. You could classify house plants. You could classify people on a bus according to their sex, weight, age, attitude, behavior, and so on.

Seventh Day. On this day select one or your worlds and note the similarities and differences you find in people, things, events. Compare or contrast two TV programs, two entertainers, two leaders, two teachers, two animals, two announcers (radio or television), two stores, two shopping malls, and so on.

Eighth Day. Take a look at causes and effects. You might want to analyze the causes or the effects of one or more of the following: good or poor self image, academic success or failure, voter enthusiasm or voter apathy, successful or failed marriages, addiction, rising or falling church attendance.

Ninth Day. As you look at your many worlds, you will soon discover that they are imperfect worlds. We human beings have the unfortunate ability to foul things up. We pollute our rivers, lakes, and streams. We destroy wildlife. We let greed determine how we behave in business, politics, and sports. All too often leaders in government, business, labor, religion, and schools operate their institutions in self-serving ways.

Take a look at what is happening in one of your worlds. List some of the issues that need to be addressed. Write down what you would do to change things. The exercise will help you later when you write an essay that persuades others that your position is valid.

Chapter 9

The Topic Sentence
and the Paragraph

In the exercises of the last seven chapters you have been writing sentences: statements that have a subject and a verb and express a complete thought. Some examples of sentences are the following:

1. There is a tradition that every March 19th, the swallows come back to the Mission of San Juan Capistrano.
2. The season of autumn is spectacular in the New England states.
3. Jane and Al have returned to San Diego after visiting their son Brett in Japan.
4. The game of golf can be frustrating.

Each of those sentences has a subject and a verb, and each expresses a complete thought.

PARAGRAPHS

A paragraph is a group of unified sentences that expresses ideas about a specific topic. Perhaps the easiest way to illustrate the definition is to imagine that someone is writing a message on the back of a postcard.

Scenario 1. Let's say that Joe has just arrived in the San Francisco airport. He's going to college there, and this is his first experience away from home. He knows that his parents will be worried about him so before he deplanes, he decides to write them a note.

> Hi! Arrived here safely a few minutes ago. The flight from Chicago was smooth all the way. No problems. The guy next to me is going to the University of San Francisco, too. We talked all the way. Will write a longer letter after I get settled in the dorm.

What's the *main idea* that Joe is expressing? It's that he arrived safely and that everything was fine on the trip.

Scenario 2.   Mary is expecting Tom, her friend, to stop by her apartment at 6:30 P.M. They are going to a rock concert at the Coliseum. At 6:00 P.M. Mary gets a frantic call from her mother, who tells her that the paramedics are taking her father to the emergency room at the Shoreland Hospital because he's been complaining of chest pains. Mary knows that Tom is on the way but she decides not to wait for him. She leaves this note on her apartment door.

> Tom. Mother just called. My dad is being taken to the emergency room of Shoreland Hospital. Chest pains. Meet me there. Mary.

What's the *main idea* that Mary is expressing in that hastily written paragraph? It's that there has been a sudden and dramatic change of plans. Certainly the paragraph can be improved, but under the circumstances Mary's paragraph is excellent.

PARAGRAPH BUILDING

The Main Idea

Although the two paragraphs above were written in a hurry, nevertheless they demonstrate a very important point about paragraphs, namely, that paragraphs must express a main point or idea. A paragraph that does not do that will leave a reader confused.

When you write your *main idea* in a sentence, that sentence is called the *topic sentence.* Usually it is the first sentence of the paragraph, but not always. Sometimes it can be the last sentence of the paragraph, and occasionally, a writer will put the topic sentence in the middle of the paragraph.

Supporting the Topic Sentence: After you express your main idea in a topic sentence, you must support that main idea with a series of unifying sentences.

Notice that in the following examples writers construct paragraphs starting with the main idea.

Example: Tom is delighted that his favorite baseball team got off to a fast start as the season began, so he uses that idea as his topic sentence:

> If the Indians continue to play as they have in the first six games, the fans are going to enjoy a fine season of baseball. (Topic Sentence)

That's a good topic sentence, but Tom needs to support that topic sentence. So he writes the following sentences:

> They have already won five games. (Supporting Sentence)

> Their pitchers have been excellent. (Supporting Sentence)

> Their hitting has been sensational. (Supporting Sentence)

> Their defense has been outstanding. (Supporting Sentence)

The Finished Paragraph. When Tom puts his topic sentence and his supporting sentences together, the results are a finished paragraph. (In the examples that follow, the topic sentence is underlined.)

> If the Indians continue to play as they have in the first six games, their fans are going to enjoy a terrific season. Already the team has won five games. The pitchers have been excellent. The hitting has been sensational, and the defense has been outstanding.

Varying the Position of the Topic Sentence

While the topic sentence is usually the first sentence of the paragraph, sometimes it is more effective when it is the last sentence. In the following example, Tom places it last:

> What's happening to the Indians this year? They are off to a fine start, having won five of their first six games. Their pitchers have been excellent, and their hitters have really been scoring a lot of runs. Moreover, their defense has been flawless. If they continue to play as they have in the first six games, their fans are going to enjoy a terrific season.

Occasionally a writer will place the topic sentence in the middle of the paragraph, as it is in the following paragraph.

> The locker room was like a morgue. No one said a word. A couple of players fought back tears. Some cried openly. The faces of a few reflected bitterness and anger. Each player had his own reaction to the defeat. Each one was playing the game again. Each one was assessing his own part in the unexpected defeat. Each one was wondering what he could say or do to soften the sting of defeat.

Implying the Topic Sentence.   Sometimes the topic sentence of a paragraph can be *implied*, that is, it is not written at all. The writer provides enough clues so that the reader gets the mood, the action, the climate, the impression that the writer is trying to create. When you are just beginning your writing career, it is best that you write out a topic sentence for your paragraphs. Once you have mastered that, then you can start writing paragraphs in which the topic sentence is implied.

PRACTICE EXERCISE 9.1
Writing Supporting Sentences

DIRECTIONS: The following are suggestions for topic sentences. Add to the topic sentence three or four sentences that will support the main idea.

1. *Topic Sentence:* The Fourth of July celebration (or some other holiday) was the best in recent memory.

First Supporting Sentence (Tell something that made it great.)

_____

_____

Second Supporting Sentence (Tell something else that made it great.)

_____

_____

Third Supporting Sentence (Write something else that made it memorable.)

_____

_____

Fourth Supporting Sentence (If necessary.)

_____

_____

2. *Topic Sentence:* Buying the right used car is a four-step process.
(*Note:* You may want to substitute *home* or *VCR* or *personal computer* for car. You may also want to write that it's a three-step process.)

First Supporting Sentence (State the first step in the process.)

_____

_____

Second Supporting Sentence (State the second step in the process.)

_____

_____

Third Supporting Sentence (State the third step in the process.)

_____

_____

Fourth Supporting Sentence (State the fourth step in the process.)

_____

_____

3. *Topic Sentence:* At rock concerts, one can observe three different kinds of fans.

First Supporting Sentence (Classify the first kind of fan.)

_____

_____

Second Supporting Sentence (Classify the second kind of fan.)

_____

_____

Third Supporting Sentence (Classify the third kind of fan.)

_____

_____

4. *Topic Sentence:* Voter (or student) apathy has three (or four) basic causes.

First Supporting Sentence (State what the first cause is.)

_____

_____

Second Supporting Sentence (State what the second cause is.)

_____

_____

Third Supporting Sentence (State what the third cause is.)

_____

_____

Fourth Supporting Sentence (If there is one.)

_____

_____

5. *Topic Sentence:* It was my experience that X City (or neighborhood) was a better place to live than Y City (or neighborhood).

First Supporting Sentence (Give a reason why it was better.)

_____

_____

Second Supporting Sentence (Give a second reason.)

_____

_____

Third Supporting Sentence (Give a third reason.)

_____

_____

6. *Topic Sentence:* A true friend can be defined in many different ways.

First Supporting Sentence (Give one definition of a friend.)

_____

_____

Second Supporting Sentence (Give another definition.)

_____

_____

Third Supporting Sentence (Give a third definition.)

_____

_____

7. *Topic Sentence:* The professor's office looked a mess.

First Supporting Sentence (Describe something that was out of place.)

_____

_____

Second Supporting Sentence (Describe something else that suggests disorder.)

_____

_____

Third Supporting Sentence (Describe something else that suggests chaos.)

_____

_____

8. *Topic Sentence:* I had every intention of studying for the exam, but unusual circumstances prevented my doing so.

First Supporting Sentence (Tell what happened first.)

_____

_____

Second Supporting Sentence (Tell what happened next.)

_____

_____

Third Supporting Sentence (Tell what happened after that.)

_____

_____

9. *Topic Sentence:* The National League should adopt the designated hitter rule for its major league baseball teams.

First Supporting Sentence (State one compelling argument.)

_____

_____

Second Supporting Sentence (Give a second argument.)

_____

_____

Third Supporting Sentence (Write a third argument for the rule change.)

_____

_____

Fourth Supporting Sentence (If necessary.)

_____

_____

SUMMARY

In our discussion thus far, we have stressed the following points in writing paragraphs:

1. A paragraph is made up of a group of unified sentences.
2. Every paragraph must have a single main idea that gives the paragraph its unity.
3. That single main idea should be expressed in a sentence called the topic sentence.
4. The topic sentence is usually the first sentence of the paragraph, but sometimes it is placed last or even in the middle of the paragraph.
5. The single main idea in the topic sentence must be developed by sentences that support the main idea.

PRACTICE EXERCISE 9.2
Placing the Topic Sentence at the Beginning of the Paragraph

DIRECTIONS: Read the following paragraph, and then answer the questions that follow.

A small fire in the lobby of the hotel caused panic among the clerks and the guests. The assistant manager was out of the hotel, so no one was in charge. The reservation clerk forgot the telephone number of the fire department. The bellhops could not find the fire extinguisher. A crystal chandelier graced the lobby. Guests were in panic. Some were yelling, "Fire!" A few were running for the phone banks. Some ran out the front door. Confusion reigned until a maid calmly poured a bucket of water over the smoking wastebasket.

1. What is gained by placing the topic sentence at the beginning of the paragraph?

_____

_____

2. What are the key words in the topic sentence?

_____

_____

3. Do all the other sentences in the paragraph support the topic sentence? Explain briefly how each sentence does or does not support the topic sentence.

_____

_____

_____

_____

_____

PRACTICE EXERCISE 9.3
The Topic Sentence

DIRECTIONS: Read the paragraph and answer the questions that follow.

On an afternoon in June, I had all kinds of reasons for not attending outdoor commencement exercises at the college where I teach. One reason was that I had attended exercises the year before, so I had already fulfilled my faculty commitment to attend exercises every other year. Another was that it was a hot and humid day. My dermatologist (who had removed three skin cancers from my face over the past six years) had advised me not to be in the sun for more than a half-hour at a time. I knew that it would take at least two hours for four hundred graduates to receive their degrees. Furthermore, dark ominous clouds began forming in the western sky and there was an occasional rumbling of thunder. Would there be a violent summer storm or possibly a tornado? The atmospheric conditions were all there, giving me yet another reason for not attending graduation exercises that Sunday afternoon.

1. Underline the topic sentence.

2. Why did the author place the topic sentence there?

_____

_____

_____

_____

3. Explain in one sentence how all the other sentences support the topic sentence.

_____

_____

_____

_____

PRACTICE EXERCISE 9.4
Planning Your Own Paragraph

DIRECTIONS: In the blanks below write a plan for your own paragraph.

Topic sentence _____

_____

_____

First supporting sentence _____

_____

_____

Second supporting sentence _____

_____

_____

Third supporting sentence _____

_____

_____

Fourth supporting sentence _____

_____

_____

PRACTICE EXERCISE 9.5
Using Your Plan to Write a Paragraph

DIRECTIONS: Using the plan you constructed, write a paragraph.

_____

_____

_____

_____

_____

_____

_____

_____

_____

_____

_____

_____

_____

_____

PRACTICE EXERCISE 9.6
Placing the Topic Sentence at the End of the Paragraph

DIRECTIONS: Read the following paragraph and answer the questions that follow.

There was an air of anticipation in the classroom. Some students stood together in small groups talking quietly. Other students sat at their desks. Some slept. Some looked through their notes and textbooks. Suddenly Professor Francis X. Cook entered the classroom. Everyone became quiet. *The dreaded statistics test was about to begin.*

1. Is the paragraph more effective because the topic sentence has been placed last? Explain.

_____

_____

_____

_____

2. What are the key words in the topic sentence?

_____

_____

_____

3. Do all the other sentences in the paragraph support the topic sentence? Explain briefly.

_____

_____

_____

_____

PRACTICE EXERCISE 9.7
Planning a Paragraph with the Topic
Sentence at the End of a Paragraph

DIRECTIONS: In the blanks that follow, plan a paragraph of your own, placing the topic sentence last.

First supporting sentence _____

_____

_____

Second supporting sentence _____

_____

_____

Third supporting sentence _____

_____

Fourth supporting sentence _____

_____

Topic sentence _____

_____

_____

_____

What are the key words in your topic sentence? _____

_____

_____

PRACTICE EXERCISE 9.8
Using Your Plan to Write a Paragraph

DIRECTIONS: Write a paragraph that follows the plan you devised in the previous exercise.

_____

_____

_____

_____

_____

_____

_____

_____

_____

_____

_____

_____

_____

_____

_____

PRACTICE EXERCISE 9.9
Placing the Topic Sentence in the Middle of a Paragraph

DIRECTIONS: Read the following paragraph, and then answer the questions that come after it.

> The young parents looked embarrassed. The waitress was somewhat amused. The other diners were annoyed. *The young child continued to scream at the top of his lungs.* It was his typical attention getter. All eyes were upon him. He was center stage and loving every minute of his performance.

1. Is anything gained by placing the topic sentence in the middle of the paragraph?

_____

_____

2. What are the key words in the topic sentence?

_____

_____

_____

3. Do all the other sentences in the paragraph support the topic sentence? Briefly explain.

_____

_____

_____

_____

_____

_____

PRACTICE EXERCISE 9.10
Planning a Paragraph with the Topic
Sentence in the Middle of the Paragraph

DIRECTIONS: In the blanks that follow, plan a paragraph of your own, placing the topic sentence in the middle.

First supporting sentence _____

_____

_____

Second supporting sentence _____

_____

_____

Topic sentence _____

_____

_____

_____

Third supporting sentence _____

_____

_____

Fourth supporting sentence _____

_____

Fifth supporting sentence _____

_____

PRACTICE EXERCISE 9.11
Using Your Plan to Write a Paragraph

DIRECTIONS: Write a paragraph that follows the plan you devised in the previous exercise.

_____

_____

_____

_____

_____

_____

_____

_____

_____

_____

_____

_____

_____

_____

_____

_____

PRACTICE EXERCISE 9.12
Additional Practice in Building Paragraphs

DIRECTIONS: Write at least three sentences to support each suggested topic sentence. In case you wish to write more than three sentences, space is provided.

1. Topic Sentence: The horses were in the starting gate.

First supporting sentence _____

_____

Second supporting sentence _____

_____

Third supporting sentence _____

_____

Fourth supporting sentence _____

_____

2. Topic Sentence: The students were anxiously awaiting their grades.

First supporting sentence _____

_____

Second supporting sentence _____

_____

Third supporting sentence _____

_____

Fourth supporting sentence _____

_____

3. Topic Sentence: The freeway traffic was backed up for five miles.

First supporting sentence _____

_____

Second supporting sentence _____

_____

Third supporting sentence _____

_____

Fourth supporting sentence _____

_____

4. Topic Sentence: The strikers at the steel plant were frustrated, cold, and angry.

First supporting sentence (Tell why they were frustrated.)

_____

_____

Second supporting sentence (Describe the conditions that made them cold.)

_____

_____

Third supporting sentence (Tell why they were angry.)

_____

_____

5. Topic Sentence: The twins were not identical because they were of different sexes, different sizes, and different personalities.

First supporting sentence (sex) _____

_____

_____

Second supporting sentence (size) _____

_____

_____

Third supporting sentence (personality) _____

_____

_____

6. Topic Sentence: Terry, Sally and Holly were extremely unhappy with their semester grades in English composition.

First supporting sentence _____

_____

_____

Second supporting sentence _____

_____

_____

Third supporting sentence _____

_____

_____

7. Topic Sentence: Traveling by plane at Thanksgiving can be a real adventure.

First supporting sentence _____

_____

Second supporting sentence _____

_____

Third supporting sentence _____

_____

Fourth supporting sentence _____

_____

8. Topic Sentence: Too many children's toys promote sexist roles for young boys and girls.

First supporting sentence _____

_____

Second supporting sentence _____

_____

Third supporting sentence _____

_____

Fourth supporting sentence _____

_____

9. Topic Sentence: There was mass confusion in the hospital's emergency room.

First supporting sentence _____

_____

Second supporting sentence _____

_____

Third supporting sentence _____

_____

Fourth supporting sentence _____

_____

10. Topic Sentence: My brother (or sister, husband, wife, neighbor, etc.) has much to learn about driving a car.

First supporting sentence _____

_____

Second supporting sentence _____

_____

Third supporting sentence _____

_____

Fourth supporting sentence _____

_____

11. Topic Sentence: Here are some easy steps to follow if you want to break the habit of smoking (or drinking).

First supporting sentence _____

_____

Second supporting sentence _____

_____

Third supporting sentence _____

_____

Fourth supporting sentence _____

_____

12. Topic Sentence: The referee and his crew let the game get out of control.

First supporting sentence _____

_____

Second supporting sentence _____

_____

Third supporting sentence _____

_____

Fourth supporting sentence _____

_____

13. Topic Sentence: I think CAR X (substitute a name) is a better automobile than CAR Y (substitute a name)

First supporting sentence _____

_____

Second supporting sentence _____

_____

Third supporting sentence _____

_____

Fourth supporting sentence _____

_____

14. Topic Sentence: The seniors were happy with their one-day bus trip to Niagara Falls.

First supporting sentence _____

_____

Second supporting sentence _____

_____

Third supporting sentence _____

_____

Fourth supporting sentence _____

_____

15. Topic Sentence: Juanita was busy preparing to open her own hair care salon.

First supporting sentence _____

_____

Second supporting sentence _____

_____

Third supporting sentence _____

_____

Fourth supporting sentence _____

_____

MODES OF PARAGRAPH DEVELOPMENT

The paragraphs you have been writing were developed in different modes or ways. Some paragraphs *informed*, some *explained*, and others *persuaded*.

Inform: Paragraphs that informed use these modes:

   narration

   description

Explain: Paragraphs that explained use these modes:

   example

   process

   classification

   comparison/contrast

   definition

   cause/effect

Persuade: Paragraphs that persuaded use this mode:

   argument

In the chapters that follow, you will learn more about these modes of presentation, not only for paragraphs, but for essays as well.

Chapter 10

The Power of the Thesis Statement

Even though we have not fully explored the many worlds that comprise our universe, we do have some convictions about what is happening or not happening in those worlds. Some of these convictions may be strongly held while others are rather tentatively held. Consider some convictions one writer has about her worlds.

World of Politics: Crooked politicians are one reason why a lot of young people do not pursue careers in government.

World of Fashion: I wish more women would refuse to follow the stupid fashion trends that help the clothing industry make a fast buck.

World of Entertainment: The great comedians are those who don't have to resort to four-letter words to get a laugh from an audience.

World of Work: I resent the fact that some guys in our company make more money than I earn simply because they are men.

World of Religion: Some television evangelists are giving organized religion a bad name.

World of Sports: Something should be done to speed up the game of baseball.

Obviously, this student has some very definite convictions on a number of subjects. We are not asking you at this time to challenge what she wrote. We only want you to note that she had the courage to state some of her convictions.

Now it's your turn to express convictions that you have about your worlds.

PRACTICE EXERCISE 10.1
Expressing Convictions

DIRECTIONS: Name a world that interests you, and then write a one-sentence statement that expresses your convictions about that world.

World of: _____

_____

_____

World of: _____

_____

_____

World of: _____

_____

_____

World of: _____

_____

_____

World of: _____

_____

_____

PRACTICE EXERCISE 10.2
Sharing and Comparing Convictions

DIRECTIONS: Share your convictions with three or four of your acquaintances and try to list the convictions that are strongly held, moderately held, half-heartedly held.

Strongly Held

_____

_____

_____

_____

Moderately Held

_____

_____

_____

_____

Half-Heartedly Held

_____

_____

_____

_____

THE THESIS STATEMENT

What you have done in Exercise 10.1 is to discover that you can write a rather good thesis statement. The statements you wrote to express your convictions about something in your worlds are thesis statements. Maybe those thesis statements are not as smooth and refined and as polished as you would like them to be. Don't worry. As you progress chapter by chapter through this book, you will learn how to express them more forcefully and more effectively. For the present, we want you to realize that there is no great problem in writing a thesis statement. You can do it. Indeed, you have already done it.

The Importance of the Thesis Statement

Did you ever have the experience of listening to a speaker ramble on endlessly? Just when you think he will show mercy and stop, he takes a deep breath and launches into another speech. Whenever that happens, you can be sure that the speaker didn't take the time to write a good thesis statement and develop a good outline. Both would have helped him make a better and briefer presentation.

Writers, like public speakers, often ramble on incoherently when they fail to write a good thesis statement and develop a good outline. They have a vague idea of what they want to say, but it never quite jells. Consequently, they quickly lose the reader. Unlike the audience of a disorganized speaker, the reader can turn to something more interesting without offending the author.

It is important to stress that *longer writing does not mean better writing.* Some people are under the impression that if they make the topic broad enough, they'll have enough "stuff" to put in to meet length requirements. That may be true, but length does not insure good writing. A thesis statement will stop you from ping-ponging all over the place and will point you in the direction of good writing.

If you can write a good thesis statement, you are well on your way to becoming a good writer. Since a thesis is critical, let's consider first what a good thesis is *not* and then look at what a good thesis *is.*

What a Thesis Is Not

1. *A good thesis is not an announcement of something that the writer is going to do.*

Example of a Poor Thesis Statement.   In this paper, I am going to describe the circumstances which made Al Capone the top mobster in this country during the 1920s.

To convert that announcement into a good thesis statement, you might write the following:

Example of a Better Thesis Statement.   Prohibition made it possible for Al Capone to become the top gangster in the country during the 1920s.

2. *A good thesis is not a statement of fact.* The following are statements of fact but are not theses:

NASA has launched manned space flights.

Bears hibernate.

Cobras are dangerous.

Americans elect a president every four years.

3. *A good thesis is not a question.* The following questions might make good titles, but they are not thesis statements.

Is NASA's manned space flight program worth the annual expenditure of billions of dollars?

Should bears be hunted when they are hibernating?

Should apartment dwellers be permitted to keep cobras in their apartments?

Is a six-year term for presidency better than a four-year term?

What a Thesis Is

1. A thesis is the controlling or main idea of an essay.
2. It is sometimes a comment on a fact.
3. Frequently, a thesis is a position that a writer takes on some arguable or controversial issue.
Here are some examples of thesis statements that you could develop from the questions listed under "What a Thesis Is Not":

1. Despite the tragic loss of seven astronauts on the space shuttle *Challenger*, mankind must continue to probe and discover the secrets of the universe.
2. There should be stiff punishment for hunters who try to trap bears in their hibernation period.
3. Since cobras are dangerous reptiles, apartment dwellers should not be permitted to keep them in their suites.

You may agree or disagree with these theses. Your statement of opposition, then, could well be your thesis statement. Regardless of the position you take, your thesis statement should tell the reader something that you believe is accurate and true or state your position on an issue.

Characteristics of a Good Thesis Statement

1. *A thesis should be restricted.* If you write that commercial air travel has become more dangerous in recent years, you may have to write volumes to prove your thesis. Restrict your thesis by saying: Three accidents and two near collisions in flight are proof enough that Jinx Airline is not concerned with passenger safety.

2. *A thesis should be unified.* Consider the above example about Jinx Airline. Suppose someone writes the following:

> Three accidents in one month and two near collisions in midair are proof enough that Jinx Airline is not concerned with passenger safety, and they also lose a lot of baggage.

Your thesis is not unified. You have enough proof to show that the airline is careless; don't get into the issue of lost baggage. Let someone else address that problem.

3. *A thesis should be specific.* Your thesis is about one specific problem about one specific airline, not many problems about an airline, and not problems of the entire industry.

If your thesis statement is restricted, unified, and specific, ordinarily you can state it in one powerful sentence. It's not always easy to put your thesis into one sentence. In fact, this might be the most difficult part of writing an essay. Nevertheless, if you can state your thesis in one sentence, you will find that your essay will have a sharp focus.

Summary. A one-sentence thesis gives sharp, clear focus to your main idea. It is the framework, the cornerstone of your essay. It is the statement that tells your reader what your essay is about.

Examples of Thesis Statements

1. Although I often rebelled against my parents when I was a teenager, I now realize that their insistence on study, their setting of curfews, and their restrictions on the family car were their ways of demonstrating tough love.

2. Fathers who do not demonstrate their affection toward their children show that they need education about parenting.

3. TV commercials can wear a variety of masks, yet they all are designed to separate people from their hard earned cash.

4. A strong desire to learn about the experiences of others, to gain up-to-date information, and to improve myself through reading have helped create in me a passion for nonfiction literature.

5. In recent years the irresponsible tactics of certain kinds of salespersons have tarnished the image of a once proud profession.

6. Because of their even temperament, their high level of intelligence, and their instinct for protecting owners, breeds of large dogs make the best pets.

7. It is my strong belief that individuals should be paid according to the worth of the contributions they make to society.

8. While Ty Cobb and Pete Rose are similar in some respects, Rose is the better athlete, because today's baseball players have greater competition.

9. Before I decide to marry a person I have been dating, I want to know his family background, his work history, and some of his personal habits.

10. That terrible monthly bill, the fear of someone stealing my credit cards, and the temptation to overspend are three reasons why I use cash instead of credit cards.

PRACTICE EXERCISE 10.3
Recognizing a Good Thesis Statement

DIRECTIONS: If the following statement is a good thesis statement, write Yes; if it is not, write No.

_____   1. The AIDS epidemic.

_____   2. In this paper I am going to tell citizens why they should pass the levy this fall.

_____   3. Mayor X should be defeated because he has used his office to hire incompetent relatives and friends.

_____   4. Gangs are a problem in this city.

_____   5. Delays in traveling by airlines.

_____   6. Windsurfing last summer.

_____   7. Cheating on exams is a widespread problem.

_____   8. Why are many high school students illiterate?

_____   9. The administration at this college should be praised for recruiting high quality teachers and for increasing security guards in the parking lots but it still needs to do something about long lines at registration.

_____   10. The nation would be better served if presidents were limited to one six-year term.

Using Freewriting to Write Tentative Thesis Statements

One writer selected the topic of "delays." Her brainstorming led her to focus on a delay that was especially irritating—a delay in traffic as she was trying to get to morning classes. She then did her freewriting and narrowed her topic to one very specific aspect of traffic jams.

Example of Freewriting

traffic jams—people late for work run out of gas—flat tire—lot of people late for work—street becomes parking lot—people blow their horns—mainstreets—freeways and narrow streets—so maybe the thesis should be on trucks that block narrow streets as they unload during rush hour. It happens especially on Market Street once or twice a week. Makes me late for classes at the college. Cars also that park near the curb—they are in the way but they don't block the street as the trucks do—so I am going to restrict this to trucks on Market Street—unloading produce during rush hour. Like to do something about those parked cars too.

Here is her thesis statement:

There should be a city ordinance that forbids trucks to unload their produce on Market Street during morning rush hours.

Notice that it is *restricted, unified,* and *specific.* If she had included parked cars, the unity of her thesis would have suffered. Wisely, she focuses on the trucks that are unloading produce on Market Street during morning rush hour. If she had written about traffic tie-ups on freeways and city streets caused by buses, cars and taxis, her thesis would be too vague. She zeroes in on a specific problem on Market Street. Once she gets that problem solved, she can go after the drivers who are parking their cars on Market Street during rush hour.

Another writer chose the topic of communications. After brainstorming, he did some freewriting to narrow the topic.

Example of Freewriting

I've been thinking a lot about communications. It's great to be able to call distant parts of the country and the world in a matter of seconds and minutes. It's great to have information at our finger tips. But there are always those who turn something good into evil for their own selfish purposes. I worry about my social security number, my bank records, my medical records. Some brainy computer hack could have access to them with the right expertise. It's like breaking and entering. It should be punished. Computer thieves should be punished just as severely as a thief who breaks into my home and steals my video recorder, my TV, or anything else. I'm in favor of laws that severely punish such thieves and invaders of my privacy. Some of these law breakers are young kids who think it's cool to break a computer code and destroy or change records. Destroying medical records could cause death or could ruin a person's reputation.

Tentative Thesis
People who use computers to destroy information or cause confusion in institutions such as hospitals and banks should be punished severely.

Another Tentative Thesis
People should be taught to respect computer property just as they are taught to respect other personal property.

And Another Tentative Thesis
Just as people are taught the dangers of using a car recklessly, so also should they be taught that using a computer can have serious consequences. (I can support this thesis with several examples: possible results of altering or wiping out medical, education, military, and financial records.)

PRACTICE EXERCISE 10.4
Writing One-Sentence Thesis Statements
That Are Restricted, Unified, and Specific

DIRECTIONS: Below is a list of general topics. Your instructor may want to suggest additional topics. Using brainstorming and freewriting, try to write one-sentence thesis statements that are *restricted, unified* and *specific*:

health _____

_____

_____

pollution _____

_____

_____

grades _____

_____

_____

computers _____

_____

_____

library _____

_____

_____

crime _____

_____

_____

entertainment _____

_____

_____

water sports _____

_____

_____

marriage _____

_____

_____

cars _____

_____

_____

Chapter 11

Using Outlines to Develop and Expand Your Thesis Statement

Most journalists can sit in front of a typewriter or word processor and type out an editorial, an opinion piece, or a serious or humorous story without writing a thesis statement, an outline, or a rough draft. That's because they have had years of practice. They are so skilled in writing that they can do thesis statements, outlines, and rough drafts in their heads. The majority of us, however, are not yet that good. Maybe with practice, we will be. For now, we go through a process that can sometimes be demanding, frustrating, and even boring.

But the process works. So have patience; you too may become so adept that you can do your prewriting in your head.

THE IMPORTANCE OF THE THESIS

Let's briefly review something that we emphasized in Chapter 10. The thesis statement is by far the most important element in the writing process. We defined a thesis as the controlling idea, the main point of an essay. It is often a comment that a writer makes about some fact or a position on some issue or arguable point. However you define a thesis, it must be *restricted, unified,* and *specific.*

A good thesis statement captures *in one or two sentences* everything that the subsequent paragraphs in the essay will develop. If properly structured, the thesis statement contains *all* of the main ideas and concepts the essay will cover and *only* those ideas and concepts.

For example, consider the writer of a letter to the editor of a daily newspaper in his city. He wants the mayor and his staff to improve city services, so he writes in his opening paragraph:

If this city intends to keep its rating as an All-American City, then the mayor and his administration should start doing something to give us more beautiful parks, cleaner streets, and safer neighborhoods.

As a thesis statement, that sentence will work just fine. It is *restricted* to one idea: that the mayor and his administration should start doing something to keep the city's high rating. It is *unified* because every idea in the sentence supports one single purpose. It is *specific* because it zeroes in on certain services that the writer wants the mayor to improve.

THE IMPORTANCE OF THE OUTLINE

Some composition teachers claim that the outline is really not necessary because it inhibits the ability to write. Furthermore, some argue that many writers do not use outlines. They just sit down at their word processors or typewriters and let the words flow.

That process works for many experienced writers. We believe that outlining is essential for you as beginning writers, because it teaches you how to organize your thoughts and develop your theses.

At the U.S. Naval Academy at Annapolis, every student has to learn how to sail a sailboat. Some may argue that the exercise is a waste of time because these men and women as officers will not be navigating sailboats but cruisers, destroyers, submarines, and other vessels with sophisticated electronic equipment. The people at Annapolis, however, discovered that the exercise in learning how to sail a boat gives the midshipman a "sense of the sea."

We believe outlining helps you develop a "sense of the sea of words." But there is another reason why we emphasize outlining. Let's go to the field of biology for an analogy.

The spinal column is one of the most important parts of the human anatomy. If the spinal column is strong and erect, a person can walk straight and do all sorts of physical exercises. Making up the spinal column are vertebrae. If these are strong the spinal column will be strong. If, however, even one vertebra starts to degenerate or becomes weak through a disease process, then the person will start having back problems.

We like to think of the thesis as the spinal column. It has to be unified, strong, solid. If it is not, the essay will have a difficult time walking.

Think of the sentences as the vertebrae that make up the spinal column. Incomplete and misplaced sentences cannot support the thesis, your essay's spinal column. In fact, they weigh heavily on it.

In treating patients with back problems, orthopedic surgeons order X-rays to give them information about the spinal column and the vertebrae. X-rays help locate troublesome vertebrae so the physician can prescribe the right treatment.

Outlines perform a similar function in writing and revising essays. A well planned outline can help the writer see which ideas support the thesis and keep it unified, and which ideas weaken it and destroy its unity.

While the primary function of an outline in essay writing is to help the writer plan the essay, some experienced writers use outlines to check their completed essays for unity and order. We strongly urge you to use at least a rough outline before you invest too much time on the writing process. When you become more confident in your writing skills, you may find that quickly outlining your rough draft is a good way to discover whether all of your sentences and paragraphs support the thesis and contribute to the unity of the essay.

SOME RULES FOR OUTLINING

Rule 1. Letters and numerals are used to show the relative value of a heading or subheading.

>*ROMAN NUMERALS*—I, II, III, IV, etc.—are used to show the most important ideas that the writer will develop. All headings that are preceded by a Roman numeral are of equal value.

>*CAPITAL LETTERS*—A, B, C, D, etc.—are used to show the next most important ideas. They are indented under the Roman numerals. All headings that are preceded by capital letters are of equal value.

>*ARABIC NUMBERS*—1, 2, 3, 4 etc.—are indented under the capital or upper case letter and show the next most important ideas. All headings that are preceded by an arabic number are of equal value.

>*LOWER CASE LETTERS*—a ,b, c, d, etc.—are indented under the arabic numbers and show the next most important ideas. All headings that are preceded by lower case letters are of equal value.

Rule 2. If you divide a piece of paper, you have at least two parts. So too, if you divide a concept like the History of America, you are going to have at least two parts and possibly three or more. This means then that in your outline you cannot have a I without a II, an A without a B, a 1 without a 2, an a without b.

Model Outline

The topic outline that follows was developed by a student who plans to write an essay on the subject "My Family." Study his outline and see how it illustrates the two rules about outlines that we just discussed.

MY FAMILY

I. My parents
    A. Father—Michael
        1. Age 45
        2. Steel worker
            a. 20 years at USX
            b. past year—unemployed
        3. Hobbies
            a. weekend golfer
            b. professional sports fan
    B. Mother—Helen
        1. Age—42
        2. Part-time secretary and housewife
        3. Hobbies
            a. Crossword puzzles
            b. bowling

II. My siblings
    A. Brother—Ted
        1. Age 16
        2. Student
            a. honor roll
            b. National Merit Scholar
        3. Hobbies
            a. chess
            b. bridge
            c. Trivial Pursuit whiz
    B. Sister—Kathy
        1. Age 12
        2. Seventh grader
            a. fair grades
            b. boy crazy
        3. Hobbies
            a. Cooking
            b. Telephoning

KINDS OF OUTLINES

A writer can develop and use different kinds of outlines such as *the scratch outline, the topic outline,* and *the sentence outline.*

Scratch Outline

It is just what it says. The writer starts scratching down—or jotting or scribbling—ideas which he or she may or may not use.

Let's say, for example, that she is writing a term paper for a political science class. She thinks that the presidential campaigns have gotten out of hand, and she wants to make a statement about them. She writes a tentative thesis statement that reads as follows:

Tentative Thesis. The presidential campaigns are too long, too expensive, and too exhausting for the candidates and the voters.

She starts scribbling on a legal pad. Her jottings follow:

Emotionally
    campaigns too long—2 years
    too much hype
    candidates exhausted
    voters exhausted

Financially
    special interest groups
    TV time expensive
    fund raising president

Politically
    first term—runs for office
    serves party, not the people
    avoids risk taking

After writing that scratch outline, the writer may have an idea on how to improve her thesis statement. The words—emotionally, financially, and politically—are the three major areas that her essay will address to support the thesis statement. She rewrites the thesis statement to address only those three major topics:

Thesis. The people of the United States would be better served emotionally, financially, and politically if the presidency were limited to one six-year term.

Topic Outline

The writer of that thesis statement is now ready to develop a topic outline. At this point, she jots down topics for each heading. The outline now looks like this:

I. Campaigns emotionally draining
   A. Too long
      1. Begins two years before leap year
      2. Intensifies during election year
   B. Too much hype
      1. PR gimmicks
      2. Television political ads
   C. Exhausting for candidates
      1. Too many debates
      2. Too many speeches each day
   D. Exhausting for public

II. Finances too important
   A. To special interest groups—money talks
   B. To political parties
   C. To president—concerned with party war chest for second term
   D. To candidates—only rich can afford to run

III. Politicking too important
   A. Too much time spent on re-election efforts
   B. President avoids risk taking
   C. Party discourages unpopular decisions

Sentence Outline

After writing the topic outline, the student may decide to write a sentence outline. That can easily be done if each topic and subtopic in the topic outline above is changed into a sentence.

I. One six-year term would be better emotionally for U.S. people.
   A. Presidential campaigns last too long.
      1. Candidates start campaigning at least two years before the general election.
      2. For at least nine months of the election year the people have to endure a lengthy series of state primaries.

    B. There is entirely too much hype in the process of electing a president every four years.
1. Every public relations gimmick is tried.
2. Style more than substance is emphasized.
3. The people are bombarded with television political ads from both major parties.
4. Issues are not always debated.

    C. Daily campaigning takes an emotional and physical toll on each candidate.
1. A long series of debates exhausts the candidates.
2. A candidate might give the same speech each day in four different states.

    D. Every four years not only are the candidates exhausted, but the public is exhausted as well.

II. The nation would be better served financially by one six-year presidential term.

    A. Since elections are costly, candidates solicit financial support from special interest groups.
1. Their agenda is often not in the public interest.
2. An incumbent president running for a second four-year term is often too dependent upon special interest groups.

    B. The president has to be concerned about his party's war chest, so he becomes a fund raiser for the party.

III. The citizens of the country would be better served politically by one six-year term.

    A. A first-term president must be concerned with re-election, so he often delays making unpopular but necessary decisions until his second term.

    B. A first term president has to spend a good part of his first term planning for re-election.

    C. A first term president, concerned with re-election, often cannot exercise bold and imaginative leadership for fear of losing political support.

In writing a draft based on the sentence outline, the writer may omit some topics or add some others. At least the sentence outline shows the writer what direction the writing is taking. It's a starting point, and that is all that an outline should be.

Note: Once you have written the sentence outline, you need not follow it to its conclusion in the writing of rough drafts and the final paper. In the course of writing a rough draft, you may think of a better way to support the thesis statement. If that happens, you should pursue that idea rather than sticking slavishly to an outline.

PRACTICE EXERCISE 11.1
Writing Outlines

DIRECTIONS: Write a scratch outline, a topic outline, and a sentence outline for one of the thesis statements you wrote in Chapter 10. If you need more practice, repeat the process using another thesis statement approved by your instructor.

Scratch Outline

These are the major points I am trying to make:

_____

_____

_____

_____

_____

_____

_____

_____

_____

_____

_____

_____

Some tentative thesis statements for my essay:

Tentative thesis #1: _____

_____

Tentative thesis #2: _____

_____

Tentative thesis #3: _____

_____

Topic Outline

Thesis: _____

_____

_____

I. First major topic: _____

_____

_____

II. Second major topic: _____

_____

_____

III. Third major topic: _____

_____

_____

_____

Sentence Outline

Thesis _____

_____

_____

Topic sentence for first major point _____

_____

_____

Supporting sentence _____

_____

Supporting sentence _____

_____

More supporting sentences _____

_____

Topic sentence for second major point _____

_____

_____

Supporting sentence _____

_____

Supporting sentence _____

_____

_____

More supporting sentences _____

_____

_____

Topic sentence for third major point _____

_____

_____

Supporting sentence _____

_____

_____

Supporting sentence _____

_____

_____

More supporting sentences _____

_____

_____

_____

Chapter 12

The Rough Draft

Published writers may have different opinions about teaching the writing process, but they generally agree on two points.

First, most published writers will tell you that *good writing is rewriting.* It rarely happens that they are ready to write the final copy after they have finished one rough draft. More than likely they are ready to cast their essays or stories into final form only after they have produced a number of rough drafts, maybe even ten or more.

Secondly, most published writers will tell you *they are never really satisfied with the final version.* They would like to work on it more, do another revision, but they cannot because a publisher's deadline has to be met. Although the reading public often proclaims these literary efforts, strangely the authors frequently do not. As true professionals, writers generally see something in the published piece that should have been worded differently or perhaps even omitted.

The conclusion of this chapter contains an excerpt from Donald Murray's essay "The Maker's Eye: Revising Your Own Manuscript." Murray, a Pulitzer prize winner, cites many writers who are never satisfied with their essays although they may have written many drafts before they produced the final copy. The pursuit of excellence drives them.

That same pursuit should also drive you.

THE ROUGH DRAFT

A rough draft is one of many attempts by a writer to cast the essay into final form. If you have written a sentence outline, then you have had some experience in organizing and developing your ideas. In the process of writing the rough drafts, you may get some new ideas or thoughts on how the material should be presented. This is a good sign, because it shows that you are continuing to think about your material. You should feel free to depart from your outline, especially when you write your second and third drafts. *Remember that the outline is merely a guide.* It is not meant to restrict you from adding to, subtracting from, or amending your drafts—or even tearing them up and starting over.

Although most people use outlines to help plan an essay, outlines can serve another function, namely, that of a checklist for unity and coherence after the essay is completed. The outline can help you check to see if the essay "hangs together." It takes only a few minutes to identify the main supporting paragraphs of your thesis and label them according to their importance—I, II, III, and so on, as well as the ideas that support the main points of your essay, labeling them A, B, C, and so on. This "X-ray" of your essay is a good tool for identifying out-of-place paragraphs and sentences. Sometimes just moving one paragraph or sentence to another place in the essay helps achieve coherence.

If you are using a word processor to write your essay, you can easily move sentences and paragraphs. If you are writing or typing your rough drafts, have a pair of scissors and some tape handy so that you can easily reorganize, using the cut and paste method. Be sure you double-space to provide adequate space for your corrections and revisions.

THE REVISION

After you have finished the rough draft or drafts, you are still not ready to write the final copy. The process of revision, at times demanding and frustrating, should not be skipped. Ask yourself the following questions:

- Are there words or phrases I can eliminate?

- Does the essay read well? (Read it aloud. Often the ear will tell you that a sentence or phrase is awkward or not smooth.)

- Is the writing simple and direct? Or are there overblown words, phrases, and sentences that make it appear pompous, like a man or woman who is overdressed?

- Are there any incomplete sentences? Run-on sentences? Dangling or misplaced modifiers? Comma splices? Mistakes in punctuation and capitalization?

- Do all the paragraphs support the thesis statement? Does each paragraph have a topic sentence, and do the sentences in each paragraph support the topic sentence?

- Does the essay show originality and imagination, or is it rather dull and flat?

- Is the essay something I want my instructor *and my peers* to read?

Use these questions as a guide to help you decide whether you need to write another rough draft. Your final essay should be a statement about you.

FINAL COPY

The final copy is really you. So if you care about your personal appearance in public, you will care about your essay. It will be neatly typed or written, and it will be free of typographical or grammatical errors. It will be ready to stand close inspection.

Student Model

Before Laurie Baumholtz chose a topic for this essay, she reviewed the brainstorming she had done at the beginning of the course. Among the many worlds she had recorded was the world of finance. Why finance? Because her financial life was in ruins after running up credit card bills beyond her budget. So the word finance was a hot button for Laurie.

Once she had chosen a general subject, she brainstormed, clustered, did some freewriting, and finally came up with a tentative thesis statement. She then developed a topic outline, followed by a sentence outline. She was then ready to write her first rough draft. Two other drafts followed, allowing her to correct her errors and revise some points. Perhaps reviewing some of the steps in Laurie's process and her final copy will help you use the same process to produce an essay worthy of you.

Freewriting

Credit cards—Wow. Go out and get what you want NOW. No money? Too bad. I can still have what I want now without waiting to save up money. Takes so long to save. Always something to use up your money before you know it it's gone. gone. Gone. Money, the root of all evil. Credit cards are evil. I hate them because after you get the things you thought were so important, you have to pay the bill. Months later, when the sweater is falling apart, the car needs repair, the microwave sits unused—the bills keep coming. I pay $25 and the finance charge is $7.89. How do I catch up. I'm going to cut all my credit cards up in little pieces. Use only cash. Then I suppose someone will rob me. Oh well, if I have only $2.00, that's all they get. What do I do when I really need credit. Got to pay off my bills so when I need credit I'll have it.

Credit cards are necessary in American society. These cards can change a person's life for better or worse. If you get credit extended and then abuse it you can be banned from future financial dealing for years. If you use credit to your advantage it can open up many doors that wouldn't open previously. Those open doors can slam shut the minute a payment isn't made. With cash a person owns something free and clear the minute you pay for it. Disadvantages to paying with cash. If you never establish credit, banks won't put faith in you when you need a loan for let's say, school, a home, or a car. They say you're not a good risk because you don't have enough—what, bills? Yes, bills, anything that keeps you there to pay the loan back. Everyone at one time or another needs to reach out for some type of credit. Possibly to start a business. I'm not sure if I can do without credit cards completely. Is that a realistic answer to my problem? A happy mix between both would be the best solution.

Topic Outline

Thesis. Monthly billing, theft, and the opportunity to overspend are just three basic reasons why I prefer using cash instead of credit cards.

I.　monthly billing

　　A. cash

　　B. credit card

II.　theft

　　A. cash

　　B. credit card

III. opportunity to overspend

　　A. cash

　　B. credit card

Sentence Outline

I.　Monthly billing is annoying.

　　A. If you use cash, there is no monthly bill.

　　B. With credit cards there is always a monthly bill.

II.　Theft can occur with cash, or credit cards.

　　A. Someone can steal only as much cash as a person is carrying.

　　B. Theft of a credit card can be damaging in several ways.

III. The opportunity to overspend is more prevalent with credit cards than it is with cash.

   A. People can only spend as much cash as they are carrying.

   B. Credit cards allow people to spend more than they can afford.

Rough Draft

Monthly billing, theft, and the opportunity to overspend are just a few basic reasons why I prefer using cash instead of credit cards.

Monthly billing is a ^/ prime example of why ~~cash is more preferable~~ *I prefer to use cash* *redundant* ~~to me. When it comes to cash there is no monthly billing!~~ Once I spend it on a particular article of worth—it's gone. The cash has then become property of the seller. ~~and I am the~~ own~~er of~~ the merchandise. ~~I so desired.~~ On the other hand, a credit card comes along with a monthly bill automatically attached to it. As far as a monthly bill goes, a credit card and a monthly bill are as one. So when a particular article is purchased with a credit card one might not have to pay at once, but rather at the end of the month. This is fine for some. [Unless you're like I was with several credit cards that had billing at the end of the month.] *Frag* I easily found myself with more bills than merchandise. ~~Now that~~ Creditors have interest ~~rates they~~ *charges* *Awk* ~~charge~~ for late pay~~ers, one~~ *ments so a credit card user* can very easily ~~end up~~ pay~~ing~~ more ~~for the~~ ~~product~~ than the cash customer did. Another thing I found out was as long as that bill kept coming, I never felt as if I owned that merchandise free and clear. There was always a doubt in the back of my mind. [A fear that one day I'd come home from work only to see the furniture store truck driving away with the entire guts of my home.] *Frag* *Too wordy and clumsy construction*

Another reason I prefer ~~the~~ *to* use ~~of~~ cash ~~as compared to the use of a~~ *rather than* credit card is ~~for the simple fact that~~ *the danger of* theft. ~~does occur. With cash,~~ When *persons are* ~~someone is~~ robbed *of their cash,* their money is gone. ~~That's the naked truth. That is~~ *Wordy* ~~also the end of it. The person is short some money. (Hoping, of course that~~ ~~they have not been physically harmed.)~~ On the other hand, ~~to~~ los~~e~~ *ing* a credit *can bring* *problem* card ~~is~~ a major ~~injustice~~ to (it's) former owner. ~~(Not to mention a royal pain~~ *omit*

~~in the butt!)~~ If the unlucky individual is wise enough to notify the company (to whom the card belongs) in so many hours <u>he/she</u> isn't liable for **Awk** ——— **Reword** anything charged on the card while it was classified as stolen. If, however, **to avoid** the victim doesn't notice the card missing for let's say 48 hours he/she is **he/she** **dilemma** then liable for 50% of anything charged on the card prior to notification of **omit** the theft. If the poor <u>sap</u> doesn't notice it gone for, let's say, a week ~~(which is a definite exaggeration on my part)~~ (he/she) is then liable for everything that was charged on it while it was considered "hot." So you tell me who's being punished for the crime in this case? I realize my examples might **SP** very well be blown out of proportion to some degree. None-the-less, the actual possibility of the victim being punished for the crime is greater than one might wish to believe.

The third reason I prefer to carry cash instead of credit cards is to prevent the opportunity to overspend. When I go into a store to buy someone a gift , I usually have a dollar figure in mind as to what I'd like to spend on him/her. By leaving home with the dollar amount in my wallet (example: $20) I am most likely going to go home with a gift of that value or of lower value for my friend. There is no way I can spend more than what I have in my wallet at the time. ~~(Unless there's a money machine in the area. That's another story all together!)~~ This is the safest way to prevent overspending on someone else or myself. On the other hand, with a credit card one can easily go over the limit they set for themselves just by signing their name by the "X." I have never found it difficult to decide to spend $20.00 on someone and then see something for $50.00 I'm sure **Not Clear** they would enjoy more. [The difference being with the cash one just thinks **Frag** of how the other person would enjoy the more expensive gift.] With the credit card one makes sure they'll see their friend's face light up with joy. It's a very easy circle to get caught up in.

I'm not suggesting credit cards to be burned in hell forever. When the idea was initially introduced someone had a very innocent thought in ～ idea of burning credit cards in hell?

mind. Like everything else there will always be people who abuse them. I am a prime example of such an abuser. I once was the proud owner of several credit cards. It took me years to slowly pull myself out of the hole. I will never do that again. As long as our ~~good~~ country keeps printing those greenbacks, I'll keep spending only as many as my budget allows.

Second Draft. We have omitted the second draft here. The primary changes involved changing the order of some ideas, adding specific and concrete incidents, and revising clumsy wording.

Final Copy

Trash the Credit Cards
Laurie Baumholtz, Cuyahoga Community College

I once was the proud owner of six credit cards: American Express, Visa, Sohio, and cards from three local department stores. It was wonderful for a few months, but the opportunity to overspend was just too tempting for me. I spent, I spent, and I spent. The bills mounted. After three years of paying for things that have begun to show signs of wear or are used up altogether, I am finally out of debt. I now use cash. Monthly billing, the fear of having my credit cards stolen, and the temptation to spend beyond my budget are the three major reasons why I prefer to use cash instead of credit cards.

Now I don't have to dread the arrival of that monthly bill. Once I pay for an article, that cash is gone. It's a simple exchange. The cash has become the property of the seller, and I am the owner of the merchandise I wanted. When I was using credit cards, however, the exchange was not simple at all. With the interest I was charged for late payments, I was spending more for my purchases than they were worth. Also, I found that I never felt as if I owned the merchandise until I had it paid for free and clear. I had a fear that one day I'd come home from work only to see the furniture store's truck driving away with the entire guts of my home.

I no longer have to worry about how I will pay for merchandise that some thief charges to my credit cards. I realize that someone could steal my cash as well, but at least I will lose only the cash I happen to be carrying at the time of the theft. If someone's credit card is stolen and the company is not notified within forty-eight hours, that person could be liable for anything charged on the card up to that time. If some poor sap doesn't notice the theft for a week, the victim could be liable for everything that was charged on the card while it was considered "hot." Who's being punished for the crime? The victim.

The most important reason I prefer to carry cash instead of credit cards is to prevent the opportunity to overspend. Formerly, when I used credit cards to buy gifts for friends, I would often go over the dollar limit I had set. I couldn't resist the thought of my friend's face lighting up with joy when presented with the more expensive gift, as if the person's face would light up twice as much with a $40 gift as with a $20 gift. What kind of friend is that, anyway? Now that I use cash, I buy the $20 gift and for no additional cost just imagine the person's delight in opening a $50 gift. No longer do I have to worry about spending beyond my budget. I have learned through experience that if I spend too much cash on something I don't need, I have to do without something that I do need until I get paid again.

I'm not suggesting that all credit cards be forever banished. I realize that in spite of my bad experience with them, I do have to establish credit so that when I need a loan for a house, a business, my education, or something else that is important to me, I will be able to get the money I need. But I will never get back in the credit card hole again. As long as our good country keeps printing those greenbacks, I'll keep spending only as many as my budget allows.

PRACTICE EXERCISE 12.1
Writing Activity

DIRECTIONS: In Chapter 10 you wrote scratch outlines, topic outlines, and sentence outlines for thesis statements. Select your best sentence outline and write a rough draft that follows your outline.

Be sure to save your outlines and your revisions. Your instructor may wish to review the process you used to achieve your final copy.

The Maker's Eye:
Revising Your Own Manuscripts

Donald M. Murray

When students complete a first draft, they consider the job of writing done—and their teachers too often agree. When professional writers complete a first draft, they usually feel that they are at the start of the writing process. When a draft is completed, the job of writing can begin.

That difference in attitude is the difference between amateur and professional, inexperience and experience, journeyman and craftsman. Peter F. Drucker, the prolific business writer, calls his first draft "the zero draft"— after that he can start counting. Most writers share the feeling that the first draft, and all of those which follow, are opportunities to discover what they have to say and how best they can say it.

To produce a progression of drafts, each of which says more and says it more clearly, the writer has to develop a special kind of reading skill. In school we are taught to decode what appears on the page as finished writing. Writers, however, face a different category of possibility and responsibility when they read their own drafts. To them the words on the page are never finished. Each can be changed and rearranged, can set off a chain reaction of confusion or clarified meaning. This is a different kind of reading, which is possibly more difficult and certainly more exciting.

Writers must learn to be their own best enemy. They must accept the criticism of others and be suspicious of it; they must accept the praise of others and be even more suspicious of it. Writers cannot depend on others. They must detach themselves from their own pages so that they can apply both their caring and their craft to their own work.

Such detachment is not easy. Science fiction writer Ray Bradbury supposedly puts each manuscript away for a year to the day and then rereads it as a stranger. Not many writers have the discipline or the time to do this. We must read when our judgment may be at its worst, when we are close to the euphoric moment of creation.

Then the writer, counsels novelist Nancy Hale, "should be critical of everything that seems to him most delightful in his style. He should excise what he most admires, because he wouldn't thus admire it if he weren't . . . in a sense protecting it from criticism." John Ciardi, the poet, adds, "The last act of the writing must be to become one's own reader. It is, I suppose, a schizophrenic process, to begin passionately and to end critically, to begin hot and to end cold; and, more important, to be passion-hot and critic-cold at the same time."

Most people think that the principal problem is that writers are too proud of what they have written. Actually, a greater problem for most professional writers is one shared by the majority of students. They are overly critical, think everything is dreadful, tear up page after page, never complete a draft, see the task as hopeless.

The writer must learn to read critically but constructively, to cut what is bad, to reveal what is good. Eleanor Estes, the children's book author, explains: "The writer must survey his work critically, coolly, as though he were a stranger to it. He must be willing to prune, expertly and hard-heartedly. At the end of each revision, a manuscript may look . . . worked over, torn apart, pinned together, added to, deleted from, words changed and words changed back. Yet the book must maintain its original freshness and spontaneity."

Most readers underestimate the amount of rewriting it usually takes to produce spontaneous reading. This is a great disadvantage to the student writer, who sees only a finished product and never watches the craftsman who takes the necessary step back, studies the work carefully, returns to the task, steps back, returns, steps back, again and again. Anthony Burgess, one of the most prolific writers in the English-speaking world, admits, "I might revise a page twenty times." Roald Dahl, the popular children's writer, states, "By the time I'm nearing the end of a story, the first part will have been reread and altered and corrected at least 150 times. . . . Good writing is essentially rewriting. I am positive of this."

Rewriting isn't virtuous. It isn't something that ought to be done. It is simply something that most writers find they have to do to discover what they have to say and how to say it. It is a condition of the writer's life.

There are, however, a few writers who do little formal rewriting, primarily because they have the capacity and experience to create and review a large number of invisible drafts in their minds before they approach the page. And some writers slowly produce finished pages, performing all the tasks of revision simultaneously, page by page, rather than draft by draft. But it is still possible to see the sequence followed by most writers most of the time in rereading their own work.

Most writers scan their drafts first, reading as quickly as possible to catch the larger problems of subject and form, then move in closer and closer as they read and write, reread and rewrite. . . .

PRACTICE EXERCISE 12.2
Discussion Questions

DIRECTIONS: In groups of four or five, discuss Donald Murray's "The Maker's Eye," using the following questions as a guide.

1. Why does Murray say that for writers the words on the printed page are never finished?

2. What does he mean when he says that writers must learn to be their own best enemies?

3. What is the great problem of most professional writers?

PRACTICE EXERCISE 12.3
Revising Activity

DIRECTIONS: Now that you have read part of Murray's essay, write another draft of the essay you developed in Exercise 12.1.

Part III

Discovering the
Power of Reading

Chapter 13

Introducing the Modes or Methods of Development

In Part II, you discovered not only the importance of prewriting exercises to help you generate ideas and topics about which you can write, but also the importance of writing topic sentences and thesis statements. We cannot stress enough our conviction, based on our classroom experience, that if you can put your ideas for an essay into a one- or two-sentence thesis statement that is restricted, unified, and specific, you are well on the way to becoming an effective writer. To be sure, the essay must be developed logically. Outlining will help you organize and develop your ideas in an orderly and logical fashion. The essay also must be readable and interesting. Revision and drafts can help make it so.

Once you have written a thesis statement that captures in a sentence or two what you want to say, you must then consider how to develop that thesis statement into an essay that will get people's attention. In Part III of *Discovery*, you will learn the various modes or methods that professional writers use to develop essays.

You already had brief encounters with the modes in Chapters 6 and 9. For example, in Chapter 6, we suggested that for your journal entries you use a different mode for each day. One day you were to narrate something that happened. On subsequent days you were directed to make journal entries in which you described, illustrated, compared or contrasted, and used other modes. In Chapter 9, you learned how paragraphs can be built through the modes.

THE IMPORTANCE OF LEARNING THE MODES

Is it important to learn these modes? We think it is for one very good reason.

In various college courses, you will be asked to write papers that call for a specific method or mode of development. In a political science course, for example, you might be asked to write an essay comparing or contrasting the differences between the two major political parties. If you are majoring in nursing or in some field of medical technology, your instructor might direct you to write a term paper in which you must explain a process such as amniocentesis. In a history class, a professor might ask for a paper on three major causes of World War I. A literature professor might want you to write a paper in which you cite specific examples to show that Hamlet was indecisive. If you are taking a sociology class, an essay question on your final exam might call for a short essay in which you classify the kinds of people in your community who are unemployed.

In this section of *Discovery*, we offer some guidelines to help you fulfill satisfactorily those writing assignments. In each chapter we include a brief section called "Writing Across the Curriculum" to make you aware of writing assignments in college courses that require students to respond to an essay question or develop an essay in a specific mode.

COMBINING THE MODES

Admittedly, these modes of development are somewhat artificial when it comes to many writing assignments. A writer for a major metropolitan newspaper, for example, doesn't sit at his word processor and say, "Well, let's see. Last week I wrote essays using methods of development such as definition, classification, and illustration. This week I should give the readers comparison, process, and narration." Usually, it doesn't work that way. If the journalist is trying to show how frustrating and complicated it is to get a driver's license renewed, he might use the mode of *process* to show all the bureaucratic nonsense the applicant has to endure. In his article, he will undoubtedly use other modes of development to prove his thesis. He might *describe* the long line of people who are angry and impatient. He might also write that the *cause* of this outdated and archaic system is political patronage. He may *argue* that if the system were simplified, some people would lose their jobs and some politicians would lose the dismissed employees' votes. Perhaps he will also *contrast* his state's method of getting a license renewal with that of a neighboring state that has streamlined the process. He combines methods with ease, and eventually so will you.

A BRIEF LOOK AT WHAT FOLLOWS

In the pages that follow, you will be learning about modes that *inform* and modes that *explain.*

Modes That Inform:

> Narration (Chapter 14)
>
> Description (Chapter 15)

Modes That Explain:

> Definition (Chapter 16)
>
> Example (Chapter 17)
>
> Process (Chapter 18)
>
> Comparison and contrast (Chapter 19)
>
> Classification and division (Chapter 20)
>
> Cause and effect (Chapter 21)

We have not included a chapter on *argument*, the mode of development that persuades, because this mode requires far more analysis and discussion than this book can give. If you know how to work with the modes we present, we think you will be in a much better position to use the argument mode later on in your writing career. You will, however, be using argument to a certain degree in any writing you do to persuade your readers to accept your position or your point of view.

We hope that the readings we have selected in the chapters that follow will help you master the modes. More importantly, we hope these readings will enlarge your vision of your universe so that you will begin to see things in those worlds that you never dreamed were there.

Each reading selection in Chapters 14 to 21 is followed by a set of the following strategies to help you relate the readings to your own experience:

> Warm-Up (an exercise to stimulate your right brain)
>
> Discovering New Words (an exercise to encourage you to discover— and use—your dictionary)
>
> Discovering the Meaning
>
> Discovering Connections

Chapter 14

How Writers
Use Narration

Writing Across the Curriculum

What you will learn in this chapter about writing a narrative essay has relevance to writing assignments in other college courses. Here are some examples of assignments that call for the narrative mode:

Nursing: Write about a visit to a pediatric ward.

Art: Write about a field trip to an art museum to view the exhibit "The Tomb Sculpture of Ancient China."

Psychology: Write about the behavior of a street gang that attacked an elderly person.

Early Childhood Education: Write about a field trip to a day-care center.

Sociology: Write about the experience of talking to a mother who has just been evicted from her apartment in a public housing project.

At an employment conference in Washington, D.C., a speaker pointed out that talented women are often denied opportunities to hold executive positions in corporations. He told this story to make his point:

> One day the governor of Nevada and his wife were driving back to the capital of the state when the governor noticed that the gas was getting low. He knew that most of the remaining three hours of travel were through desert. Just before they came to the desert, he saw an old beat-up gas station with an old beat-up hamburger stand next to it. As the governor pulled up to the pump, an old beat-up gas station attendant came out and began pumping gas.

Suddenly the governor's wife got out of the car and started talking to the old beat-up gas station attendant. They were joking and laughing and having a good time.

When the governor and his wife left the gas station, the governor said, "Darling, I noticed you talking to that old beat-up attendant. Do you know him?"

"Yes," she replied. "As a matter of fact, he and I were high school sweethearts. In fact, after we graduated, he wanted to marry me. But I went to college and married you instead."

The governor fell silent for a moment and then asked his wife if she noticed that old beat-up hamburger stand next to the old beat-up gas station. She acknowledged that she had seen it.

"Well," the governor said, "if you had married him, you would now be making hamburgers in that old beat-up stand."

"That's what you think," she said. "If I had married him, he would now be the governor of Nevada."

The audience roared its approval of that story. It was obvious that the speaker knew something about the importance of narration.

WHAT NARRATION IS

Narration is telling what happened in fact or in fiction. If you tell someone at work about an accident you witnessed that morning on the freeway, that is narration. If you tell someone the latest episode of a soap opera, that also is narration.

Narration, the telling of a story or a sequence of happenings, is often used on humorous occasions, but it is frequently used to make us think about the serious problems we face.

Guidelines for Writing Narrative Paragraphs and Essays

1. *Before you begin to write any essay, including a narrative essay, be sure to brainstorm.* Brainstorming will help you put the events and ideas into perspective so that you can choose the most important ones for your essay.
2. *Use details, but do not get bogged down in too many details or you will lose your readers.* Select only the details from your brainstorming that support the significant events and ideas you have decided to write about. Record the other details in your journal for a story you might write in the future.

3. *Decide who your audience is.* Your audience will determine your tone. If you are writing a story you hope to have published in a college newspaper or magazine, your tone will probably differ from the tone you would use if you were writing a story for children. If your audience is your peers, you will write the essay in a language and style with which they can identify.

   If your instructor is your only audience, however, your tone will probably be quite different. Many college students write only for their instructors. *We suggest that in the series of essays you write in this course, your primary audience should be your peers.*

4. *Limit the time period in your narrative.* If you were writing a novel, you would have the luxury of covering a long period of time. In an essay, you must be selective or you will lose your reader before you get to the main point.

5. *If dialogue is appropriate, use it.* From early childhood to old age, readers enjoy stories that let characters do the talking.

6. *Be consistent in your point of view.* Point of view in writing means more than the phrase "point of view" as we use it in ordinary conversation. While it refers to the writer's *tone,* it also includes the elements of *time* and *person.* The writer's *tone* can be sarcastic, humorous, informal, serious, and so forth. *Time* is indicated through words and hints that tell the reader whether the writer is referring to events, information, and actions of the past, the present, or the future.

   Person refers to the writer's choice of first, second, or third person in the narration (or any other piece of writing). Using first person (I or we) implies that the writer has a subjective view toward the ideas expressed in the essay. Second person is used when the writer addresses the reader directly, as in a letter. Third person point of view implies that the writer is attempting to write objectively about the subject. Third person is appropriate for newspaper articles, historical accounts, and other writings that call for a broader point of view than that of a single individual.

7. *Don't tell a story simply for the sake of telling a story.* Show how some issue or conflict was resolved or not resolved.

HOW WRITERS USE NARRATION

Generally speaking, in most essays you will find that writers use more than one mode to develop an idea. In the same essay you can sometimes find the modes of narration, description, example or illustration.

For example, syndicated columnists whose essays appear on opinion pages of newspapers don't sit down at word processors and say to themselves: "Well, I wrote a narrative essay last week. I suppose I should follow it up with a descriptive essay this week."

Sometimes the writer will use narration to develop a paragraph, and in the same essay may also use definition and process to develop the thesis statement. At other times, the writer may decide to use narration throughout the essay.

Read the following two paragraphs to see how the authors use narration to convey their ideas.

One does not ordinarily expect to find a human interest story on the front page of *The Wall Street Journal,* but a December 1987 issue was about a street person named Jim, who is unshaven, unkempt, and unwashed. Like so many other vagrants, he searches dumpsters each day for food. He does not interfere with people as they go to and from work, but his presence on a park bench at a busy intersection bothers them. Occasionally he becomes an uninvited guest at church weddings. He likes to sit at the back of the church and observe the marriage ceremony. When the father of a bride angrily suggested to his pastor that he evict Jim from the church, the pastor replied that he couldn't because Jim was one of the his parishioners.

The following paragraph is taken from an essay by a writer whose reflections on bobsledding as a youth convinced him that snow is a wonderful gift that contributed to his growth and development.

One year during the winter break, some college friends were visiting me. They had heard my stories about bobsledding on the Devil's Turn. Was the bobsled still in good condition? It was. Could we take it down to the valley and try out the Devil's Turn? We could, I said, but I think that we are much too heavy for the sled; but let's try it. So off we went to Devil's Turn, which that day we had to ourselves. We climbed to the very top and started down. We missed the trees and the bushes and somehow arrived safely on the valley floor. My college friends were ecstatic. It was everything that I said it was. Let's go back up. Which we did. Again we came flying down the turn barely missing a tree. As we came to the bottom, we went over a little ridge. We were going so fast that the sled left the ground, traveled some six feet in the air, and came crashing down so hard on the frozen turf that the bobsled broke in two. We went sprawling into the snow and ice, but no one was hurt. The bobsled, however, was beyond repair. We left it there and walked slowly home laughing all the way. I felt some sadness, not because of the broken bobsled, but because I realized that the incident had forever closed a wonderful chapter in my life.

In these two selections, writers narrate incidents they observed or events they experienced. While you may notice elements in their styles of writing that you would like to imitate, the aspect of their writing most worthy of imitation is simply that they had the courage to write about what is happening in their worlds. That is where all good writing begins. These selections and those you will find in the Readings and Reflections section in this and the following chapters should enlarge your vision of the universe and help you to see yourself and your worlds more clearly.

READINGS AND REFLECTIONS

Sportswriters Come to Unexpected Ends

Ira Berkow

Ira Berkow is a columnist for the New York Times. *At that newspaper, he became associated with Red Smith, one of the world's best known sports writers. Smith was widely read, even by people without a special interest in sports. They admired the literary style and grace that he brought to sports journalism.*

Berkow ends his book, Red: A Biography of Red Smith, *with this story. The story, told by Smith, was tape-recorded at a social gathering less than two years before his death.*

This is a peculiar business we work in. I have to tell you a little about what it's like. There was a sportswriter in Cincinnati years ago named Bill Phelon. He was a bachelor and a lot of people considered him eccentric because he shared his apartment in Cincinnati with a five-foot alligator. And he had a pet squirrel that he carried around the National League circuit in his topcoat pocket.

Bill Phelon loved baseball, and he was kind to animals, and above all he loved Havana. The city of Havana. As soon as the World Series was over, he would go to Havana, join up with his friend Pepe Conte, who was a sportswriter in Havana at the time, and spend as long a time there as his bankroll and the patience of his paper would allow.

And eventually the inevitable happened. Bill Phelon died. And in obedience to directions in his will, he was cremated and his ashes shipped to Pepe Conte. Pepe got a letter and a little package. And in the package was a small urn. The letter said, "Hello Pepe, this is Bill." Bill asked that Pepe rent a small plane and scatter his ashes over Morro Castle.

Pepe was deeply grieved by the loss of a friend and he took the little jug under his arm and went down to El Floridita, one of the places they had frequented, and there were a few hangers-on sitting around the joint, and Pepe put the urn up on the bar and he said to the guys, "Remember Bill Phelon?" Sure, they all remembered Bill Phelon. Pepe said, "This is to Bill Phelon. Have a drink on Bill Phelon." So they all had a drink on Bill Phelon, and Pepe tucked the jug under his arm and went on to Sloppy Joe's.

Went through the same routine. "You guys remember Bill Phelon?" "Sure." "Drink to Bill Phelon." He went on to the Plaza Bar, maybe the Angleterre, I don't know. All the spots that were favorites of Bill's and Pepe's. But somewhere on his appointed rounds, Pepe achieved a state of incandescence and he mislaid Bill Phelon.

Bill was undoubtedly swept out the next morning with the cigar butts and the empty bottles. And I tell this story to make it clear that sportswriters lead glamorous lives and come to unexpected ends. And I thank you.

WARM-UP

The story is about a sports journalist. Name some sports writers or TV sports commentators and rate them (excellent, good, fair, poor). What qualities should the ideal sports journalist have?

DISCOVERING NEW WORDS (Choose the word or phrase that best defines the word in italics.)

1. *eccentric*   (a) exciting   (b) fashionable   (c) dishonest   (d) noticeably different; unconventional

2. *circuit*   (a) electric current   (b) circle   (c) path, route   (d) schedule

3. *inevitable*   (a) bound to happen   (b) shocking   (c) boring   (d) unexplainable

4. *incandescence*   (a) happiness   (b) sadness   (c) light given off by a hot object (d) nervousness

DISCOVERING THE MEANING

Why do you think Berkow placed this chapter at the very end of his book? What does the story tell us about Red Smith?

DISCOVERING CONNECTIONS

Red Smith had a great influence on Ira Berkow. Can you think of someone who influenced you, either positively or negatively? Write a paragraph or essay about the person, narrating a particular incident that affected you in a positive or negative way. The topic of the paragraph or thesis of the essay should focus on some admirable quality or a serious failing of the person. The story you tell should support that thesis.

Sam, Be a Man

===

Robert Caro

Robert Caro is a native of New York City. He graduated from Princeton University and later became a Nieman Fellow at Harvard. For seven years, he was an investigative reporter for Newsday.

Caro's first book, The Power Broker: Robert Moses and the Fall of New York, *won both the 1975 Pulitzer Prize for Biography and the Francis Parkman Prize, awarded annually by the Society of American Historians. "Sam, Be a Man" is taken from Caro's biography of Lyndon Johnson,* Lyndon Johnson: Path to Power.

In the bleakness and boredom of Sam Rayburn's childhood, there stood out a single vivid day.

Fannin County's Congressman was Joseph Weldon Bailey, who, as Minority Leader of the House of Representatives, "dominated the Democratic minority like an overseer and conducted himself like a conqueror," and was expected, if the Democrats won control of Congress, to become Speaker. Bailey was one of the greatest of the great Populist orators. When he spoke in the House, it was said, "his tones lingered in the chamber like the echo of chimes in a cathedral." In 1894, when Sam Rayburn was twelve, Bailey spoke in Bonham, the county seat. And Sam Rayburn heard him.

He was to remember, all his life, every detail of that day: how it was raining so heavily that his mule took hours to cover the eleven miles to town; how he felt when he arrived at the covered tent "tabernacle" of the Bonham Evangelical Church, where Bailey was speaking. "I didn't go into that tabernacle. I'd never been to Bonham since we bought the farm, and I was scared of all the rich townfolks in their store-bought clothes. But I found a flap in the canvas, and I stuck there like glue while old Joe Bailey made his speech." And most vividly of all, he remembered Joe Bailey. "He went on for two solid hours, and I scarcely drew a breath the whole time. I can still feel the water dripping down my neck. I slipped around to the entrance again when he was through, saw him come out, and ran after him five or six blocks until he got on a streetcar. Then I went home, wondering whether I'd ever be as big a man as Joe Bailey."

Passing the barn the next morning, his brothers heard a voice inside. Looking through the door, they saw their little brother standing on a feeding trough, practicing a political speech. From the day he heard Joe Bailey, Sam Rayburn knew what he was going to be. Knew precisely. He told his brothers and sisters, and friends; as one recalls his words, "I'm going to get myself elected to the State Legislature. I am going to spend about three terms there and then I want to be elected Speaker. After that, I am going to run for Congress and be elected." He would be in the House of Representatives, he said, by the age of thirty. And eventually, he said, he would be its Speaker, too. Sam's ambition became a joke on the Rayburn farm; his brothers and sisters would stand outside the barn and laugh at the speeches being made inside. But the speeches went on. And in 1900, when he was eighteen years old, Sam Rayburn, standing in a field with his father one day, told him he wanted to go to college.

His father said that he had no money to send him. "I'm not asking you to send me, Pa," Sam said. "I'm asking you to let me go." The cavalryman's back was stooped from the fields now; he was old; two of his eight sons had already left the farm; the loss of a third pair of strong hands would be hard to bear. "You have my blessing," he said. On the day Sam left, his clothes rolled up and tied with a rope because he had no suitcase, his father hitched up the buggy and drove him to the railroad station. A silent man, he stood there silently until the train arrived and his son was about to board it. Then he suddenly reached out and pressed some bills into his son's hand. Twenty-five dollars. Sam never forgot that; he talked about that twenty-five dollars for the rest of his life. "God knows how he saved it," he would say. "He never had any extra money. We earned just enough to live. It broke me up, him handing me that twenty-five dollars. I often wondered what he did without, what sacrifice he and my mother made." And he never forgot the four words his father said to him as he climbed aboard the train; he was to tell friends that he had remembered them at every crisis in his life. Clutching his son's hand, his father said: "Sam, be a man!"

WARM-UP

1. In Washington, D.C., there is a government building named for Sam Rayburn. Draw a picture of a building and call it the Rayburn Building.

   On the outside walls of that building, write down the qualities that elected officials should have. Next to each quality, write down the name of a politician (living or dead) who exemplifies that quality.

2. What would be the reaction if you went home and told your family, friends or neighbors that you were thinking of running for an elected office?

Shock	Ridicule	Disbelief
Support	Laughter	Approval

DISCOVERING NEW WORDS (Choose the word or phrase that best defines the word in italics.)

1. *populist*   (a) member of Republican Party   (b) member of Democratic Party

   (c) an Independent   (d) member of a political party that sought to represent

   the interests of farmers and laborers in the 1890s.

2. *orator*   (a) speaker   (b) politician   (c) mortician   (d) farmer

3. *trough*   (a) container used to store grain   (b) container used to hold water or

   feed for animals   (c) container used to keep important papers   (d) container

   used to store perishable food

DISCOVERING THE MEANING

1. Is the story more about young Sam or his father?

2. Which of the following words describe how Sam's father felt when he saw his son get on that train for college?

Angry	Proud	Hurt
Lonely	Disappointed	Envious

3. What did the father mean when he said, "Sam, be a man."

DISCOVERING CONNECTIONS

1. Write down various words of advice that parents give to their children.

2. Recall some words of advice a parent or relative or friend gave you at a critical time of your life, and write a paragraph or an essay telling how you remembered it and valued it.

3. Young Sam didn't let ridicule and peer pressure stop him from attaining his career goal. Write a paragraph or an essay about a personal experience you had with peer pressure.

An Awakening

Helen Keller

At the age of nineteen months, Helen Keller (1880–1968) was struck with a disease that deprived her of sight and hearing. Through Anne Sullivan Macy's selfless, patient care and teaching, Keller learned the relationship between words and things. Her teacher and friend remained her companion until her death. Keller graduated from Radcliffe College cum laude *in 1904. She wrote many books about her challenges and triumphs. This selection is from* The Story of My Life.

One day, while I was playing with my new doll, Miss Sullivan put my big rag doll into my lap also, spelled "d-o-l-l" and tried to make me understand that "d-o-l-l" applied to both. Earlier in the day we had had a tussle over the words "m-u-g" and "w-a-t-e-r." Miss Sullivan had tried to impress it upon me that "m-u-g" is *mug* and that "w-a-t-e-r" is *water*, but I persisted in confounding the two. In despair she had dropped the subject for the time, only to renew it at the first opportunity. I became impatient at her repeated attempts and, seizing the new doll, I dashed it upon the floor. I was keenly delighted when I felt the fragments of the broken doll at my feet. Neither sorrow nor regret followed my passionate outburst. I had not loved the doll. In the still, dark world in which I lived there was no strong sentiment or tenderness. I felt my teacher sweep the fragments to one side of the hearth, and I had a sense of satisfaction that the cause of my discomfort was removed. She brought me my hat, and I knew I was going out into the warm sunshine. This thought, if a wordless sensation may be called a thought, made me hop and skip with pleasure.

We walked down the path to the well-house, attracted by the fragrance of the honeysuckle with which it was covered. Someone was drawing water and my teacher placed my hand under the spout. As the cool stream gushed over one hand she spelled into the other the word *water*, first slowly, then rapidly. I stood still, my whole attention fixed upon the motions of her fingers. Suddenly I felt a misty consciousness as of something forgotten—a thrill of returning thought; and somehow the mystery of language was revealed to me. I knew then that "w-a-t-e-r" meant the wonderful cool something that was flowing over my hand. That living word awakened my soul, gave it light, hope, joy, set it free! There were barriers still, it is true, but barriers that could in time be swept away.

I left the well-house eager to learn. Everything had a name, and each name gave birth to a new thought. As we returned to the house every object which I touched seemed to quiver with life. That was because I saw everything with the strange, new sight that had come to me. On entering the door I remembered the doll I had broken. I felt my way to the hearth and picked up the pieces. I tried vainly to put them together. Then my eyes filled with tears; for I realized what I had done, and for the first time I felt repentance and sorrow.

I learned a great many new words that day. I do not remember what they all were; but I do know that *mother, father, sister, teacher* were among them— words that were to make the world blossom for me. . . .

I recall many incidents of the summer of 1887 that followed my soul's sudden awakening. I did nothing but explore with my hands and learn the name of every object that I touched; and the more I handled things and learned their names and uses, the more joyous and confident grew my sense of kinship with the rest of the world.

WARM-UP

Act out how Helen might have communicated the following concepts:

1. I am ill.

2. I am hungry.

3. Where is my new doll?

Act out how Helen's teacher, Anne Sullivan Macy, might have communicated the following ideas to Helen:

1. You are eating too fast.

2. Your mother is ill and must go to the hospital.

DISCOVERING NEW WORDS (Choose the word or phrase that best defines the word in italics.)

1. *confounding*   (a) confusing   (b) throwing   (c) dismissing   (d) wanting

2. *hearth*   (The "ea" sound rhymes with the "ea" sound in heart.)

    (a) kitchen floor   (b) the floor of a fireplace, usually extending into

    a room   (c) lobby floor   (d) porch floor

3. *vainly*   (a) proudly   (b) sadly   (c) without success   (d) quickly

4. *repentance*   (a) sorrow for something one has done   (b) success   (c) joy

    (d) annoyance

DISCOVERING THE MEANING

Rank your agreement with the following statements from 1 to 5, (1, Agree completely; 5, Disagree completely).

_____   1. Helen was mentally impaired.

_____   2. Helen's temper was caused primarily by her parents spoiling her.

_____   3. Helen exaggerated the importance of words in her life.

_____   4. Anne Sullivan Macy's success with Helen was due mainly to her patience and dedication.

DISCOVERING CONNECTIONS

1. Have you ever felt so frustrated about a failure that you wanted to throw things? (Crumpling up an essay you are working on and throwing it on the floor? Feeling like punching out a classmate who gets A's without even trying? Smashing the basketball when it refuses to obey your commands?) If so, you can identify to some degree with Helen's frustration at being isolated from others because of her inability to communicate. Write a narrative paragraph or essay about how you or someone you know achieved a goal in spite of repeated frustration and obstacles.

    Hints: Decide what point you want to make, then select details that support that point or thesis. Use dialogue if possible, being careful to correctly punctuate quotations. Try to make smooth transitions from one point to another so that the reader can easily follow the progression of events. Sometimes this can be achieved by using words such as "then," "next," and "finally."

Salvation

====

Langston Hughes

Langston Hughes is one of the most important writers in the development of black literature in America. Although he was at first criticized by other black writers for using the black dialect in his poetry, stories and novels, he eventually attained universal recognition for his achievements in literature. "Salvation" is a chapter from the author's book, The Big Sea.

I was saved from sin when I was going on thirteen. But not really saved. It happened like this. There was a big revival at my Auntie Reed's church. Every night for weeks there had been much preaching, singing, praying, and shouting, and some very hardened sinners had been brought to Christ, and the membership of the church had grown by leaps and bounds. Then just before the revival ended, they held a special meeting for children, "to bring the young lambs to the fold." My aunt spoke of it for days ahead. That night I was escorted to the front row and placed on the mourners' bench with all the other young sinners, who had not yet been brought to Jesus.

My aunt told me that when you were saved you saw a light, and something happened to you inside! And Jesus came into your life! And God was with you from then on! She said you could see and hear and feel Jesus in your soul. I believed her. I had heard a great many old people say the same thing and it seemed to me they ought to know. So I sat there calmly in the hot, crowded church, waiting for Jesus to come to me.

The preacher preached a wonderful rhythmical sermon, all moans and shouts and lonely cries and dire pictures of hell, and then he sang a song about the ninety and nine safe in the fold, but one little lamb was left out in the cold. Then he said: "Won't you come? Won't you come to Jesus? Young lambs, won't you come?" And he held out his arms to all us young sinners there on the mourners' bench. And the little girls cried. And some of them jumped up and went to Jesus right away. But most of us just sat there.

A great many old people came and knelt around us and prayed, old women with jet-black faces and braided hair, old men with work-gnarled hands. And the church sang a song about the lower lights are burning, some poor sinners to be saved. And the whole building rocked with prayer and song.

Still I kept waiting to *see* Jesus.

Finally all the young people had gone to the altar and were saved, but one boy and me. He was a rounder's son named Westley. Westley and I were surrounded by sisters and deacons praying. It was very hot in the church, and getting late now. Finally Westley said to me in a whisper:

"God damn! I'm tired o'sitting here. Let's get up and be saved." So he got up and was saved.

Then I was left all alone on the mourners' bench. My aunt came and knelt at my knees and cried, while prayers and songs swirled all around me in the little church. The whole congregation prayed for me alone, in a mighty wail of moans and voices. And I kept waiting serenely for Jesus, waiting, waiting— but he didn't come. I wanted to see him, but nothing happened to me. Nothing! I wanted something to happen to me, but nothing happened.

I heard the songs and the minister saying: "Why don't you come? My dear child, why don't you come to Jesus? Jesus is waiting for you. He wants you. Why don't you come? Sister Reed, what is this child's name?"

"Langston," my aunt sobbed.

"Langston, why don't you come? Why don't you come and be saved? Oh, Lamb of God! Why don't you come?"

Now it was really getting late. I began to be ashamed of myself, holding everything up so long. I began to wonder what God thought about Westley, who certainly hadn't seen Jesus either, but who was now sitting proudly on the platform, swinging his knickerbockered legs and grinning down at me, surrounded by deacons and old women on their knees praying. God had not struck Westley dead for taking his name in vain or for lying in the temple. So I decided that maybe to save further trouble, I'd better lie, too, and say that Jesus had come, and get up and be saved.

So I got up.

Suddenly the whole room broke into a sea of shouting, as they saw me rise. Waves of rejoicing swept the place. Women leaped in the air. My aunt threw her arms around me. The minister took me by the hand and led me to the platform.

When things quieted down, in a hushed silence, punctuated by a few ecstatic "Amens," all the new young lambs were blessed in the name of God. Then joyous singing filled the room.

That night, for the last time in my life but one—for I was a big boy twelve years old—I cried. I cried, in bed alone, and couldn't stop. I buried my head under the quilts, but my aunt heard me. She woke up and told my uncle I was crying because the Holy Ghost had come into my life, and because I had seen Jesus. But I was really crying because I couldn't bear to tell her that I had lied, that I had deceived everybody in the church, that I hadn't seen Jesus, and that now I didn't believe there was a Jesus any more, since he didn't come to help me.

WARM-UP

Imagine that you are a preacher at a religious revival. What themes would you stress and what hymns would you select to support your themes?

DISCOVERING NEW WORDS (Choose the word or phrase that best defines the word in italics.)

1. *dire*   (a) tired   (b) having terrible consequences   (c) successful
   (d) wonderful

2. *gnarled*   (a) knotty or misshapen   (b) crabby   (c) diseased   (d) standing tall

3. *serenely*   (a) nervously   (b) calmly   (c) mistakenly   (d) joyfully

4. *knickerbockered*   (a) wearing old clothes   (b) wearing a basketball uniform
   (c) wearing blue jeans   (d) wearing pants that are cut full and banded just
   below the knees.

5. *in vain*   (a) irreverently   (b) jealously   (c) keenly   (d) without success.

6. *deacons*   (a) members of a congregation who assist the minister in various
   functions   (b) nuns   (c) politicians   (d) beggars

7. *ecstatic*   (a) sad   (b) giddy   (c) delighted; enraptured   (d) irreverent

DISCOVERING THE MEANING

1. What does young Langston Hughes think will happen to him at the revival meeting? On what does he base this belief?

2. Why does he finally decide to say that Jesus had come to him?

3. Why does he cry later that night?

DISCOVERING CONNECTIONS

Have you ever been pressured to say that you agreed with someone when you either disagreed or had doubts? Write a paragraph or an essay about an incident that caused you pain because you were not true to your beliefs, your opinion, your friend, your family. Try to use dialogue to re-create the incident.

SUGGESTED TOPICS FOR NARRATIVE
PARAGRAPHS AND ESSAYS

Below are some suggested topics for your consideration in writing narrative paragraphs and essays. The brainstorming and freewriting you did in Chapters 1 and 2 about you and the many worlds in your universe may suggest other topics. In every one of your worlds there is at least one narrative story for you to discover.

1. Write about some success experience in your life such as conquering a fear, winning a game, making a team, getting a job.

2. Write about some incident wherein you experienced failure, disappointment, rejection, or discrimination. Maybe you were cut from the team, rejected when you asked someone for a date, or suffered because someone (perhaps a parent or teacher) did not deliver on a promise. Or maybe you experienced discrimination because of your color, gender, religion, or ethnic origin.

3. Recall your first experience with sadness, pain, or death, and write about it.

4. Write about a memorable conflict or confrontation you had with a parent, a teacher, a neighbor, a classmate, a bully, or a coworker.

5. Write about some memorable experience involving a parent, a brother or sister, grandparents, or someone else.

6. Recall an embarrassing experience that was painful at the time but which you can laugh at now.

7. Recall some humorous experience that happened on some solemn occasion such as a church service.

8. Recall a story that you heard as a child and expand upon it.

9. Write about your experiences in learning how to drive or having your first accident.

Chapter 15

How Writers
Use Description

Writing Across the Curriculum

What you will learn in this chapter about writing a description essay has relevance to writing assignments in other college courses. Here are some examples of assignments that call for the description mode:

Biology: Write a paragraph describing what you saw when a drop of drinking water was placed under a microscope.

Nursing: Describe the activity in the emergency room of your local hospital.

Gerontology: Describe the patients sitting in the lobby of a nursing home.

Hospitality Management: Describe the activity going on behind the counter of a Wendy's, McDonald's, Burger King, or some other fast-food restaurant.

Description is the careful and selective use of words to convey the sense of sight, sound, smell, taste, and touch. Through the use of words that appeal to the senses, writers attempt to bring about in the reader the same sense of awe, joy, sadness, anger, fear, anxiety, or other emotion that they experienced when they encountered some person, place, or event in one of their worlds.

Guidelines for Using Description in Paragraphs and Essays

1. *Use words that appeal to the reader's senses* (sight, sound, smell, taste, and touch) to convey a vivid impression of what you are describing.

2. *Use words that are concrete rather than abstract.* Abstract words such as kindness, beauty, justice, and so forth, refer to ideas that cannot be seen, heard, smelled, tasted, or touched. Instead of telling your reader that someone is beautiful, just, or kind, give details that *show* the reader in what way that person is beautiful, just, or kind.

Compare the following descriptions. Which ones appeal to the senses and convey more vivid pictures?

Abstract: The boat race was beautiful to watch.
Concrete: Sailboats with colorful spinnakers glided through the white-capped waters of Lake Chautauqua in the first race of the season.

Abstract: The furniture was worn.
Concrete: The fabric of the once lovely sofa was faded and frayed.

Abstract: A computer was on the desk.
Concrete: A battered computer lay half buried on the writer's litter-strewn desk.

If you need practice in using specific, concrete words, do Exercise 15.1.

PRACTICE EXERCISE 15.1
Using Specific and Concrete Words and Phrases

DIRECTIONS: In the first column are words that are *general*. Try to find three ways to make the term more specific and more appealing to your senses.

Example:
music: jazz, sounds of a live band, a piano concerto

	I	II	III
food	_____	_____	_____
clothing	_____	_____	_____
art	_____	_____	_____
school	_____	_____	_____
books	_____	_____	_____

DIRECTIONS: Replace the following abstract adjectives with concrete descriptive phrases:

Example:
beautiful: long-lashed sparkling blue eyes, soft unblemished skin, graceful shapely legs

tired: _____

odd: _____

smart: _____

humorous: _____

Improve the following sentences with specific, concrete details that help the reader *see, hear, taste, feel,* or *smell* what you are describing:

1. I ate cereal for breakfast.

_____

_____

2. He was dressed in an odd way.

_____

_____

3. My first apartment was small.

_____

_____

4. When we stepped off the elevator, we smelled someone's dinner cooking.

_____

_____

5. I held the puppy in my arms.

_____

_____

    3. *In describing some person or thing, follow some kind of logical order.* In describing a scene, for example, move from the background to the foreground or vice versa. In describing an event, move from the beginning to the end; or for dramatic effect, start with the conclusion.

    4. *Focus on details that support the impression you are trying to create.* It is wise to avoid overwhelming the reader with many details unless you are striving to create a certain effect.

    5. *Keep your audience in mind.* We discussed this point in Chapter 14, and it may be helpful for you to review what was said there. Keeping your audience in mind applies in whatever mode of development you use.

READINGS AND REFLECTIONS

Death of a Star

Lance Morrow

Lance Morrow won the National Magazine Award in 1981 for his essays in Time. *Among his books are* The Chief, America, *and* Fishing in the Tiber.
In a Time *article, Morrow describes that awful moment in January, 1986, when the* Challenger *exploded over the Atlantic Ocean. He begins with a descriptive passage.*

The eye accepted what the mind could not: a sudden burst of white and yellow fire, then white trails streaming up and out from the fireball to form a twisted Y against a pure heaven, and the metal turning to rags, dragging white ribbons into the ocean. A terrible beauty exploded like a primal event of physics—the birth of a universe; the death of a star; a fierce, enigmatic violence out of the blue. The mind recoiled in sheer surprise. Then it filled with horror.

WARM-UP

Scenario: You are attending the final meeting of a committee appointed by your city council to decide on a fitting memorial for the astronauts who died in the *Challenger* accident. Ideas being considered are (1) erecting a monument on the public square (2) starting a scholarship fund (3) commissioning a painting for the lobby of City Hall. Decide which idea you will recommend and provide concrete, specific details for those who will carry out your recommendation.

DISCOVERING NEW WORDS (Choose the word or phrase that best defines the word in italics.)

1. *primal*   (a) first ever   (b) easy   (c) bookish   (d) beautiful

2. *enigmatic*   (a) ugly   (b) strong   (c) puzzling   (d) easily explained

3. *recoiled*   (a) wound up again   (b) shrank back   (c) jumped   (d) pondered

DISCOVERING THE MEANING

Notice the many specific, concrete details Morrow supplies to make the reader see and feel what he saw and felt.

Morrow organizes the details according to a time sequence: first "a sudden burst . . . ," then "white trails . . . ," then more details. Had he described the explosion without regard to the order in which details appeared, what would be the overall effect on the paragraph?

DISCOVERING CONNECTIONS

Have you ever witnessed an event that filled you with horror, such as an automobile accident, a robbery, a sudden illness? Or an event that filled you with joy, such as a victory at a sports event, the birth of a child, an unexpected visit from someone you love? Describe one of those events from your own life in your journal. Use your journal account as the basis for a paragraph or essay.

Steve's Mom
====

Fielding Dawson

Fielding Dawson was born in 1930 in New York City. He grew up in Kirkwood, Missouri, and now writes and paints in New York City. Tiger Lilies *is filled with memories of Dawson's childhood and adolescence just before and just after World War II. This selection from* Tiger Lilies *is about Dawson's remembrance of the mother of one of his friends.*

Steve's mom was lean with crystal gray eyes and short choppy brown and gray hair. She wore Levis, moccasins, and shirts that looked like men's shirts, tucked in flat under a beaded belt. I was generally afraid of her, and she knew it. She knew just about everything about me, and as we walked and ran up and down the mounds and through the tall dry scrub toward the smoke and flame, I had the sensation I was moving alongside a lithe, silent, fox-like, plain, and utterly beautiful creature.

WARM-UP

Try to exercise your creativity (a right-brain function) by drawing a rough sketch of Steve's mother, or if you lack confidence to try that, describe a sketch you would draw if you were an artist. What would Steve's mom be doing in your sketch? What background would you use?

DISCOVERING NEW WORDS

If there are any words you do not understand, consult a dictionary.

DISCOVERING THE MEANING

1. The main idea of this paragraph is not expressed in a topic sentence. What is the main idea that Dawson conveys?

2. Would the paragraph have been more effective if the author had written a topic sentence and placed it first in the paragraph?

3. Jot down the words or phrases that describe Steve's mother.

DISCOVERING CONNECTIONS

Write a description of someone you remember from childhood. Remember to give specific, concrete details so that your readers will "see" what you saw, "hear" what you heard, "smell" what you smelled, and so forth.

Sleek as a Beaver

Tom Wolfe

Tom Wolfe has written several bestsellers, among them The Right Stuff, *a nonfiction account of the lives of America's first astronauts.* Bonfire of the Vanities, *a novel with a Wall Street setting, reveals sharp contrasts between the rich and the poor and between the powerful and the powerless.*

Watch for concrete and specific descriptive words and phrases in this paragraph from Tom Wolfe's novel, Bonfire of the Vanities.

Back in the big silent kitchen, with the door open, Sherman could hear Pollard clanging up the metal treads of the fire stairs. Soon he came into view, puffing, from his climb of all of two flights, but impeccable. Pollard was the sort of plump forty-year-old who looks tonier than any athlete the same age.

His smooth jowls welled up from out of a white shirt of a lustrous Sea Island cotton. A beautifully made gray worsted suit lay upon every square inch of his buttery body without a ripple. He wore a navy tie with the Yacht Club insignia and a pair of black shoes so well cut they made his feet look tiny. He was as sleek as a beaver.

WARM-UP

Sketch Pollard in your journal—or find a picture in a magazine of someone who fits Wolfe's description of Pollard.

DISCOVERING NEW WORDS (Choose the word or phrase that best defines the word in italics.)

1. *impeccable*   (a) improbable   (b) loud   (c) flawless   (d) sloppy

2. *tonier*   (a) having firmer muscles   (b) in better mental shape   (c) wearing flashier clothes   (d) better at playing cards

3. *jowls*   (a) lower jaw and cheeks   (b) neck   (c) shoulders   (d) eyelids

4. *lustrous*   (a) dull   (b) sickly   (c) glowing   (d) foolish

5. *worsted*   (a) silk   (b) plaid   (c) black and white checkered   (d) firm-textured woolen fabric

DISCOVERING THE MEANING

1. What is the main idea of this paragraph?

2. What overall impression does Wolfe attempt to create about Pollard?

3. What details indicate that Pollard is wealthy?

4. What details describe Pollard's physique?

5. What words does Wolfe use to involve our sense of hearing?

DISCOVERING CONNECTIONS

Write a short description of someone you know. Select one particular trait or one aspect of your impression of the person, and support that impression with several concrete, specific details.

Cotton Picking Time

Maya Angelou

Maya Angelou—poet, actress, novelist, teacher, dancer—writes power-fully about the black experience. In both her poetry and her autobiographical books, among them I Know Why the Caged Bird Sings, *from which this selec-tion is taken, Angelou reflects her capacity to confront adversity, to triumph over it, and to grow in spite of, or because of it.*

Each year I watched the field across from the Store turn caterpillar green, then gradually frosty white. I knew exactly how long it would be before the big wagons would pull into the front yard and load on the cotton pickers at daybreak to carry them to the remains of slavery's plantations.

During the picking season my grandmother would get out of bed at four o'clock (she never used an alarm clock) and creak down to her knees and chant in a sleep-filled voice, "Our Father, thank you for letting me see this New Day. Thank you that you didn't allow the bed I lay on last night to be my cooling board, nor my blanket my winding sheet. Guide my feet this day along the straight and narrow, and help me to put a bridle on my tongue. Bless this house, and everybody in it. Thank you, in the name of your Son, Jesus Christ, Amen."

Before she had quite arisen, she called our names and issued orders, and pushed her large feet into homemade slippers and across the bare lye-washed wooden floor to light the coal-oil lamp.

The lamplight in the Store gave a soft make-believe feeling to our world which made me want to whisper and walk about on tiptoe. The odors of onions and oranges and kerosene had been mixing all night and wouldn't be disturbed until the wooded slat was removed from the door and the early morning air forced its way in with the bodies of people who had walked miles to reach the pickup place.

"Sister, I'll have two cans of sardines."

"I'm gonna work so fast today I'm gonna make you look like you standing still."

"Lemme have a hunk uh cheese and some sody crackers."

"Just gimme a coupla them fat peanut paddies." That would be from a picker who was taking his lunch. The greasy brown paper sack was stuck be-hind the bib of his overalls. He'd use the candy as a snack before the noon sun called the workers to rest.

In those tender mornings the Store was full of laughing, joking, boasting and bragging. One man was going to pick two hundred pounds of cotton, and another three hundred. Even the children were promising to bring home fo' bits and six bits. The champion picker of the day before was the hero of the dawn. If he prophesied that the cotton in today's field was going to be sparse and stick to the bolls like glue, every listener would grunt a hearty agreement. The sound of the empty cotton sacks dragging over the floor and the murmurs of waking people were sliced by the cash register as we rang up the five-cent sales.

If the morning sounds and smells were touched with the supernatural, the late afternoon had all the features of the normal Arkansas life. In the dying sunlight the people dragged, rather than their empty cotton sacks. Brought back to the Store, the pickers would step out of the backs of trucks and fold down, dirt-disappointed, to the ground. No matter how much they had picked, it wasn't enough. Their wages wouldn't even get them out of debt to my grandmother, not to mention the staggering bill that waited on them at the white commissary downtown.

The sounds of the new morning had been replaced with grumbles about cheating houses, weighted scales, snakes, skimpy cotton and dusty rows. In later years I was to confront the stereotyped picture of gay song-singing cotton pickers with such inordinate rage that I was told even by fellow Blacks that my paranoia was embarrassing. But I had seen the fingers cut by the mean little cotton bolls, and I had witnessed the backs and shoulders and arms and legs resisting any further demands.

Some of the workers would leave their sacks at the Store to be picked up the following morning, but a few had to take them home for repairs. I winced to picture them sewing the coarse material under a coal-oil lamp with fingers stiffening from the day's work. In too few hours they would have to walk back to Sister Henderson's Store, get vittles and load, again, onto the trucks. Then they would face another day of trying to earn enough for the whole year with the heavy knowledge that they were going to end the season as they started it. Without the money or credit necessary to sustain a family for three months. In cotton-picking time the late afternoons revealed the harshness of Black Southern life, which in the early morning had been softened by nature's blessing of grogginess, forgetfulness and the soft lamplight.

WARM-UP

Work in groups. First, be sure that everyone in the group understands the word "stereotype." Then decide on a people group that you would like to discuss, e.g., teachers, basketball players, nurses, librarians, various ethnic groups, mentally retarded people, rich people, or some other group. Allow five minutes or less for each person to jot down his or her own stereotyped word picture of the people group, then compare your results with one another. In the following five minutes, record as many reasons you can think of to explain why people tend to stereotype groups and the effects stereotyping can have on both those who are stereotyped and those who do the stereotyping.

DISCOVERING NEW WORDS (Choose the word or phrase that best defines the word in italics.)

1. *cooling board*   (a) ironing board   (b) place to rest when overcome by the heat   (c) resting place for a corpse   (d) cupboard used to store perishable food.

2. *winding sheet*   (a) sheet used on a water bed   (b) designer sheet   (c) material used to make ship sails   (d) material used to wrap a corpse

3. *bridle*   (a) a check or restraint   (b) flowers worn by a bride   (c) seasoning for food   (d) good words

4. *fo' bits*   (a) four rabbits   (b) four pieces of cotton   (c) four quarters, or one dollar   (d) fifty cents

5. *six bits*   (a) six cents   (b) six dimes   (c) sixty cents   (d) seventy-five cents

6. *prophesied*   (a) swore   (b) predicted   (c) feared   (d) hoped

7. *sparse*   (a) small in quantity   (b) plentiful   (c) ripe   (d) fluffy

8. *commissary*   (a) commissioner's office   (b) store for a company or the military   (c) court house   (d) post office

9. *stereotyped*   (a) musical   (b) created on a typewriter   (c) original   (d) conventional

10. *inordinate*   (a) not coordinated   (b) inadequate   (c) exceeding reasonable limits   (d) embarrassing

11. *paranoia*   psychological condition in which a person feels   (a) sad   (b) treated unfairly   (c) unusually happy   (d) underpaid

12. *winced*   (a) made an involuntary facial expression showing distress   (b) became angry   (c) tried   (d) cried

13. *vittles*   (a) vitamins   (b) work clothes   (c) food   (d) oil

DISCOVERING THE MEANING

1. What is the main idea in the selection from Maya Angelou's biography?

2. How does Angelou's description of the people she knew who picked cotton differ from the stereotyped picture she describes?

3. Compare the description of the cotton pickers in the morning as they prepare to go to the fields with the description of them returning in the evening from the fields.

DISCOVERING CONNECTIONS

Write a paragraph or essay describing one of the following people groups:

1. Every city has groups who work hard at their jobs despite their low pay. Can you name any such group? What importance does that group have to the commerce of your city?

2. What groups of workers are being exploited?

3. Are children being exploited today for their labor? If so, who are they and where are they? What is being done to prevent this exploitation?

SUGGESTED TOPICS FOR DESCRIPTIVE
PARAGRAPHS AND ESSAYS

1. Describe some scene of beauty that you remember.

2. Describe your feelings when you saw a newborn child.

3. Describe one of the following: your parents, a brother or a sister, your house, your neighborhood, your city, town, or village.

4. Describe a crowd at a prize fight, or a professional hockey, football, soccer, or basketball game.

5. Describe a cemetery scene where you watched the burial of a close relative or friend.

6. Describe an elderly person such as your grandfather, grandmother, or great grandparent.

7. Describe your feelings while watching a memorable movie, concert, play, or ballet performance.

8. Describe the confusion following a traffic accident.

9. Describe the devastation caused by the San Francisco earthquake of October 14, 1989.

10. Describe an important event in your life: a wedding, a Bar Mitzvah or Bas Mitzvah, a graduation, becoming engaged, becoming a parent.

11. Describe the countryside in autumn or some other season.

12. Describe a family scene such as a mother sending her child off to school for the first time, a father teaching a child to ride a bike, a child learning to walk.

13. Describe a restaurant counter at 7:00 A.M.

14. Describe a student rushing to be on time for an early morning class.

15. Describe a moment in a sports event such as a quarterback changing signals at the line of scrimmage; a wide receiver fumbling the ball after being hit by linebackers; making a hole-in-one; winning a diving competition.

Chapter 16

How Writers
Use Definition

Writing Across the Curriculum

What you will learn in this chapter about writing a definition essay has relevance to writing assignments in other college courses. Here are some examples of assignments that call for the definition mode:

Biology: Write a paragraph defining hematology.

Business Administration: Write paragraphs in which you define one of the following terms: annuity, quality control, productivity.

Dietetic Technology: Write a paragraph in which you define one of the following terms: digestion, ingestion, etiology.

Labor Studies: Write a paragraph or an essay in which you define one of the following terms: collective bargaining, grievance, binding arbitration.

Definition is the mode of writing that attempts to clarify a word, a concept, an idea, or an issue. Failure to define terms and clarify issues is often the reason why communication problems arise in business, government, religion, labor, education, and even in basic institutions such as the family.

During the early 1980s, women's groups tried to get two-thirds of the states to ratify the Equal Rights Amendment (ERA). Some of the ERA's strongest supporters did not always make a good case for ERA because they failed to define clearly what it meant and and what it did not mean, what it would do and what it would not do. Failure to define the amendment clearly gave opponents of ERA an opportunity to define ERA in ways that were sometimes dishonest and ludicrous.

QUALITIES OF A GOOD DEFINITION

Good definitions get to the truth of an issue, the heart of the matter. A good definition is precise; it clearly states the main qualities of a concept, issue, idea, or word. It sets limits and boundaries, distinguishing the word or concept from all other words and concepts.

Extended Definitions

It is relatively easy to define some words in a short concise manner. Other words, such as kindness, justice, love, require extended definitions.

Definitions Can Be Formal or Informal

Some definitions become apparent through context; others do not. When you come across an unfamiliar word in your reading and you cannot figure out its meaning by the way it is used, you consult a dictionary. The dictionary meaning is a *formal* definition.

We often use *informal* definitions in our conversations and in our writing to clarify the meaning of words. For example, you may say to a friend, "Is that guy smart!" Then you explain what you mean by smart. "He finished the final in twenty minutes, and the rest of us struggled for two hours."

HOW WRITERS USE DEFINITION

Defining Key Terms

When authors write essays on complex topics they usually define key terms. Consider, for example, the problem of defining "illiteracy," a popular topic. Parents and educators sometimes complain that many high school students are functionally illiterate. What exactly does that term mean? To whom does it apply and not apply? Does the term "functional illiterate" apply, for example, to the high school dropout who reads at the third grade level? Compared to his classmates who have gone on to college or to responsible jobs in the workplace, some would argue that the term could apply. But wait. The dropout has a steady job as a maintenance man in a factory. He has a driver's license, pays taxes, and obeys the laws of the community in which he lives. Is he a functional illiterate? Of course not.

Defining in this case means telling who *does not* come under the umbrella of functional illiteracy. That done, the writer can then tell his readers what group *does* come under the umbrella.

Now reverse the term. Who is functionally literate? Certainly, the high school graduate who has gone on to college and done well in his studies. But what about the high school graduate who has not gone to college? He is certainly functionally literate. In fact, in some ways he may be more culturally literate than his fellow classmates who have gone on to college if he has had more exposure to cultural programs and events and done more reading.

Five Ways to Define

Writers define words, concepts, and issues in five ways: classification, negation, example, synonym, comparison/contrast.

Defining by Classification.   This means that the writer assigns the term to a class or category and then tells how the term differs from other members in that class. Some examples will make this clear.

TERM	CLASS	DIFFERENCES
TV anchor	Newscaster	who begins and ends the TV news program
Obituary	A newspaper report	that announces the death of a prominent community person
Balk	An illegal motion	made by a pitcher before throwing a baseball
Debate	A formal contest of argumentation	in which two opposing sides attack and defend a given proposition

Defining by Negation.   Sometimes writers define something by telling what it is not. For example, in the chapter on thesis, we defined the term thesis by saying that it is *not* a title, it is *not* an announcement, it is *not* a question. Then we defined it positively by saying that it is a statement that reflects the writer's point of view or a position that a writer takes on a controversial or arguable issue.

Defining by Example or Illustration.   If a writer is trying to define the term *superstar,* he or she can make the definition more understandable by giving examples: Luciano Pavorotti (opera), Kevin Mitchell (baseball), Kevin Costner (movies), Betsy King (golf), Eddie Murphy (comedy), Florence Griffith-Joyner (track).

Definition by Synonym.   Sometimes writers find that synonyms help them define a subject more clearly. If a writer is defining someone as a statesman, the synonyms "conciliator, negotiator, compromiser, unifier, leader" could be helpful in defining the statesmanlike qualities the person has.

Definition by Comparison and Contrast.   If the writer is trying to define an average businessman, an average actor or actress, an average ball player, he may compare or contrast that average person with other better known people in that field who were average, above average or below average in performance.

Guidelines for Writing Definition Paragraphs and Essays

1. Short dictionary definitions may serve a purpose in an essay, but they should be used sparingly.
2. An extended definition is more appropriate for the definition essay, since it expands on the dictionary definition to clarify the meaning more precisely.
3. Your use of definition will depend upon your audience. If you are defining the baseball term *double play* for a group of students from a foreign country, you will probably have to give a long and detailed explanation. If, however, your audience is a group of American students, you can safely assume that most, if not all, know what the term is. You will insult their intelligence if you try to define the obvious.

READINGS AND REFLECTIONS

Tell Me About Me
===

William Sloane

William Sloane had a distinguished career as an editor, publisher, and writer of both fiction and nonfiction. After his death in 1974, his wife completed The Craft of Writing *from chapter headings he had written and selections from his collection of lecture notes and outlines. The book is addressed to writers. A short selection follows in which he defines "reader."*

I am not sure how many readers are left today in the very large society in which we live. By reader I mean another human being who is not professionally or personally involved with writers. Who is this reader I am talking about? The first thing about him is that he has learned to read. There is any God's quantity of books about this process, the problems it's making in our society, and how very, very scarred and crippled the reader may have become in the process of being taught. Let's skip over all of that, and assume he has mastered this skill to a certain extent. He is capable of looking at a printed page and finding communication in it. Let us hope he is a voluntary reader. The great mass of students who are reading fiction in this country are captive readers. It is assigned to them: Poe one day and Melville the next. This is not the kind of reader I want to talk about. The reader I am concerned with is the one who bought a magazine with your story in it, bought a book you wrote, paperback perhaps—he waited for it to come out in paperback—but in any event, he is reading whatever it is you have written, voluntarily.

The next thing about your reader that's interesting is that he doesn't care at all about you. If he's attending a class or course, he has to care at least nine sentences' worth, which can be stated later in a term paper or on an examination. But the genuine reader doesn't care whether he's reading a book written by a man or a woman, by somebody young or old, or if it was written yesterday or two hundred years ago. Furthermore, he isn't there to be improved by you. He isn't saying, "Tell me, dear author, about yourself and what you think about the world, art, life, the eternal verities." What he is saying is so frightening that I urge you not to think about it while you are writing—you may get a kind of palsy. What he is saying is, "Tell me about me. I want to be more alive. Give me *me.*" All the great fiction of the world satisfies this need: it tells me about me. That's what's good about Shakespeare and it's also what's good about Homer. Shakespeare—except when you get hold of a book called "The Doctored Works of Shakespeare" or something of the sort—tells you absolutely nothing about himself. You can't learn anything about Shakespeare in Shakespeare. He, himself, is in dispute among scholars and critics to this very day because all he ever wrote about was you and me. Tell me about me.

WARM-UP

Think about some books you have read. What books do you remember best? Why? Does the "Tell me about me" factor have anything to do with your choices? In small groups, discuss ways your favorite books made you see yourself in a new light or told you something about yourself.

DISCOVERING NEW WORDS (Choose the word or phrase that best defines the word in italics.)

1. *verities*   (a) virtues   (b) arguments   (c) truths   (d) politics

2. *palsy*   (a) friendliness   (b) condition marked by loss of power to feel or to

   control movement   (c) emotional illness   (d) nervousness

DISCOVERING THE MEANING

Underline the parts of the selection that define *reader.* What need of the reader does Sloane believe all great fiction fulfills?

DISCOVERING CONNECTIONS

Select for your journal two or three pieces of writing that caused you to have the "Tell me about me" experience.

The Company Man

Ellen Goodman

Ellen Goodman is a syndicated columnist for the Boston Globe. *Formerly she worked for* Newsweek *and the* Detroit Free Press. *"The Company Man" is taken from* Close to Home, *a collection of Goodman's essays.*

He worked himself to death, finally and precisely, at 3:00 A.M. Sunday morning.

The obituary didn't say that, of course. It said that he died of a coronary thrombosis—I think that was it—but everyone among his friends and acquaintances knew it instantly. He was a perfect Type A, a workaholic, a classic, they said to each other and shook their heads—and thought for five or ten minutes about the way they lived.

This man who worked himself to death finally and precisely at 3:00 A.M. Sunday morning—on his day off—was fifty-one years old and a vice-president. He was, however, one of six vice-presidents, and one of three who might conceivably—if the president died or retired soon enough—have moved to the top spot. Phil knew that.

He worked six days a week, five of them until eight or nine at night, during a time when his own company had begun the four-day week for everyone but the executives. He worked like the Important People. He had no outside "extracurricular interests," unless, of course, you think about a monthly golf game that way. To Phil, it was work. He always ate egg salad sandwiches at his desk. He was, of course, overweight, by 20 or 25 pounds. He thought it was okay, though, because he didn't smoke.

On Saturdays, Phil wore a sports jacket to the office instead of a suit, because it was the weekend.

He had a lot of people working for him, maybe sixty, and most of them liked him most of the time. Three of them will be seriously considered for his job. The obituary didn't mention that.

But it did list his "survivors" quite accurately. He is survived by his wife, Helen, forty-eight years old, a good woman of no particular marketable skills, who worked in an office before marrying and mothering. She had, according to her daughter, given up trying to compete with his work years ago, when the children were small. A company friend said, "I know how much you will miss him." And she answered, "I already have."

"Missing him all these years," she must have given up part of herself which had cared too much for the man. She would be "well taken care of."

His "dearly beloved" eldest of the "dearly beloved" children is a hard-working executive in a manufacturing firm down South. In the day and a half before the funeral, he went around the neighborhood researching his father, asking the neighbors what he was like. They were embarrassed.

His second child is a girl, who is twenty-four and newly married. She lives near her mother and they are close, but whenever she was alone with her father, in a car driving somewhere, they had nothing to say to each other.

The youngest is twenty, a boy, a high-school graduate who has spent the last couple of years, like a lot of his friends, doing enough odd jobs to stay in grass and food. He was the one who tried to grab at his father, and tried to mean enough to him to keep the man at home. He was his father's favorite. Over the last two years, Phil stayed up nights worrying about the boy.

The boy once said, "My father and I only board here."

At the funeral, the sixty-year-old company president told the forty-eight-year-old widow that the fifty-one-year-old deceased had meant much to the company and would be missed and would be hard to replace. The widow didn't look him in the eye. She was afraid he would read her bitterness and, after all, she would need him to straighten out the finances—the stock options and all that.

Phil was overweight and nervous and worked too hard. If he wasn't at the office, he was worried about it. Phil was a Type A, a heart-attack natural. You could have picked him out in a minute from a lineup.

So when he finally worked himself to death, at precisely 3:00 A.M. Sunday morning, no one was really surprised.

By 5:00 P.M. the afternoon of the funeral, the company president had begun, discreetly of course, with care and taste, to make inquiries about his replacement. One of three men. He asked around: "Who's been working the hardest?"

WARM-UP

A friend who is a workaholic confides in you, saying, "My spouse and three children are no longer close to me. Why?" Discuss what changes in lifestyle you would suggest to the friend.

DISCOVERING NEW WORDS (Choose the word or phrase that best defines the word in italics.)

1. *obituary*   (a) notice of death   (b) doctor's report   (c) hospital report

   (d) last will and testament

2. *coronary thrombosis*   (a) heart attack   (b) gall bladder attack   (c) flu

   (d) automobile accident

3. *discreetly*   (a) quietly, prudently   (b) loudly, openly   (c) angrily   (d) shyly

DISCOVERING THE MEANING

1.   Why were the neighbors embarrassed when Phil's son asked them what his father was like?

2.   Type A, a phrase coined by San Francisco cardiologists Meyer Friedman and Ray Rosenman, has become a popular label for people who are extremely competitive, impatient, and almost always in a hurry. List several ways Phil and other Type A people you know fit this definition.

DISCOVERING CONNECTIONS

Goodman defines the term "company man" by giving examples of the way Phil related to his family and his job. Define *noncompany man or noncompany woman* through five examples that show how such a person relates to family and job.

I Want a Wife

Judy Syfers

Judy Syfers earned a bachelor of fine arts degree in painting at the University of Iowa. In "I Want a Wife," Syfers tempers anger with ironic humor to strike an effective blow to the stereotypical male view of the role of a wife. The essay was first published in Ms *magazine in 1972.*

I belong to that classification of people known as wives. I am A Wife. And, not altogether incidentally, I am a mother.

Not too long ago a male friend of mine appeared on the scene fresh from a recent divorce. He had one child, who is, of course, with his ex-wife. He is obviously looking for another wife. As I thought about him while I was ironing one evening, it suddenly occurred to me that I, too, would like to have a wife. Why do I want a wife?

I would like to go back to school so that I can become economically independent, support myself, and, if need be, support those dependent upon me.
I want a wife who will work and send me to school. And while I am going to
school I want a wife to take care of my children. I want a wife to keep track
of the children's doctor and dentist appointments. And to keep track of mine,
too. I want a wife to make sure my children eat properly and are kept clean.
I want a wife who will wash the children's clothes and keep them mended. I
want a wife who is a good nurturant attendant to my children, who arranges
for their schooling, makes sure that they have an adequate social life with
their peers, takes them to the park, the zoo, etc. I want a wife who takes care
of the children when they are sick, a wife who arranges to be around when
the children need special care, because, of course, I cannot miss classes at
school. My wife must arrange to lose time at work and not lose the job. It may
mean a small cut in my wife's income from time to time, but I guess I can
tolerate that. Needless to say, my wife will arrange and pay for the care of the
children while my wife is working.

I want a wife who will take care of *my* physical needs. I want a wife who
will keep my house clean. A wife who will pick up after me. I want a wife
who will keep my clothes clean, ironed, mended, replaced when need be, and
who will see to it that my personal things are kept in their proper place so
that I can find what I need the minute I need it. I want a wife who cooks the
meals, a wife who is a *good* cook. I want a wife who will plan the menus, do
the necessary grocery shopping, prepare the meals, serve them pleasantly,
and then do the cleaning up while I do my studying. I want a wife who will
care for me when I am sick and sympathize with my pain and loss of time
from school. I want a wife to go along when our family takes a vacation so
that someone can continue to care for me and my children when I need a rest
and change of scene.

I want a wife who will not bother me with rambling complaints about a
wife's duties. But I want a wife who will listen to me when I feel the need to
explain a rather difficult point I have come across in my course of studies.
And I want a wife who will type my papers for me when I have written them.

I want a wife who will take care of the details of my social life. When my
wife and I are invited out by my friends, I want a wife who will take care of
the babysitting arrangements. When I meet people at school that I like and
want to entertain, I want a wife who will have the house clean, will prepare
a special meal, serve it to me and my friends, and not interrupt when I talk
about the things that interest me and my friends. I want a wife who will have
arranged that the children are fed and ready for bed before my guests arrive
so that the children do not bother us. I want a wife who takes care of the
needs of my guests so that they feel comfortable, who makes sure that they
have an ashtray, that they are passed the hors d'oeuvres, that they are offered

a second helping of the food, that their wine glasses are replenished when necessary, that their coffee is served to them as they like it. And I want a wife who knows that sometimes I need a night out by myself.

I want a wife who is sensitive to my sexual needs, a wife who makes love passionately and eagerly when I feel like it, a wife who makes sure that I am satisfied. And, of course, I want a wife who will not demand sexual attention when I am not in the mood for it. I want a wife who assumes the complete responsibility for birth control, because I do not want more children. I want a wife who will remain sexually faithful to me so that I do not have to clutter up my intellectual life with jealousies. And I want a wife who understands that *my* sexual needs may entail more than strict adherence to monogamy. I must, after all, be able to relate to people as fully as possible.

If, by chance, I find another person more suitable as a wife than the wife I already have, I want the liberty to replace my present wife with another one. Naturally, I will expect a fresh, new life; my wife will take the children and be solely responsible for them so that I am left free.

When I am through with school and have a job, I want my wife to quit working and remain at home so that my wife can more fully and completely take care of a wife's duties.

My God, who *wouldn't* want a wife?

WARM-UP

On a scale of 1 to 5 (1, not important; 5, very important), rate the importance of the following qualities in a spouse.

1. _____ Good looking

2. _____ Humorous

3. _____ Smart

4. _____ Hard-working

5. _____ Rich

6. _____ Kind

7. _____ Generous

8. _____ Same ethnic background as yours

9. _____ Same religious affiliation as yours

10. _____ Same political affiliation as yours

DISCOVERING NEW WORDS

Instead of taking a self-test and finding the correct responses at the end of the chapter, practice your skill at defining words. Write a short definition of each word in the list you already know and compare it with the dictionary definition. Look up the meaning of the words you do not know.

nurturant: _____

peers: _____

rambling: _____

hors d'oeuvres: _____

replenished: _____

entail: _____

adherence: _____

monogamy: _____

DISCOVERING THE MEANING

1. Classify the duties mentioned by Syfers in this selection according to occupation. Example:

Child care worker	*Secretary*	*Housekeeper*
take care of children	keep track of appointments	pick up after family
_____	_____	_____
_____	_____	_____
_____	_____	_____

2. With the help of a dictionary or a literary glossary, define *satire*. Does this selection fit into that category of literature? Explain.

3. This selection first appeared in *Ms* magazine in 1971. In what ways have role expectations in marriage changed since then?

4. In a sentence or two, state the thesis of the selection.

DISCOVERING CONNECTIONS

1. In spite of the largely accepted view that working wives do most of the home and child care, that is not always the case. You might want to write a paragraph or an essay from a husband's point of view, especially if you are male, using satire to make your case. In your prewriting, be sure to brainstorm about the duties husbands traditionally perform.

2. Write a paragraph or an essay that defines the husband/wife relationship in an ideal marriage. Satire would probably not be a good vehicle for essay on this topic; humor, on the other hand, could keep it from taking on a preachy tone.

Hymn of Love

St. Paul, 1 Cor. 13 (Edited by J. B. Phillips)

One of the most interesting figures in the New Testament is St. Paul, who was born around 10 A.D. After the death of Jesus, he spent many adventurous years spreading Christianity and was put to death in the year 67.

The New Testament contains several letters which were either written by or are attributed to Paul. In this letter, St. Paul defines love. Reading the selection in contemporary language helps people understand what St. Paul meant by love, or charity. The selection is taken from the revised edition of The New Testament in Modern English, *edited by J. B. Phillips, who has put into contemporary English many books of the Bible.*

Christian love—the highest and best gift

If I speak with the eloquence of men and of angels, but have no love, I become no more than blaring brass or crashing cymbal. If I have the gift of foretelling the future and hold in my mind not only all human knowledge but the very secrets of God, and if I also have that absolute faith which can move mountains, but have no love, I amount to nothing at all. If I dispose of all that I possess, yes, even if I give my own body to be burned, but have no love, I achieve precisely nothing.

This love of which I speak is slow to lose patience—it looks for a way of being constructive. It is not possessive: it is neither anxious to impress nor does it cherish inflated ideas of its own importance.

Love has good manners and does not pursue selfish advantage. It is not touchy. It does not keep account of evil or gloat over the wickedness of other people. On the contrary, it shares the joy of those who live by the truth.

Love knows no limit to its endurance, no end to its trust, no fading of its hope; it can outlast anything. Love never fails.

All gifts except love will be superseded one day

For if there are prophecies they will be fulfilled and done with, if there are "tongues" the need for them will disappear, if there is knowledge it will be swallowed up in truth. For our knowledge is always incomplete and our prophecy is always incomplete, and when the complete comes, that is the end of the incomplete.

When I was a little child I talked and felt and thought like a little child. Now that I am a man I have finished with childish things.

At present we are men looking at puzzling reflections in a mirror. The time will come when we shall see reality whole and face to face! At present all I know is a little fraction of the truth, but the time will come when I shall know it as fully as God has known me!

In this life we have three lasting qualities—faith, hope and love. But the greatest of them is love.

WARM-UP

Use Figure 16.1 to brainstorm about the *love* relationships in your life. Write your name in the center circle, and the names of people whom you love and who love you in the other circles. On the basis of those relationships, attempt to define at least two different types of love.

DISCOVERING NEW WORDS (Choose the word or phrase that best defines the word in italics.)

1. *eloquence*   (a) loudness   (b) fluency   (c) anger   (d) tone

2. *prophecy:*   (a) wisdom   (b) a long life   (c) prediction   (d) kindness

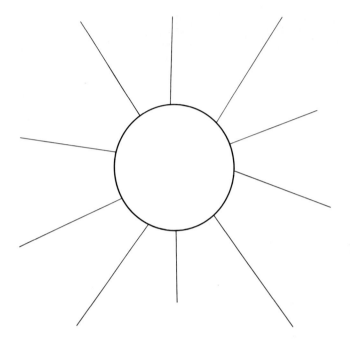

FIGURE 16.1   You and Your Love Relationships

DISCOVERING THE MEANING

Sometimes it is easier to define what something is not than what it is. Explain in a sentence or two what these phrases from the selection mean:

(a) "Love is never boastful . . ."
(b) "Love keeps no score of wrongs . . ."
(c) (Love) "does not gloat over other men's sins . . ."

DISCOVERING CONNECTIONS

Write a definition of "friend." Start with a thesis which includes two or three qualities that you look for in a friend. Support the thesis by further defining those qualities.

SUGGESTED TOPICS FOR DEFINITION
PARAGRAPHS AND ESSAYS

In addition to the topics suggested here, you may wish to suggest some of your own.

1. Define friend.
2. Define "nerd."
3. Define "wimp."
4. Define Christmas spirit.
5. Define fashion.
6. Define peer pressure.
7. Define excellence.
8. Define mother, father, sister, brother, grandmother, grandfather.
9. Define *chutzpah*.
10. Define Ramadan.
11. Define morale.
12. Define integrity.
13. Define "high five."

Chapter 17

How Writers
Use Examples

Writing Across the Curriculum

What you will learn in this chapter about writing an example essay has relevance to writing assignments in other college courses. Here are some examples of assignments that call for the example mode:

English: In a short essay give some examples of modern female writers whose female characters are women with strong personalities.

Biology: In a paper give specific examples of vegetation that can be found in your locality.

Humanities: Write a paper in which you cite at least three works of art which reflect the struggle of human beings to maintain their individuality.

Law Enforcement: Write a paper in which you give examples of poor police procedures that can easily antagonize minority groups.

Psychology: Write a paper in which you give examples of people whose behaviors demonstrate extreme paranoia.

USING EXAMPLES IN CONVERSATION

We use examples frequently in our conversation. If we are describing an unusual piece of architecture we happened to see while vacationing, we use examples of local architecture to help our listener visualize what we saw.

If we are trying to convince a friend to vote for a candidate we are supporting, we use examples to show why that particular candidate deserves our vote.

When we are called in for a job interview, we arm ourselves with examples of the skills we can bring to the job and examples of how we have performed well in the past.

USING EXAMPLES IN WRITING

Using examples effectively in your writing is a good skill to cultivate. You will need it in responding to essay questions in assignments and in tests. Using examples is a good way to illustrate your understanding of an issue and to support your convictions.

Writers use examples—anecdotes, figures, facts, events—to support a thesis, to clarify an issue, to support general statements. Concrete examples can make complex information understandable.

Jonathan Shell wrote a best-selling book to show what would happen if an atomic bomb were dropped on a major city like New York. He could have written the book in terms that only scientists could understand. Instead, he chose to write in language that anyone could understand. He gave examples of what would happen when the bomb hit and what would happen in the wake of the aftershocks that would follow the first explosion. He gave examples of what would happen to buildings and bridges, what would happen to the communications and transportation systems, and what would happen to the inhabitants. It was a bleak and frightening picture. It would not have been that, however, had he not used such good examples to illustrate his thesis that a civilized society must do all in its power to eliminate destructive nuclear devices from the face of the earth.

Guidelines for Writing Paragraphs and Essays That Illustrate by Use of Example

1. *Use only the number of examples needed to support your thesis statement.* Sometimes one example will be sufficient; at other times, two or three examples might be too few.

If you are arguing that the police response time in your city is too slow, a few examples from one district of the city would not be enough. You would need examples from all of the districts in the city. Or if you are arguing that the superintendent of your school district should have his contract renewed because of his outstanding leadership, you will convince others if you give many concrete examples of his leadership. If you give only a couple of examples, you will not prove your case.

2. *Make sure that the examples you are using are representative of the group you are talking about.*

If you contend that the professional football players on your city's team are civic-minded individuals who give their time to raising money for charities or to tutoring illiterate youths, you need to give many examples to prove your point. If only three or four are civic minded, you cannot use them to make a sweeping statement about the entire team.

3. *Arrange your examples in such a way that they will have the greatest impact upon your readers.*

Suppose you are writing an essay showing that a professional football player is truly civic-minded. He spends three hours a week tutoring illiterate youths; he and his wife have opened their home to children waiting for adoption; he frequently speaks to high school students on the dangers of chemical dependency. Opening his home to children awaiting adoption is the most striking example of his civic and human concern for people, but don't mention that first. Save it for the last, because it will make the greatest impact on your readers.

4. *Remember this Latin saying: "Omnia exempla claudicant."* (All examples limp). The way you use examples and the way you position them in an essay will determine how slight or how pronounced the limp is.

READINGS AND REFLECTIONS

A Friend for Life

Robert Caro

You have already been introduced to Robert Caro in Chapter 14. In this paragraph, also excerpted from Lyndon Johnson: The Path to Power, *Caro illustrates what being a friend meant to Sam Rayburn, a Texas Democrat who was Speaker of the House from 1940 to 1961.*

The four words of advice alluded to in the selection are, "Sam, be a man." You may remember that Sam's father addressed those words to Sam as he was leaving for college.

He campaigned on a little brown cow pony, riding from farm to farm. Unable to make small talk, he discussed farm problems, a short, solid young man with a hairline that was already receding, and earnest brown eyes. At each farm, he asked who lived on the next farm, so that when he got there, he could call them by name. Two incidents in the campaign showed that he had not forgotten his father's four words of advice. A man approached him one day and said that a ten-dollar contribution to an influential farmer would ensure the votes of the farmer's relatives. "I'm not trying to buy the office," Rayburn replied. "I'm asking the people to give it to me." He and his opponent, Sam Gardner of Honey Grove, became friends and, near the end of the campaign, rode from town to town together in a one-horse buggy; arriving in a town, they would take turns standing in the back of the buggy and speaking. In one town, Gardner became ill and spent three days in bed. Although Gardner appeared to be leading, Rayburn didn't use the three days to campaign; he spent them with Gardner, nursing him. Gardner was to be a friend of Sam Rayburn's all his life.

WARM-UP

List all the characteristics that you expect to find in a friend. Write down the names of persons who have all or most of those characteristics.

DISCOVERING NEW WORDS

If there are any unfamiliar words in the selection, look them up in the dictionary. Write sentences in which you use the words.

DISCOVERING THE MEANING

1. What is the topic sentence of Caro's paragraph?

2. When Sam Rayburn left home to start college, his father said to him, "Sam, be a man." State in your own words the two examples the author uses to show that Rayburn had not forgotten his father's advice.

DISCOVERING CONNECTIONS

Rayburn revealed his character when he chose caring for his opponent over continuing the campaign. Write a paragraph or essay about an occasion in your life or in the life of someone else when friendship called for personal sacrifice.

Fear Is Like Fire

A few years ago, Charles Kuralt's CBS *Sunday Morning featured boxing heavyweight trainer Cus D'Amato in a segment titled "Fire Out of Fear." In the interview, D'Amato said that every kid, including his protege Mike Tyson, who wanted to be a fighter, has a sense of fear. Fear is like fire, he explained. If fire is out of control, it can do terrible things. But if it is controlled, it can cleanse and illuminate. The writer of the following paragraph uses D'Amato's analogy in an essay that shows how fear of aging can be paralyzing to some and successfully challenged by others.*

So it is with fear. If fear is not controlled, it can paralyze and intimidate. For example, fear of growing old and losing one's job keeps some in a constant state of anxiety. A sixty-year-old secretary fears that a younger woman will replace her. A fifty-year-old salesman is concerned because of his company's accent on youth. A forty-year-old automobile worker is fearful that a robot will soon take his job. Each knows that it's time to start retraining for another job. But another kind of fear grips them. They know that they should go to college and gear up for another career. But they are afraid of failure. They are afraid of looking foolish before a classroom of young kids.

WARM-UP

List some of the fears you had as a child growing up or list the fears that you have today. List the fears you have overcome and list the fears that still remain.

DISCOVERING NEW WORDS (Choose the word or phrase that best defines the word in italics.)

1. *intimidate*   (a) punish   (b) threaten   (c) make poor   (d) anger

2. *anxiety*   (a) worry   (b) forgetfulness   (c) anger   (d) poverty

DISCOVERING THE MEANING

1. What is the topic sentence of this paragraph?

2. List the examples the author uses to support the topic sentence.

DISCOVERING CONNECTIONS

1. Think about one of your major fears. Illustrate with examples how that fear has affected your life.

2. List some examples of the ways you can turn your fear into "fire."

3. Write an essay about yourself in which you tell through examples how you were able to overcome some irrational fear.

Roses for Some Mothers on Father's Day

=====

In the following paragraph taken from an essay published on the opinion page of a newspaper, the author illustrates his thesis by giving several examples of how some mothers "have stepped in and done a father's job."

It is right that the nation set aside a day to honor fathers—men who have given life and nourished it. But a grateful country should not forget that vast army of women who because of circumstances—death, desertion, divorce— have stepped in and done a father's job. They have worked to support families, often in entry-level jobs because raising a family did not count as "previous work experience." They managed to pay mortgages and taxes even though they generally have earned far less than their male counterparts in comparable jobs. They have clothed and fed children, calmed their fears, and acted as their advocates when they were delinquent or disruptive at school. They have taken them on camping trips and have read the sports pages in order to discuss and enjoy the games with their fatherless sons. They have been house painters, plumbers and electricians. They have stood their ground when their peer-pressured sons and daughters heaped verbal abuse upon them. They have done all these things alone. At times they have lived on the edge of madness, but somehow most of them have remained sane. A nation celebrating Father's Day should also remember that some of its best fathers are mothers.

WARM-UP

The author addresses mothers who play a father's role in addition to their role as mother. It's also true, however, that some of the nation's best mothers have been fathers. Can you think of men in your family or neighborhood who have had to assume the duties of motherhood when a spouse was hospitalized or when a spouse died or when the wife worked outside the home and the male was a "househusband?" List some things normally done by the mother that the fathers had to do for their children.

DISCOVERING NEW WORDS (Choose the word or phrase that best defines the word in italics.)

1. *nourished*   (a) consumed   (b) used   (c) lost   (d) tended

2. *advocates*   (a) accusers   (b) defenders   (c) sources of cash   (d) teachers

DISCOVERING THE MEANING

1. What is the topic sentence of this paragraph?

2. List the examples the author uses to support the topic sentence.

DISCOVERING CONNECTIONS

Write an essay based on one of the two following thesis statements. Give examples to support your position.

1. Marriages would be happier if women would stay at home and raise children.

2. Marriages would be happier if spouses re-defined the roles that have been traditionally assigned to men and to women, to husbands and to wives.

If They Really Had a Nice Day

Richard Cohen

Richard Cohen is a Washington Post *columnist and a member of the* Washington Post Writers Group. *His columns appear in newspapers throughout the country. In this essay, he supports his thesis through example after example.*

One day they finished building Washington. All over town there were no cranes, no construction sites and nowhere was the traffic congested. You could drive anywhere you wanted and know for sure that construction would not be blocking a lane and no truck would be pulling out in traffic. It was a wonderful day.

It was the same day that a kid came into the park with a boom-box and asked everyone nearby if it was all right if he played it. He asked if they wanted to hear classical or pop music, rock or country music. And when they could not decide, he said that it would probably be better if he just kept the thing turned off. With that, he took out a candy bar, unwrapped it and put the wrapper in a trash can. What a day it was.

Other wonderful things happened that day. All the cabdrivers started saying thank you when they were tipped and repeated the destination when it was given so you knew they understood what you had said. Many of them put little signs in their cabs saying the customer was always right and that they would take any route requested. It was a wonderful day.

That same day the garbagemen did not come early in the morning, but later. They said they would never again come before everyone was awake and admitted that they themselves could never figure out why they had always started so early. Anyway, they picked up the cans and quietly put them down and when it was time to tell the driver to move on, they did not yell "Yo!" at the top of their lungs. They merely pressed a button for a buzzer that was heard by only the driver in the cab. That was the kind of day it was.

All over town incredible things were happening. Cars no longer ran red lights, drivers signaled before turning and pedestrians did not run into the street with a I-dare-you-to-hit-me look on their faces. Daredevil messengers on bikes decided that pedestrians were people, too, and slowed down and all the kids who had colored their hair purple and mutilated their bodies ran into Brooks Brothers and came out looking, well, different. This was some day.

On this particular day I took an airplane flight. I drove to the airport and had no trouble finding a parking space. Then I walked to the terminal and did not get accosted by someone insulting Jane Fonda. I walked right on the plane, and the person in front of me did not have a double-bass that he was trying to get into the overhead rack.

When we took off I asked for a drink, gave the stewardess a $20 bill and she said she had change. She said that from that day on all the stewards and stewardesses were going to carry change and quit pretending that an airplane was really something other than a flying saloon. This is what she said and then she said that there would be no announcement about frequent-flyer clubs. I went to sleep and when I awoke, my pants were not creased. What a day!

On this wonderful day there were no stories about floods in India or soccer riots in Europe. Nothing happened in Beirut, there were no stories in the newspaper about Madonna, Florida did not execute anyone and I had actually heard of everyone mentioned in *People* magazine. Rosemary Clooney was on the cover. Prince Charles was ignored, Princess Diana gave birth to a hat, and

Frank Sinatra received the first annual Amadeus Award. It goes to someone whose character is in inverse proportion to his talent.

Wonderful, even magical, things happened that day. My son came home from school and right away did all his homework. The carpenter who had built a bookcase years ago just appeared without being summoned and said he would replace the warped shelves. The painter came and opened the window he had painted shut years ago and the electrician returned, he said, just to check things out.

Later, I took the car to the repair shop, and the mechanic said the problem resulted from mistakes he had made in an earlier visit. Sorry—and no charge.

At the end of the day, I sat back in satisfaction, pleased that I had had such an experience and that, hardest to believe of all, no one had said "Have a nice day." They had actually done something about it.

WARM-UP

Discuss or record in your journal the things people do that cause you to have a *not-so-nice* day. Do some of things that bother Cohen, the author of the essay, also bother you? How do you deal with people who annoy you with offensive behavior?

DISCOVERING NEW WORDS (Choose the word or phrase that best defines the word in italics.)

1. *congested*   (a) sick   (b) crowded   (c) loud   (d) impolite

2. *boom-box*   (a) explosive device   (b) tool box   (c) radio   (d) record player

3. *double bass*   (a) stringed musical instrument   (b) large fish   (c) radio
   (d) trombone

4. *accosted*   (a) approached and spoken to   (b) insulted   (c) snubbed   (d) lied to

NOTE: *Brooks Brothers:* a proper noun; name of a clothing store that caters to upper income men.

DISCOVERING THE MEANING

1. What is the thesis of this essay?

2. Richard Cohen uses innumerable examples to support his thesis. Most of them could be simply stated using this formula: We would all have a better chance at having a nice day if _____

List at least five examples to complete the statement.

3. Describe the author's tone. How does the tone help Cohen convey his thesis?

DISCOVERING CONNECTIONS

List some examples you would include if you were writing an essay with a thesis similar to Cohen's.

What If Peace Stormed the Earth?
===

George Eppley

George Eppley is one of the authors of Discovery. *In this essay, which was first published in the* Plain Dealer *in April, 1986, Eppley uses a variety of examples to illustrate the high price of war.*

And so one day peace came upon Earth. It came so quickly that it caught the nations of the world by surprise. It came, not because the superpowers decided there would be peace or because diplomats skillfully negotiated an end to wars. Peace happened because the youth of the United States, the Soviet Union, and the countries of Europe, the Middle East, Africa, Latin America, and Asia stood together and demanded peace.

The peace movement began slowly and met with opposition and hatred. But it endured and gathered momentum like a ripple that grows into a tidal wave, covering the Earth.

It could not have happened in an earlier age. But with telecommunications and television, the youths of one nation were in contact with the youths of other nations. Satellites enabled them to hold simultaneous rock concerts for peace which were viewed by millions of people. Student exchanges were commonplace. Bargain airfares made it possible for youths to travel and to study in foreign lands, and they did so in great numbers.

The youth movement grew also because young women of all nations got involved. They had seen the grief and agony that war had visited on their mothers and grandmothers. Many had seen their brothers and fathers, their friends and lovers go off to war and never return. They believed that it was time for the women of the world to stop this madness. And with one voice they said so.

The students of the world learned that because they could trust each other there was no need to arm. This was in marked contrast to the leaders of nations, who distrusted each other and therefore were armed.

The celebration of world peace was the greatest in history. It was like Armistice Day, VE Day and VJ Day, only it lasted much longer. Euphoria reigned, and people were reluctant to leave its warm glow.

Unbelievable things happened everywhere.

In the United States and in Russia, the process of reducing nuclear weapons to zero began.

In Afghanistan the Russians and the Afghans threw down their arms and embraced. In Iraq, Iranians and Iraqui troops mingled freely and extended to one another the hand of fellowship. Libya and other countries noted for terrorist activities renounced them and vowed never to support terrorism again. The Ethiopian government stopped its policy of genocide and allowed shipments of food and clothing to reach starving people. In South Africa, whites welcomed blacks into their cities and homes. Apartheid was denounced by whites who had previously supported it.

In Berlin, East Germans and West Germans began to tear down the Wall. Berliners moved freely from the one part of the city to the other without a permit and without fear of being cut down by machine gun fire. In Poland, the government held free elections. Lech Welesa was elected president by an overwhelming margin. Solidarity no longer was underground. Democracy and freedom had triumphed.

In Central America the story was much the same. The Sandinistas and the contras were at peace in Nicaragua. In El Salvador, the fighting and killing stopped. Peasants were given their own land. Soviet advisers left Cuba, and Castro and the United States agreed to exchange ambassadors.

Wonderful things happened in the Middle East. Israelis and Arabs settled the Palestinian question. Gone were intrigue and suspicion, revenge and retaliation. These were replaced by forgiveness and reconciliation. In Lebanon warring factions forgave and forgot the past and began rebuilding that once-beautiful city of Beirut.

Peace came to Northern Ireland. Catholics and Protestants held services in their churches where they asked forgiveness for the divisions that had devastated their land.

Some Christians believed that the second coming of Christ was imminent. At daybreak people would gather in churches to wait and watch and wonder. But the time was not yet.

Not everyone was happy with peace on Earth. After a few months, restlessness and anxiety came over many people in the major countries of the Western world. Peace had come so silently and so suddenly that no one knew how to make the transition from a wartime economy to a peacetime economy. Millions of people had been engaged either in making the weapons of war or in building defense systems for peace.

Now these systems were gone. Men and women found themselves competing in a job market in which there were no jobs. These included employees of companies that had huge defense contracts, munitions makers and arms merchants, military personnel, spies, double agents, and hi-tech scientists who had done research for offensive and defensive space weapons.

These were not the only ones affected. Stockholders who held shares in companies that depended upon defense contracts saw their stocks fall to new lows. The makers of steel, cars, trucks, tanks, warships, submarines, and fighter planes were hurting too.

Even the makers of military toys found that their supplies were a thousand times greater than the demand. Parents were not buying toy tanks, soldiers, machine guns, and war games. Instead, they were buying their kids pens and pencils and books. Hell, the toy makers said, a kid could poke out his eye with a pen and could go blind reading books. Can an Einstein doll ever have the appeal of a Rambo?

It was not that these people liked war. It was rather that they had not been prepared for peace. For years they lived in an economy predicated on military might. Now suddenly they had to live in an economy predicated on peace and justice. The consequences were frightening. A global depression appeared imminent.

The youth leaders of every nation gathered for a conference. They debated whether their nations should go back to the old ways, the old systems, and the old arrangements. After seven days and seven nights they concluded the conference and issued a statement to the world, which is the moral of this fable:

If people will not pay the high price of peace, they will inevitably pay the higher price of war.

WARM-UP

Try to suggest a theme for a fantasy. Begin your fantasy with the words "What if . . . ." For example,

> "What if this were the end of the 16th century?"
> "What if no one ever died?"
> "What if men had babies?"
> "What if there were no television or radio?"

DISCOVERING NEW WORDS (Choose the word or phrase that best defines the word in italics.)

1. *euphoria* (a) drunkenness (b) unbelief (c) feeling of great happiness (d) elected officers

2. *renounced* (a) rejected (b) accepted (c) blamed (d) forgave

3. *genocide* (a) systematic annihilation of a racial, political or cultural group (b) suicide (c) killing of the sick and infirm (d) rejection of the elderly

4. *apartheid* (a) policy of racial segregation (b) murder (c) punishment (d) wealth

5. *denounced* (a) adopted (b) forgotten (c) required (d) openly condemned

6. *intrigue* (a) interesting stories (b) secret scheming (c) hatred (d) murder

7. *retaliation* (a) forgiveness (b) revenge (c) returning favors (d) retail selling

8. *reconciliation* (a) re-establishing friendship (b) replacement of stolen money (c) establishment of new rules (d) guesswork

9. *factions* (a) soldiers (b) conflicting groups (c) nations (d) veterans

10. *imminent* (a) important (b) silly (c) lasting (d) about to happen

11. *predicated* (a) copied (b) preserved (c) based (d) dependent

DISCOVERING THE MEANING

1. State the thesis of the essay in one sentence.

2. What examples does the author use to support the thesis?

DISCOVERING CONNECTIONS

1. What is the importance of hope? Can people live without it? Use your journal to record your thoughts about hope.

2. List the things for which you hope. Are these things attainable or unattainable? Give reasons for your answers in a paragraph, an essay, or a journal entry.

3. Is it possible to attain a better world or should we be reconciled to the fact that war is part of the human condition? Write about your reflections in a paragraph, an essay, or in your journal.

SUGGESTED TOPICS FOR EXAMPLE PARAGRAPHS AND ESSAYS

Write a paragraph or an essay using one of the following topics or one suggested by your instructor. Brainstorming will help you think of good examples you can use in your essay.

1. Discipline was my parents' way of demonstrating tough love.

2. The school calendar should be lengthened (or shortened).

3. The teachers I remember were the ones who were most demanding.

4. Athletic rivalries among high schools are getting out of hand.

5. Fear of failure often keeps people from taking risks or doing their best.

6. Some fashion designers are ripping off young consumers.

7. My high school experience prepared me for the demands of college.

8. Professor X is an inconsistent grader.

9. I have a good self concept because in the process of growing up I was praised, affirmed, and rewarded.

10. Peer pressure often leads people to do things they soon regret.

11. More young people would enter politics if their political leaders were better role models.

12. There's too much violence in children's cartoons.

13. People have a right not to marry, but that right is not always respected.

Chapter 18

How Writers
Use Process

In a process paragraph or essay, the writer explains either how to do something or how something was done. The essay is *instructional* if the writer is explaining how to do something such as wallpaper a bedroom, change a tire, reduce stress, or fix a leaky faucet. But the essay is *informational* if the writer is explaining how something was done, for example, in what manner a particular tornado formed and moved through an area, how a pearl was formed, or how a dictator was overthrown.

Examples of Process Writing

Some people are making fortunes writing about processes. If you need proof of that, go into your college bookstore. You will probably find that one large section has all kinds of "how to" books—how to lose weight, how to write well, how to study for exams, how to take notes, how to travel in a country on $25 per day, how to become an antique collector, how to improve one's self-image, how to become assertive, how to dress for success, how to climb the corporate ladder. The list of process instructional books goes on and on.

Process informational books are in the bookstore, too. You can find volumes explaining how a presidency was won or lost, how a battle was won or lost, how a treaty was made, how a nation gained its independence, how an assassin's plot was foiled, how an accused person was acquitted or convicted.

The reading selections in this chapter will help you understand the difference between process essays that are instructional and those that are informational.

Guidelines for Writing Process
Paragraphs and Essays

1. *Before explaining a process to someone else, be sure you understand the process thoroughly yourself.*

Have you ever asked for directions in a strange town? You are lost and you want to find a motel where you have reservations. You stop someone on the street and get directions. Sometimes those directions are perfect because that person knows the route. Occasionally, however, you might ask someone who pretends to know the way but really does not. Nothing can be more annoying than driving in a strange city with incorrect directions.

2. *Define any terms or concepts with which the reader may be unfamiliar.*

Some years ago, before buying our first personal computer, we took a basic course in understanding the language and the functions of the computer. With advice from our instructor, we bought a computer that would fit our needs. We wanted to use it primarily for word processing. After making the purchase, we hurried home to unpack it. Everything was in good order. Next, we started reading the operator's manual. After three hours, we could not get the word processor to work. Frustrated, we called a friend who is a computer specialist. Fortunately, he was free and came right over.

When we told him that we followed directions to the letter and showed him the manual, he laughed and said, "This manual was written by some engineer who thinks that you have the same understanding of how computers work that he does." Our friend put down the manual and walked us through the steps. In fifteen minutes we completely understood the process. We never referred to the manual again.

We learned a lesson from this. It is important to explain the steps of the process in language that the average person can understand.

3. *Before you begin to explain the process, make sure that you tell your readers what materials, formulas, ingredients, and tools they will need to complete the process successfully.*

This common sense rule is important whether a husband and wife are attempting to wallpaper their living room, or someone is explaining to a friend how to bake cookies.

4. *Arrange the process into a series of chronological or logical steps so that the reader can easily complete the process.*

If a mother is teaching her young daughter how to bake her first cake, the mother will follow a chronological sequence. Making the frosting for the cake and applying it will be the last step in the process and not the first, as her young daughter might insist.

5. *In explaining the process, try to alert the reader to the points in the process that may cause some difficulty.*

One night we watched a very interesting program on a public television station. A talented instructor at a community college was teaching a class the art of glass blowing. Since the students were working near a furnace giving off intense fire and heat, he constantly reminded them of the danger. In addition, there were times when he warned them of special difficulties and how to manage them. He did not want his students to experience any surprises. In explaining a process to your readers, make sure they do not have any surprises—unless they are a part of the process.

6. *Transitional words and phrases* such as *first, second, next,* and *then* will help inform your reader that a new step in the process is beginning.

READINGS AND REFLECTIONS

Requiem for an Elephant
==

Cynthia Moss

After graduating from Smith College, Cynthia Moss worked as a reporter/ researcher for Newsweek. *In 1968 she moved to Africa, where she devoted herself to the study of elephant life. Moss has published numerous articles about elephants in scientific journals and popular magazines. In this selection, taken from* Elephant Memories, *Chapter X, "Life Cycle and Death," Moss describes the process elephants use in attempting to identify an elephant carcass.*

Elephants may not have a graveyard but they seem to have some concept of death. It is probably the single strangest thing about them. Unlike other animals, elephants recognize one of their own carcasses or skeletons. Although they pay no attention to the remains of other species, they always react to the body of a dead elephant. I have been with elephant families many times when this has happened. When they come upon an elephant carcass they stop and become quiet and yet tense in a different way from anything I have seen in other situations. First they reach their trunks toward the body to smell it, and then they approach slowly and cautiously and begin to touch the bones, sometimes lifting them and turning them with their feet and trunks. They seem particularly interested in the head and tusks. They run their trunk tips along the tusks and lower jaw and feel in all the crevices and hollows in the skull. I would guess they are trying to recognize the individual.

WARM-UP

This selection describes the process that elephants use to identify and react to their dead. Discuss the ways that people show respect for their dead.

DISCOVERING NEW WORDS (Choose the word or phrase that best defines the word in italics.)

1. *crevices* (a) bumps (b) scars (c) holes (d) narrow cracks

2. *hollows* (a) cavities (b) bumps (c) scars (d) large cracks

DISCOVERING THE MEANING

1. Notice that the author uses words such as *when, first, then, sometimes* to guide the reader through the process she is explaining.

2. What is the main idea of the paragraph?

3. What details of the process support the main idea of the paragraph?

DISCOVERING CONNECTIONS

Observe some process in nature and write about it in your journal. Examples: a summer rain or a snow storm; growth of a flower, a potted plant, or grass; lifting of fog; birds searching for food; changes in a body of water.

We use the process mode when we tell someone how to prepare food. Ordinarily, recipes list the required ingredients with specific amounts, then explain how to combine the ingredients and produce the finished product. Sometimes just a simple explanation of the process is all that is necessary. In the following paragraph, someone explains how to cook carrots.

Experimenting with Carrots

My husband and I have always liked carrots—raw, boiled, and mixed with nutmeg and butter, sauteed, in soup, in stir-fry dishes—just about any way you can imagine. Recently, I decided on a whim to experiment with carrots, using my new food processor. I suppose someone will tell me that they have been preparing carrots this way for years; nevertheless, I discovered it myself. First, pare or scrape the carrots (after cutting off the green tops, of course), then cut them lengthwise in narrow strips. Cook the carrots to the degree of tenderness you like. Then put them in the food processor or blender with a dash of nutmeg and some fresh parsley. For two generous servings I use three dashes of nutmeg and about three sprigs of parsley. Turn on the food processor for about three seconds, then turn it off and scrape the sides of the mixing container. Repeat the three-second processing two or three more times. One advantage to serving carrots this way is that you can prepare them ahead of time and re-heat them in a microwave or conventional oven when you are ready to serve the rest of the meal.

WARM-UP

Imagine that you are going to give a dinner for the rest of the class. Each person is responsible for bringing one dish to the banquet that represents his or her ethnic or regional heritage. Discuss the process for staging such a dinner.

DISCOVERING NEW WORDS

If you are uncertain about the meaning of any words, consult a dictionary.

DISCOVERING THE MEANING

Explaining processes clearly is a skill that is in demand in a technical world. Manuals are needed for hundreds of products—computers, toys, VCRs, food processors, and so forth. List some jobs that require the ability to explain processes.

DISCOVERING CONNECTIONS

In a paragraph or essay explain one of the following processes:

1. How to use chopsticks.

2. How to cook a hamburger on an outdoor grill.

3. How to eat spaghetti.

4. How to make your favorite dip or frosting.

How to Write with Style

Kurt Vonnegut

Kurt Vonnegut is a contemporary writer of novels, plays and short fiction. Two of his most popular novels are Cat's Cradle, *and* Slaughterhouse Five, *written in the 1960s. "How to Write with Style" was first published in International Paper's "Power of the Word" series.*

Newspaper reporters and technical writers are trained to reveal almost nothing about themselves in their writings. This makes them freaks in the world of writers, since almost all of the other inkstained wretches in that world reveal a lot about themselves to readers. We call these revelations, accidental and intentional, elements of style.

These revelations tell us as readers what sort of person it is with whom we are spending time. Does the writer sound ignorant or informed, stupid or bright, crooked or honest, humorless or playful—? And on and on.

Why should you examine your writing style with the idea of improving it? Do so as a mark of respect for your readers, whatever you're writing. If you scribble your thoughts any which way, your readers will surely feel that you care nothing about them. They will mark you down as an egomaniac or a chowderhead—or worse, they will stop reading you.

The most damning revelation you can make about yourself is that you do not know what is interesting and what is not. Don't you yourself like or dislike writers mainly for what they choose to show you or make you think about? Did you ever admire an empty-headed writer for his or her mastery of the language? No.

So your own winning style must begin with ideas in your head.

1. FIND A SUBJECT YOU CARE ABOUT

Find a subject you care about and which you in your heart feel others should care about. It is this genuine caring, and not your games with language, which will be the most compelling and seductive element in your style.

I am not urging you to write a novel, by the way—although I would not be sorry if you wrote one, provided you genuinely cared about something. A petition to the mayor about a pothole in front of your house or a love letter to the girl next door will do.

2. DO NOT RAMBLE, THOUGH

I won't ramble on about that.

3. KEEP IT SIMPLE

As for your use of language: Remember that two great masters of language, William Shakespeare and James Joyce, wrote sentences which were almost childlike when their subjects were most profound. "To be or not to be?" asks Shakespeare's Hamlet. The longest word is three letters long. Joyce, when he was frisky, could put together a sentence as intricate and as glittering as a necklace for Cleopatra, but my favorite sentence in his short story "Eveline" is this one: "She was tired." At that point in the story, no other words could break the heart of a reader as those three words do.

Simplicity of language is not only reputable, but perhaps even sacred. The *Bible* opens with a sentence well within the writing skills of a lively fourteen-year-old: "In the beginning God created the heaven and the earth."

4. HAVE THE GUTS TO CUT

It may be that you, too, are capable of making necklaces for Cleopatra, so to speak. But your eloquence should be the servant of the ideas in your head. Your rule might be this: If a sentence, no matter how excellent, does not illuminate your subject in some new and useful way, scratch it out.

5. SOUND LIKE YOURSELF

The writing style which is most natural for you is bound to echo the speech you heard when a child. English was the novelist Joseph Conrad's third language, and much that seems piquant in his use of English was no doubt colored by his first language, which was Polish. And lucky indeed is the writer who has grown up in Ireland, for the English spoken there is so amusing and musical. I myself grew up in Indianapolis, where common speech sounds like a band saw cutting galvanized tin, and employs a vocabulary as unornamental as a monkey wrench.

In some of the more remote hollows of Appalachia, children still grow up hearing songs and locutions of Elizabethan times. Yes, and many Americans grow up hearing a language other than English, or an English dialect a majority of Americans cannot understand.

All these varieties of speech are beautiful, just as the varieties of butterflies are beautiful. No matter what your first language, you should treasure it all your life. If it happens not to be standard English, and if it shows itself when you write standard English, the result is usually delightful, like a very pretty girl with one eye that is green and one that is blue.

I myself find that I trust my own writing most, and others seem to trust it most, too, when I sound most like a person from Indianapolis, which is what I am. What alternatives do I have? The one most vehemently recommended by teachers has no doubt been pressed on you, as well: to write like cultivated Englishmen of a century or more ago.

6. SAY WHAT YOU MEAN TO SAY

I used to be exasperated by such teachers, but am no more. I understand now that all those antique essays and stories with which I was to compare my own work were not magnificent for their datedness or foreignness, but for saying precisely what their authors meant them to say. My teachers wished me to write accurately, always selecting the most effective words, and relating the words to one another unambiguously, rigidly, like parts of a machine. The teachers did not want to turn me into an Englishman after all. They hoped that I would become understandable—and therefore understood. And there went my dream of doing with words what Pablo Picasso did with paint or what any number of jazz idols did with music. If I broke all the rules of punctuation, had words mean whatever I wanted them to mean, and strung them together higgledy-piggledy, I would simply not be understood. So you, too, had better avoid Picasso-style or jazz-style writing, if you have something worth saying and wish to be understood.

Readers want our pages to look very much like pages they have seen before. Why? This is because they themselves have a tough job to do, and they need all the help they can get from us.

7. PITY THE READERS

They have to identify thousands of little marks on paper, and make sense of them immediately. They have to *read,* an art so difficult that most people don't really master it even after having studied it all through grade school and high school—twelve long years.

So this discussion must finally acknowledge that our stylistic options as writers are neither numerous nor glamorous, since our readers are bound to be such imperfect artists. Our audience requires us to be sympathetic and patient teachers, ever willing to simplify and clarify—whereas we would rather soar high above the crowd, singing like nightingales.

That is the bad news. The good news is that we Americans are governed under a unique Constitution, which allows us to write whatever we please without fear of punishment. So the most meaningful aspect of our styles, which is what we choose to write about, is utterly unlimited.

8. FOR REALLY DETAILED ADVICE

For a discussion of literary style in a narrower sense, in a more technical sense, I commend to your attention *The Elements of Style,* by William Strunk, Jr., and E. B. White (Macmillan, 1979). E. B. White is, of course, one of the most admirable literary stylists this country has so far produced.

You should realize, too, that no one would care how well or badly Mr. White expressed himself, if he did not have perfectly enchanting things to say.

WARM-UP

In telling beginning writers how to develop their own style, Vonnegut writes: "Find a subject you care about and which you in your heart feel others should care about. It is this genuine caring, and not your games with language, which will be the most compelling and seductive element in your style."

List some subjects you care about and which you would write about if you were a famous author and didn't have to worry about writing essays for a composition class.

DISCOVERING NEW WORDS (Choose the word or phrase that best defines the word in italics.)

1. *reputable*   (a) well thought of, honorable   (b) disgraceful   (c) damaging

    (d) legal

2. *piquant*   (a) clumsy   (b) pleasantly spicy   (c) boring   (d) useless

3. *locutions*   (a) noises   (b) locomotives   (c) rhymes   (d) styles of speaking

4. *unambiguously*   (a) clearly   (b) unemotionally   (c) correctly   (d) orally

DISCOVERING THE MEANING

1. Read the section at the beginning of this chapter titled Guidelines for Writing Process Essays. Does Vonnegut follow any or all of the guidelines?

2. How did Vonnegut's teachers help him say what he means to say?

3. What does Vonnegut mean by "Pity the readers"?

4. Why is Vonnegut's advice on rambling effective?

5. What does Vonnegut advise about revising your writing?

DISCOVERING CONNECTIONS

1. According to Vonnegut, why did his teachers have him read "antique essays and stories" with which he was to compare his own work?

2. Do you think that the selections in this textbook are helping you in your writing become "understandable and therefore understood?" If not, what suggestions would you make to the authors about selections for future editions?

3. Write an essay whose thesis is the following:

    "Antique essays and stories with which I am to compare my writing are (are not) helping me become understandable and therefore understood."

Careful You Don't Cut Yourself

Patrick E. McManus

A monthly columnist for Outdoor Life *magazine, Patrick F. McManus has published stories in many other periodicals including* Field & Stream, Sports Illustrated, Audubon, *and* Reader's Digest. *This selection is taken from "First Knife," a chapter in* The Grasshopper Trap.

Your response to the question of whether you had a knife on you had been thought through months and possibly years in advance. If you were fortunate enough to be chewing on a toothpick, you would reach up slowly, deliberately, and remove the toothpick, then flick it back over your shoulder, possibly creating the impression in the adult that you couldn't chew a toothpick and reach for a knife at the same time, but no matter. There was a right way to do a thing and a wrong way, and this was the right way. Next you bent sideways from the hips, furrowed your brow slightly, and dug your hand into the pocket of your jeans, your fingers expertly sorting through such items as throwing rocks, a dried frog, a steel marble, your reserve wad of bubble gum, and the like, until they closed around the knife, *your* knife, the one that had been requested by an adult. You withdrew your knife with slow deliberation and expertly opened it, always selecting the big blade, of course. Then you handed it to the adult, who probably would have preferred to open the knife himself. And finally, at long last, you got to say it, not smugly or disrespectfully, of course, but matter-of-factly, *maturely,* and possibly with just the slightest touch of pride:

"Careful you don't cut yourself—that blade is razor sharp."

WARM-UP

In their efforts to be responsible, parents and teachers often repeat certain warnings and bits of advice to young people so often that children know exactly what the advice will be even before the adults open their mouths to speak. Recall three or four of those warnings. Record some of them in your journal for future reference.

DISCOVERING NEW WORDS

If there are any words in the selection that you cannot define, consult a dictionary.

DISCOVERING THE MEANING

1. According to the author, what steps are necessary to correctly perform the process of lending someone a knife?

2. What words does the author Patrick McManus use to indicate a transition between some of the steps in the process of lending someone a knife?

DISCOVERING CONNECTIONS

Write a paragraph or essay in which you describe a process you used as a child: playing a game; talking your way out of a scolding; getting out of a responsibility; performing a dreaded task; doing your homework.

SUGGESTED TOPICS FOR PROCESS
PARAGRAPHS AND ESSAYS

Write about some process with which you are familiar from personal experience. The list below is meant to help you recall some process activities you may have experienced. Your instructor may suggest other topics.

1. How you learned to drive.

2. How to prepare a meal.

3. How you survived working for a tough boss.

4. How you learned to swim or ski (water, snow).

5. How to build an aquarium.

6. How to ask for a date or how to decline a date invitation.

7. How to get a loan from a bank.

8. How to take good pictures or how to develop your own film.

9. How you entertained small children without TV.

10. How to buy a used car.

11. How to wallpaper a room.

12. How to become a wise shopper.

13. How to become an antique collector or a stamp collector.

14. How to administer CPR (cardiopulmonary resuscitation).

15. How to fireproof your home.

16. How to discipline a child without using corporal punishment.

17. How to fish for salmon or walleye, or some other species of fish.

18. How to become a better putter.

19. How to waste time creatively.

20. How to care for a pet.

Chapter 19

How Writers Use
Classification and Division

<hr>

Writing Across the Curriculum

What you will learn in this chapter about writing a classification/division essay has relevance to writing assignments in other college courses. Here are some examples of assignments that call for the classification or division mode:

Law Enforcement: Write a paper in which you classify the kinds of weapons drug gangs are using against the police.

Labor Studies: Write a paper in which you classify current attitudes toward the labor movement.

Dietetic Technology: Write a paper in which you show how at least three kinds of diets can be dangerous to one's health.

Physical Education: Write a paper in which you recommend three kinds of physical education that will benefit elementary school children.

<hr>

Classification is using a single identifiable criterion to analyze information about people, events, and things so that the information will be more understandable.

To illustrate, let us suppose that an editor has assigned a reporter to write a review of all the major news stories that came across the wire in the past month. The reporter can simplify her life and her task if she classifies the stories according to some criterion, for example, *newsworthy.* Her categories might be *newsworthy, more newsworthy,* and *headline grabber.*

Division is another technique a writer can use to analyze a subject. While classification puts things into categories, division analyzes the component parts of a subject.

For example, we classify newspapers according to different criteria. One criterion might be frequency of publication: daily, weekly, bi-weekly, monthly. But if we analyze a newspaper according to its component parts, we are using the principle of division. Many newspapers provide this analysis for its readers. On the front page is a little box listing the major parts of the newspaper such as news, features, editorials, obituaries, sports, comics, and classified.

You can see that *classification* and *division* are closely related. In fact, *division* is really a form of *classification* and will be treated as such in this chapter.

Guidelines for Writing Classification/Division Paragraphs and Essays

1. *Use a single identifiable criterion to categorize your information.* If, for example, you choose the criterion of religious affiliation to classify the members of your class, you would use categories such as Protestant, Catholic, Jewish, Hindu, Moslem, Buddhist. Including *Mexican* in your categories would be incorrect, because *Mexican* defines nationality, not religious affiliation.

2. *The classification should be inclusive, or complete.* If, for example, you are classifying General Motors cars according to model, your categories must include Cadillac, Buick, Pontiac, Oldsmobile, and Chevrolet. If you omit one class, the classification is incomplete.

3. *The classification should have some purpose or reason.* Your purpose might be to show that certain kinds of models have many mechanical problems, while other models from the same manufacturer do not. Another purpose might be to show that families with small children prefer certain kinds of vans or station wagons, or that older persons prefer certain kinds of sedans.

4. *A thesis statement, although not strictly necessary in a classification/division essay, will invariably strengthen your essay.* Consider, for example, this thesis:

> Greedy athletes, selfish athletes, and drug-addicted athletes are giving professional sports a bad name.

That statement is certainly more provocative than saying simply that some athletes are greedy, some are selfish, and some are drug-addicted.

5. *Classification and division are effective strategies for narrowing a subject.* For example, should you wish to write an essay on the increase in automobile accidents, it would probably be helpful to use classification and division to help you decide what aspect of the problem you are going to consider. You could consider the ages of the drivers involved or the types of cars involved. Or you could limit your discussion to accidents that are drug-related and those that are not. Or you might write about accidents involving insured and noninsured motorists.

READINGS AND REFLECTIONS

Usually when one writes a classification/division essay, it's a good idea to write an introductory paragraph in which the thesis statement paragraph is either stated or implied. Consider, for example, these opening paragraphs of an essay by Stephanie L. Clark, a student. She saves her thesis statement for the end of the second introductory paragraph.

Punk Music

Stephanie L. Clark

"Turn that awful noise down or off!" my mother snarls across the room. When I heatedly protest that what she is listening to, namely punk, is more than just noise, that it has a fascinating history and many different styles, my words fall on deaf ears. It will always be "that noise" to her. This is perfectly understandable. For the ordinary listener, punk is obnoxious.

To anyone, however, who has paid attention to the music trends of the last decade or so, punk is regarded as a vital force that has influenced music styles, fashion and attitudes. The preponderance of black clothing is an effect of punk. That stale, unchanging musical dinosaur called Heavy Metal has not escaped its influence. Many different musical styles go under the heading punk, for example, thrash. The most important component of punk, however, is attitude. Punk can be divided into three categories on this basis: classic, peace punk, and neo-Nazi.

Writers—even student writers such as Stephanie L. Clark—develop their own style. They use various techniques to indicate that they are putting persons, places or things into categories so that the reader can more easily follow their logic in developing their thesis statements. The following essays by well known writers begin differently, but both writers use the mode of classification to develop their thesis. One is about handshakes; the other is about the city of New York.

How to Press Flesh

Glen Waggoner

Glen Waggoner is Senior Writer for Esquire *magazine. He earned a B.A. at Southern Methodist University and an M.A. and Ph.D. at Columbia University. He is the author of several books. In "How to Press Flesh," Waggoner classifies people according to the way they shake hands.*

A handshake tells you a lot about a man. For one thing, it tells you that he's probably an American. Europeans hug when they greet each other, the English nod, the Japanese bow, but Americans shake hands. And that's the way it is.

Extending an empty hand to show that you have no weapon, grasping another's hand to signify your human bond—you have to admit the handshake has impeccable symbolic credentials. Too bad that it has become so commonplace as to have lost much of its original meaning. Anyway, it's our way of saying hello, so we might as well get straight once and for all the main kinds of handshake, especially the only one that is correct.

The Politician's Pump. A familiar face with a toothy grin that materializes out of a crowd as its owner grabs your right hand in a firm grip, while simultaneously seizing your right forearm in his left hand. Two short, strong shakes and you find yourself being moved sideways as Teeth swivels to mug the next voter. (Also known as the Receiving-Line Two-Hand when practiced by college presidents.)

The Preemptive Squeeze. All fingers and thumb. Your extended hand is caught just short of its target by a set of pincers that encloses your four fingers at the second knuckle and leaves your thumb pointing west. No palm contact whatsoever. One quick squeeze, a side-to-side waggle, and your hand is unceremoniously dropped, leaving it utterly frustrated. .

The Limp Fish. The most hated of all. Someone puts his fingers in your hand and leaves them there. Excusable in foreigners, who are still grappling with a language where *gh* and *f* sound alike (as in "tough fish"). For others, unacceptable.

The Macho Man. The old bone-crusher, the familiar signature of the emotionally insecure but physically strong. If you're alert, you can see this one coming in time to take countermeasures. The best defense is a good offense: grab his hand toward the base of the palm, cutting down on his fingers' leverage, and start your grip before he starts his. Of course, if he's strong enough and macho enough, it won't work, and he'll bond your individual digits into a single flipper for trying to thwart him.

The Preacher's Clasp. As your right hands join, his left folds over the top and immobilizes them both (okay, all three, but who's counting?). Always accompanied by steady eye contact (no way you won't be the first to blink), and usually by a monologue delivered two inches closer to your face than is really necessary. Once the exclusive province of Presbyterian ministers, the Clasp is now practiced by a broad spectrum of the relentlessly sincere, including motivational speakers and honors graduates of weekend-therapy marathons. The worst thing about it is that it makes your hand sweat.

The Right Way. A firm, full-handed grip, a steady squeeze, and a definite but understated downward snap (but no up-and-down pumping, unless you're contemplating a disabling karate move), followed at once by a decisive release accompanied by eye contact and performed only if both parties are standing (the ritual implies mutual respect and equality, after all). Sounds easy enough, but how frequently do you encounter a really good one?

Footnote: Shaking Hands with Women. No difference in grip (the Right Way is always right), but convention has it that you should wait for her to extend her hand first. These days, chances are good she will.

WARM-UP

Consider all the ways you greet people. If you were writing a story about yourself, how would you describe the greeting you would use at a casual meeting of some of the following people: your father or mother, your girlfriend or boyfriend, your younger brother or sister, your grandmother, your best friend, your senior high school English teacher, an acquaintance you would like to know better.

DISCOVERING NEW WORDS (Choose the word or phrase that best defines the word in italics.)

1. *impeccable*   (a) historic   (b) friendly   (c) faultless   (d) silly

2. *preemptive*   (a) seizing before anyone else gets a chance   (b) exclusive   (c) ordinary   (d) distasteful

3. *province*   (a) tactic   (b) habit   (c) territory   (d) greeting

4. *spectrum*   (a) range   (b) habit   (c) tactic   (d) greeting

DISCOVERING THE MEANING

1. What is the thesis of "How to Press Flesh?"

2. Why doesn't Waggoner include in his essay the "high five?"

3. The title, "How to Press Flesh," suggests that the essay is a *process* essay. What characteristics indicate that the author uses the classification/division mode of development to analyze his subject?

DISCOVERING CONNECTIONS

Write a paragraph, essay, or entry in your journal that classifies the way people perform some ordinary action such as expressing thanks when someone holds a door or performs some other courtesy; saying goodbye; asking a stranger for directions; ordering a meal in a restaurant; greeting family or friends at the airport after a vacation; making introductions; or performing some other activity.

The Three New Yorks
E. B. White

E. B. White is well known for Elements of Style, *which he co-authored with William Strunk, and the classic children's book,* Charlotte's Web. *For many years his articles were a regular feature of the* New Yorker.

In "The Three New Yorks," an essay published in The Essays of E. B. White, *the author writes about three distinct types of New Yorkers. In the following introductory paragraphs, he clearly states his thesis.*

There are roughly three New Yorks. There is, first, the New York of the man or woman who was born here, who takes the city for granted and accepts its size and its turbulence as natural and inevitable. Second, there is the New York of the commuter—the city that is devoured by locusts each day and spat out each night. Third, there is the New York of the person who was born somewhere else and came to New York in quest of something. Of these three trembling cities the greatest is the last—the city of final destination, the city that is a goal. It is this third city that accounts for New York's high-strung disposition, its poetical deportment, its dedication to the arts, and its incomparable achievements. Commuters give the city its tidal restlessness, natives give it solidity and continuity, but the settlers give it passion. And whether it is a farmer arriving from Italy to set up a small grocery store in a slum, or a young girl arriving from a small town in Mississippi to escape the indignity of being observed by her neighbors, or a boy arriving from the Corn Belt with a manuscript in his suitcase and a pain in his heart, it makes no difference: each embraces New York with the intense excitement of first love, each absorbs New York with the fresh eyes of an adventurer, each generates heat and light to dwarf the Consolidated Edison Company.

The commuter is the queerest bird of all. The suburb he inhabits has no essential vitality of its own and is a mere roost where he comes at day's end to go to sleep. Except in rare cases, the man who lives in Mamaroneck or Little Neck or Teaneck and works in New York, discovers nothing much about the city except the time of arrival and departure of trains and buses, and the path to a quick lunch. He is desk-bound, and has never, idly roaming in the gloaming, stumbled suddenly on Belvedere Tower in the Park, seen the ramparts rise sheer from the water of the pond, and the boys along the shore fishing for minnows, girls stretched out negligently on the shelves of the rocks; he has never come suddenly on anything at all in New York as a loiterer, because he has had no time between trains. He has fished in Manhattan's wallet and dug out coins but has never listened to Manhattan's breathing, never awakened to its morning, never dropped off to sleep in its night. About 400,000 men and women come charging onto the island each weekday morning, out of the mouths of tubes and tunnels. Not many among them have ever spent a drowsy afternoon in the great rustling oaken silence of the reading room of the Public Library, with the book elevator (like an old water wheel) spewing out books onto the trays. They tend their furnaces in Westchester and in Jersey but have never seen the furnaces of the Bowery, the fires that burn in oil drums on zero winter nights. They may work in the financial district downtown and never see the extravagant plantings of Rockefeller Center—the daffodils and grape hyacinths and birches and the flags trimmed to the wind on a fine morning in spring. Or they may work in a midtown office and may let a whole year swing round without sighting

Governors Island from the sea wall. The commuter dies with tremendous mileage to his credit, but he is no rover. His entrances and exits are more devious than those in a prairie-dog village, and he calmly plays bridge while buried in the mud at the bottom of the East River. The Long Island Rail Road alone carried forty million commuters last year, but many of them were the same fellow retracing his steps.

The terrain of New York is such that a resident sometimes travels farther, in the end, than a commuter. Irving Berlin's journey from Cherry Street in the Lower East Side to an apartment uptown was through an alley and was only three or four miles in length, but it was like going three times around the world.

WARM-UP

Discuss the city or town or region in which you live. Try to classify the kinds of people, the kinds of religion, the kinds of architecture, the kinds of businesses you find.

Or imagine you are starting a model city. Where would it be located? How large would it be? Would you strive for racial and ethnic diversity?

DISCOVERING NEW WORDS (Choose the word or phrase that best defines the word in italics.)

1. *turbulence*   (a) cloudiness   (b) state of turmoil   (c) peace   (d) beauty

2. *quest*   (a) search   (b) conquest   (c) deserting   (d) payment

3. *deportment*   (a) achievements   (b) genius   (c) manner in which people conduct themselves   (d) dedication

4. *tidal*   (a) watery   (b) wave-like   (c) monumental   (d) tidy

5. *gloaming*   (a) twilight   (b) roaming   (c) midnight   (d) subway

6. *spewing*   (a) gushing   (b) idly dropping   (c) sorting   (d) carrying

7. *devious*   (a) deep   (b) important   (c) not straightforward, shifty   (d) confusing

8. *terrain*   (a) a special train   (b) sidewalks   (c) side streets   (d) the character of the land

DISCOVERING THE MEANING

1. Is "The Three New Yorks" a classification essay or a division essay? Explain.

2. Which New York does White prefer? Why?

3. What negative comments does White make about the New York commuter?

DISCOVERING CONNECTIONS

1. Who were the founders of your city, town or village? Why did they choose your particular location to establish the community? Write an essay about some facet of your city's origin.

2. If you have visited a large city such as New York, Chicago, Los Angeles, Toronto, or London, write an essay about the kinds of people you saw there, or the kinds of restaurants you patronized or would like to have patronized, the kinds of monuments or museums you visited, the kinds of street people you saw.

SUGGESTED TOPICS FOR CLASSIFICATION AND DIVISION PARAGRAPHS AND ESSAYS

Using a single criterion such as age, height, religion, competence, attitude, develop a classification essay by analyzing one of the following topics and breaking it down into at least three categories.

1. Teachers
2. Athletes
3. Classmates in college or in high school
4. Priests, ministers or rabbis (their personalities or their sermons)
5. Fashions
6. Detective stories
7. TV commercials
8. Landlords
9. Hunters
10. Nurses
11. Doctors
12. Lawyers
13. Sports cars
14. Talk show hosts
15. Comedians
16. Friends
17. Smokers
18. Boaters
19. Drivers
20. Movies

Chapter 20

How Writers Use Comparison/Contrast

Writing Across the Curriculum

What you will learn in this chapter about writing a comparison/contrast essay has relevance to writing assignments in other college courses. Here are some examples of assignments that call for the comparison and contrast mode:

Sociology: Compare or contrast two religions, or two neighborhoods, or two families or ethnic groups living in the same neighborhood.

Music: Compare or contrast the musical contribution of two artists or two orchestras or two rock groups.

Nursing: Compare or contrast natural childbirth and a birth by Caesarean section.

Business Administration: Compare or contrast the management styles of two chief executives or two managers.

Political science: Compare or contrast the leadership styles of President Bush and President Reagan.

Speech: Compare or contrast the oratorical abilities of Dr. Martin Luther King, Jr., and the Rev. Jesse Jackson.

Why do we choose to drive to work using one route rather than another? Why do we choose to associate with one group of people rather than with another? Why do we choose one make of car over another? Or choose to go to one movie over another? Or why do we go to one doctor or dentist rather than going to another who may be in the same building or even in the same office complex? Why do we choose to live in one part of town rather than in another? Why do we choose to belong to one political party rather than to another?

The answer in most cases is that we have done some comparing and contrasting and have made some decisions. *Comparing means looking at similarities. Contrasting means looking at the differences.*

Writers compare and contrast in both fiction and nonfiction writing. At times they use *comparison* to show how persons, places and things are similar; and at other times they use *contrast* to show how persons, places and things are different.

Guidelines for Writing Comparison/Contrast Paragraphs and Essays

1. *Use a thesis statement* to help you put your essay into sharper focus. Your reader will know immediately what you are going to compare and contrast, and it will help you avoid making statements that may be interesting but which do not support the thesis. If, for example, you are contrasting identical twins, you could write: Although Joe and Jim are identical twins, they have different temperaments.

2. *Avoid comparing or contrasting trivial things.* For example, there may be some similarities or differences between a golf tee and a place kicker's tee, but not too many readers are interested in finding out what they are.

3. *If two subjects are very similar, you might want your essay to focus on the differences; if they are very different, it might be wise to concentrate on their similarities.* For example, if two cities are somewhat similar because they have the same kinds of industries, the same ethnic groups, and the same natural resources, write about their differences. Contrast their educational opportunities, their cultural opportunities, or some other quality that makes them significantly different.

4. *Two basic structures are helpful in organizing comparison/contrast essays: subject-by-subject development, or point-by-point development.* The student model that follows demonstrates how subject-by-subject development or point-by-point development can be used to structure an outline for a comparison/contrast essay.

Student Model

Thesis. Magazine X is a better weekly than Magazine Y because it has better investigative reporting, more interesting reporting, and more objective reporting.

Subject-by-subject outline:

   I. Magazine Y (subject)

      A. Investigative reporting

      B. Interesting reporting

      C. Objective reporting

  II. Magazine X (subject)

      A. Investigative reporting

      B. Interesting reporting

      C. Objective reporting

Point-by-point outline:

    I. Investigative reporting (point)

      A. Magazine Y

      B. Magazine X

   II. Interesting reporting (point)

      A. Magazine Y

      B. Magazine X

  III. Objective reporting (point)

      A. Magazine Y

      B. Magazine X

    5. *When the comparison or contrast is necessarily long or somewhat complex, use point-by-point development; when it is short, use subject-by-subject development.* For example, if you are writing a term paper in which you are comparing or contrasting the leadership style of the president of the United States with that of the secretary general of the Soviet Union, use point-by-point development. If, however, you have only thirty minutes in an essay test to show the differences between the two major political parties, use subject-by-subject development.

    6. *Devote equal time and space to each of the subtopics you are comparing or contrasting.* For example, if you favor Magazine X over Magazine Y, don't let your bias lead you to shortchange Magazine Y. Give fair and equal treatment to each magazine.

READINGS AND REFLECTIONS

Doctors and Nurses
===

Martha Weinman Lear

Martha Weinman Lear has been an editor with The New York Times Magazine *and has written numerous articles for other major magazines.*
   In her novel Heart-Sounds, *Lear uses comparison and contrast to show how her husband, a prominent surgeon, changed his point of view toward doctors and nurses after he was hospitalized following a massive heart attack.*

Who would have believed, for example, that the nurses were so much more important to sick people than the doctors were? Doctors didn't know that at all. As a doctor, he had always thought of the nurse—it astonished him now that he could have been so dense—as a sort of executive secretary. If she (always she) kept an orderly desk, knew what was going on with the patients, took orders efficiently and gave the right pill to the right patient at the right time, she was a good nurse.

But now that he was a patient, he could see that the nurses were . . . angels! Angels of mercy!

They were with him constantly, these woman figures. They were gentle and good. They fixed his pillow. They came when he called for help. They said, "This will make you feel better" and "There, isn't that better?" They touched him with their hands, flesh to flesh. His succor. His lifesavers. His lifelines.

The male figures were with him for ten minutes a day. They were marginal figures, shadowy and cold. They touched him with instruments—stethoscopes, blood-pressure gadgets. They had condescending airs. They asked him many curt questions and grunted at him. He did not like them.

WARM-UP

Brainstorm for three minutes to produce a list of professions that we associate with compassion, caring, and kindness. Brainstorm about professions we associate with competence, toughness and aggressiveness.

   Discuss what would happen to productivity if people in the professions on the second list added compassion, caring, and kindness to their qualities of competence, toughness, and aggressiveness.

DISCOVERING NEW WORDS

If there are any words you do not understand, consult a dictionary.

DISCOVERING THE MEANING

In a sentence or two, express the main difference between doctors and nurses from the point of view of the patient in this selection.

DISCOVERING CONNECTIONS

1. Think about your family doctor. Does he have the same cold qualities of the doctors and interns who attended Dr. Lear? Or does he have some of the qualities that Lear attributes to the nurses who looked after his needs? Write a paragraph or an essay about a doctor or nurse you know.

2. Think about nurses who have attended you when you were hospitalized. Were they angels of mercy? Or were they cold, tough, and aggressive? Write about the experience.

3. There is a shortage of nurses in the country. Do you think that doctors' attitudes towards nurses may be a contributing factor? Write a paragraph or essay comparing or contrasting the attitudes of doctors and nurses or two other groups of professionals.

Elderly — or Old?
===

Dorothea S. Greenbaum

Sculptor and writer, Dorothea S. Greenbaum, was eighty-eight years old when her essay "Elderly, Then Old" was published on the op-ed page of the New York Times. In the following excerpt from the essay, Greenbaum uses comparison and contrast to write about significant differences between being old and being elderly.

There is a difference between being "old" and being "elderly." When you're old, you relinquish the battle to prolong the appearance of youth. The days of face-lifting and hair-coloring are over. You don't have to try so hard. You cling to things rather than to people. Things express one's personality and ask nothing in return.

To the young, old and elderly seem much alike. But there is a basic difference: The old have given up; the elderly are still in the race. They do have something in common, however. Old and elderly play the same game, a dreary competition: "I am sicker than you are." A cataract operation is measured against someone else's broken hip, a heart attack against a stroke, and so on and on. I find myself in the competition with my bad eyes and ears.

The borderline between old and elderly is indistinct. People on both sides occasionally wander across the line. Sensible old people make few plans. Their day-to-day lives depend on health, unexpected visits from friends, the weather—even favorite television programs. But the elderly have projects: different hairdos, walks around the block to keep their muscles in shape, plans for travel, and visits to their children.

WARM-UP

Imagine that you are having a party for senior citizens in your neighborhood. Whom would you invite? What age groups would you include? What would you serve? What kind of entertainment would you plan?

DISCOVERING NEW WORDS (Choose the word or phrase that best defines the word in italics.)

1. *relinquish*   (a) begin   (b) fight   (c) give up   (d) relish

2. *prolong*   (a) lengthen the duration   (b) shorten the duration   (c) pretend

   (d) regret

DISCOVERING THE MEANING

Greenbaum distinguishes between being old and being elderly. In the first column, list traits she attributes to the old. In the second column list traits she attributes to the elderly:

OLD	*ELDERLY*
_____	_____
_____	_____
_____	_____
_____	_____

DISCOVERING CONNECTIONS

Make a list of persons you know who are old and another list of persons whom Greenbaum would call elderly. Write a paragraph or an essay in which you describe how one from the "old" list contrasts with a person from the "elderly" list.

That Lean and Hungry Look

Suzanne Britt

Suzanne Britt's essays and columns have appeared in several newspapers and magazines. "That Lean and Hungry Look," was published originally in the "My Turn" column of Newsweek.

Caesar was right. Thin people need watching. I've been watching them for most of my adult life, and I don't like what I see. When these narrow fellows spring at me, I quiver to my toes. Thin people come in all personalities, most of them menacing. You've got your "together" thin person, your mechanical thin person, your condescending thin person, your tsk-tsk thin person, your efficiency-expert thin person. All of them are dangerous.

In the first place, thin people aren't fun. They don't know how to goof off, at least in the best, fat sense of the word. They've always got to be adoing. Give them a coffee break, and they'll jog around the block. Supply them with a quiet evening at home, and they'll fix the screen door and lick S&H green stamps. They say things like "there aren't enough hours in the day." Fat people never say that. Fat people think the day is too damn long already.

Thin people make me tired. They've got speedy little metabolisms that cause them to bustle briskly. They're forever rubbing their bony hands together and eyeing new problems to "tackle." I like to surround myself with sluggish, inert, easygoing fat people, the kind who believe that if you clean it up today, it'll just get dirty again tomorrow.

Some people say the business about the jolly fat person is a myth, that all of us chubbies are neurotic, sick, sad people. I disagree. Fat people may not be chortling all day long, but they're a hell of a lot *nicer* than the wizened and shriveled. Thin people turn surly, mean, and hard at a young age because they never learn the value of a hot-fudge sundae for easing tension. Thin people don't like gooey soft things because they themselves are neither gooey nor soft. They are crunchy and dull, like carrots. They go straight to the heart of the matter while fat people let things stay all blurry and hazy and vague, the way things actually are. Thin people want to face the truth. Fat people know there is no truth. One of my thin friends is always staring at complex, unsolvable problems and saying, "The key thing is . . . ." Fat people never say that. They know there isn't any such thing as the key thing about anything.

Thin people believe in logic. Fat people see all sides. The sides fat people see are rounded blobs, usually gray, always nebulous and truly not worth worrying about. But the thin person persists. "If you consume more calories than you burn," says one of my thin friends, "you will gain weight. It's that simple." Fat people always grin when they hear statements like that. They know better.

Fat people realize that life is illogical and unfair. They know very well that God is not in his heaven and all is not right with the world. If God was up there, fat people could have two doughnuts and a big orange drink anytime they wanted it.

Thin people have a long list of logical things they are always spouting off to me. They hold up one finger at a time as they reel off these things, so I won't lose track. They speak slowly as if to a young child. The list is long and full of holes. It contains tidbits like "get a grip on yourself," "cigarettes kill," "cholesterol clogs," "fit as a fiddle," "ducks in a row," "organize," and "sound fiscal management." Phrases like that.

They think these 2,000-point plans lead to happiness. Fat people know happiness is elusive at best and even if they could get the kind thin people talk about, they wouldn't want it. Wisely, fat people see that such programs are too dull, too hard, too off the mark. They are never better than a whole cheesecake.

Fat people know all about the mystery of life. They are the ones acquainted with the night, with luck, with fate, with playing it by ear. One thin person I know once suggested that we arrange all the parts of a jigsaw puzzle into groups according to size, shape, and color. He figured this would cut the time needed to complete the puzzle by at least 50 percent. I said I wouldn't do it. One, I like to muddle through. Two, what good would it do to finish early? Three, the jigsaw puzzle isn't the important thing. The important thing is the fun of four people (one thin person included) sitting around a card table, working a jigsaw puzzle. My thin friend had no use for my list. Instead of joining us, he went outside and mulched the boxwoods. The three remaining fat people finished the puzzle and made chocolate, double-fudged brownies to celebrate.

The main problem with thin people is they oppress. Their good intentions, bony torsos, tight ships, neat corners, cerebral machinations, and pat solutions loom like dark clouds over the loose, comfortable, spread-out, soft world of the fat. Long after fat people have removed their coats and shoes and put their feet up on the coffee table, thin people are still sitting on the edge of the sofa, looking neat as a pin, discussing rutabagas. Fat people are heavily into fits of laughter, slapping their thighs and whooping it up, while thin people are still politely waiting for the punch line.

Thin people are downers. They like math and morality and reasoned evaluation of the limitations of human beings. They have their skinny little acts together. They expound, prognose, probe, and prick.

Fat people are convivial. They will like you even if you're irregular and have acne. They will come up with a good reason why you never wrote the great American novel. They will cry in your beer with you. They will put your name in the pot. They will let you off the hook. Fat people will gab, giggle, guffaw, gallumph, gyrate, and gossip. They are generous, giving, and gallant. They are gluttonous and goodly and great. What you want when you're down is soft and jiggly, not muscled and stable. Fat people know this. Fat people have plenty of room. Fat people will take you in.

WARM-UP

Individually or in a group brainstorm about the word *thin*. Try to think of as many words as you can that are related to thinness. Suppose that everyone in the world were thin. Try to think of the jobs that would be lost.

DISCOVERING NEW WORDS (Choose the word or phrase that best defines the word in italics.)

1. *condescending* (a) reverent (b) sassy (c) in a superior manner (d) angrily

2. *metabolisms* Definition: the complex of physical and chemical processes involved in living organisms.

3. *inert* (a) active (b) sick (c) lifeless (d) nervous

4. *chortling* (a) snarling (b) snorting, joyful chuckle (c) giggle (d) disturbing cry

5. *wizened* (a) pudgy (b) skinny (c) shriveled (d) wise

6. *nebulous* (a) vague (b) important (c) ridiculous (d) crabby

7. *elusive* (a) well-defined (b) easy to obtain (c) difficult to define or describe (d) silly

8. *convivial* (a) crabby (b) serious (c) smart (d) friendly

DISCOVERING THE MEANING

1. Why does Britt like fat people better than thin people? Is Britt herself biased?

2. Is there a bias in our society against people who are fat?

3. What careers in television are open to thin people? Would fat people be considered as commentators, newscasters or anchors for a television news show? Why or why not?

4. Is it true that fat people are more "generous, giving, and gallant" than thin people or is Britt saying this tongue in cheek?

5. Britt writes: "Thin people are downers." Based on your experience, is that true?

6. Does Britt's essay conform to the guidelines for writing comparison/contrast essays suggested earlier in this chapter?

DISCOVERING CONNECTIONS

1. Perhaps you know some person who has experienced discrimination because of obesity. Record your thoughts in your journal.

2. Perhaps you know someone who is anorexic (so obsessed with being thin that he or she can't eat). Record your thoughts about that.

3. Write a paragraph or an essay in which you compare or contrast two friends, one who is overweight and one who is thin.

4. Someone once said that in every fat man there is a thin man wildly signaling to get out. Write a paragraph or an essay in which you defend or attack that statement.

A Grateful Society Will Celebrate

George Eppley

George Eppley is one of the authors of Discovery. *This essay originally appeared on the opinion page of the* Plain Dealer.

I am not an Ansel Adams when it comes to taking pictures of people or scenery. Even with a nifty little Minolta that has a computer inside to read light and measure distance, I sometimes goof. Recently, however, I took a picture of which I am proud. It's not going to win any prize, but for me it's the best image of 1986.

It's a picture of my 92-year-old mother-in-law, Edna Campbell Dixon, holding a three-month-old baby girl named Kathleen Dunbar Cook. The picture is important because the past and the future come together so nicely in the present. It's about what was, what is and what will be. It's about the changing roles of women in our society.

Edna Campbell's life began in 1895 when horses and buggies were clogging and polluting city streets. She was born in an era when men dominated the domestic and political scene. It was a time when it was unthinkable that women could hold political office because until 1920 they were not permitted to vote. She grew up at a time when family roles were rigidly defined. Division of labor kept women in second-class situations. Young women were expected to marry and raise a family.

If women didn't marry, society called them "spinsters" and "old maids." If they sought to embark on a career, they became secretaries, teachers or librarians. It was tough for a woman to gain acceptance by the powerful white male club that dominated government, business, industry, education, medicine, law and journalism. Talented female writers often took male pseudonyms in order to get their works published. Career choices for millions of talented women like Edna Campbell Dixon were extremely limited. How unfortunate for them and for the country.

How fortunate that Kathleen Dunbar Cook was born in 1986 because her career choices will be almost limitless when she reaches the age of 21. They include not only homemaker and spouse but also lawyer (like her father), department store executive (like her mother), teacher, doctor, astronaut, engineer, scientist, TV anchor person, priest and hundreds of other careers where she can feel productive and fulfilled. She could become a movie actress who uses her career to win the presidency, causing some men to remark that an excellent actress could never be a good president (although they once believed that a mediocre actor could).

We should never forget that the multiple career choices, denied to Edna Campbell Dixon and open to Kathleen Dunbar Cook, have not come about because of the generosity of the white male establishment but because courageous women for more than a century have battled relentlessly for equal rights. I was reminded of this the other day when I came across a remarkable essay titled "In Defense of the Equality of Men," written by Lorraine Hansberry, the author who gave us in 1959 the powerful drama "A Raisin in the Sun."

Hansberry notes that "a whole generation have come to maturity believing that feminists . . . were strident, ludicrous creatures in incongruous costumes of feathered hats and oversized bloomers who marched about, mainly through the saloons of the land, conking poor, peaceful, beer-guzzling males over the head. The image successfully erases a truer and more cogent picture. In deed and in oratory, in their recognition of direct political action as opposed to parlor and bedroom wheedling of husbands and fathers as the true key to social transformation, American feminist leaders, in particular, set a path that a grateful society will undoubtedly, in time, celebrate."

In her essay, Hansberry pays special tribute to one of those feminists, Susan B. Anthony, by quoting a portion of the speech that Anthony addressed to the court where she was being sentenced to jail for voting in the state of New York in 1879:

"Your denial of my right to vote is the denial of my right of consent as one of the governed, the denial of my right of representation as one of the taxed, the denial of my right to a trial by a jury of my peers. . . . But yesterday, the same man-made form of law declared it a crime punishable with a $1,000 fine and six months imprisonment for you, or me, or any of us, to give a cup of cold water, a crust of bread, or a night's shelter to a panting fugitive as he was tracking his way to Canada. And every man or woman in whose veins coursed a drop of human sympathy violated that wicked law, reckless of consequences, and was justified in doing so. As then, the slaves who got their freedom must yet take it over, or under, or through the unjust forms of law, precisely so now must women, to get their right to a voice in this government, take it; I have taken mine, and mean to take it at every possible opportunity." ("*The Norton Anthology of Literature by Women.*")

What Kathleen Dunbar Cook will become, I do not know. I hope that some day she will enter the political arena to fight for the rights of women, children, the elderly and other groups who need fearless advocates in government. Edna Campbell Dixon will not be on Earth to see her do that, but I am sure that in eternity with Susan B. Anthony, Lorraine Hansberry and a vast multitude of women, she will be cheering her on.

WARM-UP

1. Individually or in groups make a list of changes that have occurred in the twentieth century that have changed the way we view women in society. What changes in women's roles do you think will occur in twenty-first century America?

2. In groups, discuss your responses to the following questions:

   • If you needed a by-pass operation, which would you want the chief surgeon to be—a man or a woman?

   • If you were in an accident, would you want two policemen or two policewomen to respond to the 911 call?

- If you had the choice of working for a male boss or a female boss, which would you choose if the pay and the benefits were the same?

DISCOVERING NEW WORDS (Choose the word or phrase that best defines the word in italics.)

1. *pseudonym*   (a) legal name   (b) fictitious name   (c) maiden name

   (d) strange name

2. *strident*   (a) harsh   (b) soft   (c) quiet   (d) shaky

3. *ludicrous*   (a) beautiful   (b) ugly   (c) obese   (d) ridiculous

4. *incongruous*   (a) not corresponding, inconsistent   (b) colorful, gaudy

   (c) stylish, chic   (d) old-fashioned

5. *cogent*   (a) serene   (b) colorful   (c) intellectually appealing   (d) innocent

6. *wheedling*   (a) carving   (b) singing   (c) persuading by flattery   (d) shouting

DISCOVERING THE MEANING

1. A century ago the male attitude toward women in this country could be expressed in a German saying; "küche, kinder, und kirche." (Women should concern themselves with the kitchen, children, and church.) Does this attitude toward women still exist among males today? If so, give examples to support your position.

2. The media years ago depicted feminists as "strident, ludicrous creatures in incongruous costumes of feathered hats and oversized bloomers who marched about mainly through the saloons of the land, conking poor, peaceful, beer-guzzling males over the head." Do the media today depict feminists in an exaggerated way?

DISCOVERING CONNECTIONS

1. List the names of women who have achieved prominence in medicine, law, religion, education, aviation, literature, journalism. If you know either through reading or through contact with these women that their gender or sex worked against them, write an essay or a paragraph about it.

2. At a recent political convention, the woman keynote speaker said that the famous dancer Ginger Rogers did everything her partner Fred Astaire did only "backwards and in high heels." Write about something that women can do as well as or better than men. Or write about a profession in which men excel over women.

Lake Highlands and Tremont

Stephanie L. Clark

Stephanie L. Clark is the pen name of the student who wrote the selection that follows. She lived in the Tremont area in Cleveland, Ohio while she attended Cuyahoga Community College and worked at Sane Nuclear Freeze, an organization dedicated to stopping the proliferation of nuclear weapons. At the time of publication of this textbook, she was enrolled in a Texas university.

"This could never happen in Lake Highlands," I thought to myself as the hillbillies, all thirty of them, ceased their verbal sparring and started punching. It was 3:00 A.M. and drunken patrons of "The Red Baron Tavern" had decided that it was an appropriate time for a little street fighting. They blocked up traffic and made a tremendous amount of noise. Peace was restored to our neighborhood fifteen minutes later when the police arrived, but I couldn't fall back asleep for another hour. I lay in bed and mused on one of my favorite topics: the radical differences between two neighborhoods where I've lived—Lake Highlands in Dallas and Tremont in Cleveland. Both are subsections of large metropolitan areas that are about the same in size and population, but the similarities stop right there. Tremont is ethnic, diverse, lower class, and always interesting; Lake Highlands is homogeneous, upper class, and boring.

In Tremont on my street alone there are Puerto Ricans, Middle Easterners, Poles, Italians, Egyptians, Greeks, blacks, Irish, Ukrainians, you name it. The ethnic diversity is best exemplified by one small stretch of West 14th Street that contains a Greek Orthodox church, a Russian church, a Baptist church, and a Korean Catholic church. In Lake Highlands you would be hard pressed to find someone who isn't white and Protestant, much less Korean Catholic. For someone like me, who thinks ethnic diversity enhances an area, it makes Tremont attractive.

The diversity is not limited to ethnic groups. In Tremont one can find artists, yuppies, working class families, and on the down side, drug dealers and other criminals. In Lake Highlands there are only upper middle class families headed by professionals. These professionals include doctors and lawyers, and it is not surprising that Lake Highlands is well to do. The residents have taken steps to keep it that way. A few years ago they passed an ordinance that prohibits construction of housing under a certain value, effectively barring most people from living there. Tremont, on the other hand is economically mixed. There are a lot of poor; Sam at Food City told me he deals mostly in food stamps rather than cash. Negative consequences of poverty include bad schools and crime. Lake Highland's crime rate is zilch, and its school system is consistently rated among the best in the nation by the people who do that sort of thing. I don't want to give the impression that Tremont is a slum and hotbed of criminal activity. It isn't. Rather its income level is diverse and it has both projects and condos.

If all the people were suddenly sucked out of Tremont and the neighborhood completely emptied, it would still be an interesting place because of the layout and old architecture. The beautiful red brick building next door was built in 1897, and there are many buildings nearby that are older than that. The old churches and store fronts impart a sense of character and history missing from the Lake Highlands, where you would be hard pressed to find a building constructed before 1965. Lake Highlands is shiny new and clean, but all the houses look exactly the same. The architecture varies only with an occasional new 7-11 store. Because Tremont is older, it is set up for walking. The Food City Market, a florist shop, a photography studio, an art gallery, a park, six churches, and the Auburn Deli are all within walking distance. It is a genuine neighborhood, a community, not just a place for people to sleep.

In an age that values cookie cutter housing and newness above everything, I am glad such communities as Tremont still exist.

WARM-UP

Discuss the features of your neighborhood, village, town, or city that make it unique.

DISCOVERING NEW WORDS

Discuss the student's use of slang in the essay. Does it add or detract from her style?

DISCOVERING THE MEANING

1. What elements of Tremont give it diversity?

2. Does Clark use subject-by-subject development or point-by-point?

3. Does Clark balance her treatment of the two areas she contrasts?

DISCOVERING CONNECTIONS

1. Compare or contrast the neighborhood in which you now live with a neighborhood in which you formerly lived.

2. Take a walk through your neighborhood, looking at people and places with the eyes of the writer or the artist in you. Describe or sketch a scene that is characteristic of your neighborhood.

3. Write a journal entry, a paragraph, or essay about a person, event, or place in your neighborhood.

SUGGESTED TOPICS FOR COMPARISON/CONTRAST PARAGRAPHS AND ESSAYS

Compare or contrast:

1. Your mother and father in their parenting roles

2. Your brothers or sisters

3. Two friends or relatives

4. Two cities or neighborhoods where you have lived

5. Two job experiences or two bosses for whom you worked

6. Two teachers

7. Two cars you have owned

8. Life at high school and at college

9. Two trips you have taken

10. Two books, movies, or television programs

11. Two orchestras or rock groups

12. Two ballerinas, or two professional athletes, or two writers

13. Two computers or word processors

Chapter 21

How Writers Analyze
Causes and Effects

Writing Across the Curriculum

What you will learn in this chapter about writing a cause-and-effect essay has relevance to writing assignments in other college courses. Here are some examples of assignments that call for the cause-and-effect mode:

Nursing: Write a paper in which you indicate three things that might cause a patient to go into cardiac arrest.

Law Enforcement: Write a paper in which you explain at least three of the major causes of juvenile delinquency.

Labor Studies: Write a paper in which you discuss some of the major causes for decline in membership of labor unions.

Economics: Write a paper showing some of the immediate effects of a cut in the capital gains tax.

Business: Write a paper in which you discuss the major reasons why many companies go into bankruptcy.

When we analyze why something happened, we are looking for *causes.* When we consider the consequences of what happened, we are looking at the *effects.*

For example, it is not uncommon for television viewers to turn on the evening news and learn that a business establishment, a supermarket, an apartment complex, or a home has been gutted by a fire of unknown origin. Once the fire is out, police, firefighters, and insurance investigators look for causes of the fire. Was it caused by a careless smoker? Children playing with matches? An arsonist? An owner trying to collect insurance? Faulty electrical wiring? A fire in the trash compactor? Sometimes it takes months and even years of investigation to determine the exact cause or causes of the fire.

While the causes of a major fire may be hard to determine, the effects of the blaze are immediately apparent. Loss of property, loss of merchandise, and loss of valuables are just some effects that are readily seen. Sometimes fires cause personal injury or death to the occupants of the building and to firefighters.

Guidelines for Writing Cause-and-Effect Paragraphs and Essays

1. *Give careful consideration to a number of causes and effects to help you decide which to include in your essay.* Sometimes the most significant causes and effects are those which do not immediately meet the eye. For example, just as a fire inspector will look long and hard at the possible causes of a fire before ruling that careless smoking was the cause, so an insurance investigator will look carefully at the effects of an accident before offering a settlement.

A wise foreman will consider many factors for an employee's poor performance, especially if it differs from past performance. The basic cause may be laziness and motivation, but there could be other more significant causes such as marital problems, sickness of a child, and financial obligations.

2. *Distinguish between proximate and remote causes.* For example, a college student, away from home for the first time, may fail several courses, because he prefers an active social life to study. While his partying could be the *proximate* cause of his failure, perhaps the *remote* cause is his lifelong failure to discipline himself.

3. *Avoid "post hoc ergo propter hoc" reasoning, which translated, means that because Event B followed Event A, Event A caused Event B.* For example, (1) A black family moves into an affluent white neighborhood. Shortly afterwards some homes in the neighborhood are burglarized. Some people immediately blame the black family for the rash of crime. Concluding that the minority family is responsible for the crimes is *post hoc propter hoc* reasoning, which is illogical reasoning at its very worst.

(2) An unemployed auto worker and his sixteen-year-old daughter have an argument because she habitually comes home at one, two, and three o'clock in the morning. Her father grounds her for a month and will not let her use the family car. She responds by giving her father the silent

treatment. A week later her father commits suicide. Because his suicide followed her misbehavior, she reasons that her misbehavior caused his suicide. Unfortunately, faulty reasoning of this kind could cause the young lady to experience guilt and depression.

(3) A young brother and sister are constantly fighting with one another, much to the annoyance of their parents. One day they learn that their parents are getting a divorce. They may mistakenly reason that their fighting caused the divorce. It's hard for them to realize that the causes of their parents' divorce are more complex than occasional fights between a brother and a sister.

4. *In analyzing causes and effects, strive to give fair and objective views.* For example, (1) perhaps one of the reasons your favorite baseball team did not win the pennant was injuries to key players. Fairness, however, demands that you also mention that some of the other players were selfish and lazy.

(2) Some politicians are adept at avoiding the real causes behind their defeats. They blame the media or the fact that special interest groups contributed heavily to their opponents' campaigns. Rarely do we hear politicians blame themselves, admitting that they were arrogant, lazy, overconfident, or that the voters had accurately assessed them as unqualified for the jobs.

5. *Select the causes or effects that will have the greatest impact on your reader.* To do that, you must be aware of your reader's point of view. For example, suppose you are writing an essay supporting legislation to subsidize child care for working parents. If the bill cannot pass without support from retired people in the community, you will have to include some effects of the legislation that would benefit the entire community, not just working parents. You might point out that many mothers on welfare could become tax-paying citizens if they had adequate day care for their children.

6. *Express your point of view in a thesis statement.* Your essay will be more effective, if besides analyzing causes and effects, you take a stance and clearly state your point of view. Let's say that you have analyzed your baseball team's poor showing during the past season. You have determined that the basic causes are poor pitching, poor defense and poor managerial decisions. If you believe that the major cause of the team's poor performance lies with the manager, then let your thesis express that opinion, as follows:

> *Poor pitching, poor defense and especially poor decisions by the manager are the basic reasons why the Blue Devils occupied the cellar for all of last season.*

Some Examples of Cause-and-Effect Paragraphs

In *The Secret Life of the Unborn Child,* Dr. Thomas Verny makes some interesting observations on how an expectant mother can influence her child's life well before the baby's birth. He is writing about causes and effects.

Considering his acute hearing, it should come as no surprise that the unborn child is also capable of learning a bit about music. A four- or five-month-old fetus definitely responds to sound and melody—and responds in very discriminating ways. Put Vivaldi on the phonograph and even the most agitated baby relaxes. Put Beethoven on and even the calmest child starts kicking and moving.

Of course, personality is much more than the sum of what we learn—in or out of the womb. My point is that since we have finally identified some of the early experiences which shape future traits and characteristics, a woman can now begin actively influencing her child's life well before birth. One way is by giving up, or cutting back on, cigarettes during pregnancy. Another way is by talking to the child. He really does hear; and, even more importantly, he responds to what he hears. Soft, soothing talk makes him feel loved and wanted. Not because he understands the words; obviously, they are well beyond his comprehension. But the tone of what is being said isn't. He is mature enough intellectually to sense the emotional tone of the maternal voice.

It's even possible to begin teaching an unborn baby. At the very least, a pregnant woman who spends a few minutes each day listening to soothing music could make her child feel more relaxed and tranquil. At most, that early exposure might create in the child a lifelong musical interest. It did for Boris Brott, conductor of the Hamilton (Ontario) Philharmonic Symphony.

Verny then relates how Brott was mystified as to why he knew certain cello lines of music and could play them sight unseen. The mystery was solved when Brott's mother told him that when she was pregnant with him she used to play on the cello those very same songs and music.

In the summer of 1988, *Newsweek* magazine's cover story dealt with the problem of pollution in the oceans and in the lakes of the nation. In comprehensive articles such as this, it is not unusual for a writer to treat both causes and effects.

The lead paragraph deals primarily with some of the causes of the pollution, and a later paragraph deals primarily with the effects of ocean pollution.

With 9 million people competing for a place in the sun, New Yorkers are used to a little hassle—and a little mess—with their summertime fun at the beach. But this year is different: for the past several weeks, beaches from Staten Island to the eastern Long Island resort towns have been intermittently shut down by a trickle of potentially hazardous medical waste—sutures, hypodermic needles, catheter bags and vials of blood. Where the debris came from is anybody's guess, and frustrated state and city officials have been quarreling about the likely source. But the beach-going public, fearful of the fact that several of the mysterious blood samples have tested positive for AIDS, is observing New York's latest garbage crisis by staying home in droves. . . .

. . . 'Black mayonnaise': The problem for most landlubbers, of course, is that most of the effects of coastal pollution are hard to see. Bays and estuaries that are now in jeopardy—Boston Harbor, for example, or even San Francisco Bay—are still delightful to look at from shore. What is happening underwater is quite another matter, and it is not for the squeamish. Scuba divers talk of swimming through clouds of toilet paper and half-dissolved feces, of bay bottoms covered by a foul and toxic combination of sediment, sewage and petrochemical waste appropriately known as "black mayonnaise." Fishermen haul in lobsters and crab covered with mysterious "burn holes" and fish whose fins are rotting off.

In lengthy discussions such as the article from *Newsweek,* writers can deal effectively with both causes and effects. In shorter pieces, however, a writer may choose to write about causes only or effects only for various reasons.

For example, in a report to faculty and parents, a high school principal may dwell only with the causes, not the effects, of a dramatic rise in the school's SAT and ACT scores: a better reading program at the lower grades, better communications with parents, and better faculty morale. Those who listen to the report already know what the effects will be. Why dwell on the obvious?

READINGS AND REFLECTIONS

A Symbol of Stability and Strength

William O. Douglas

William O. Douglas was appointed to the U.S. Supreme Court by Franklin D. Roosevelt in 1939. During his long tenure there, he was considered one of the most liberal members of the Court. He wrote more than thirty books, many of them about civil liberties.

In the first chapter of his autobiography, Go East, Young Man, *Douglas tells about how the death of his father affected him, a six-year-old child. His father had undergone surgery for stomach ulcers, was apparently doing well, and was expected home shortly. He writes:*

Instead, he never returned. He was present one day and then he was gone forever. There would never be another to lift me high in the air, to squeeze my hand and give me masculine praise. There were no longer any pockets I could search for nuggets of maple sugar. The step in the hallway, the laugh, the jingle of coins in the pockets—these had gone as silently as the waters of the great Columbia. He never would return. At first I could not believe his absence was so complete.

Douglas's father was buried in Yakima, Washington. Douglas writes about other effects on his emotions: the minister's words to him, his mother's fear and loneliness, and the towering strength of Mount Adams:

. . . As I stood by the edge of the grave a wave of lonesomeness swept over me. Then I became afraid—afraid of being left alone, afraid because the grave held my defender and protector. These feelings were deepened by the realization that Mother was afraid and lonely too. My throat choked up and I started to cry. I remembered the words of the minister, who had said to me, "You must now be a man, sonny." I tried to steel myself and control my emotions.

Then I happened to see Mount Adams towering over us on the west. It was dark purple and white in the August day and its shoulders of basalt were heavy with glacial snow. It was a giant whose head touched the sky.

As I looked, I stopped sobbing. My eyes dried. Adams stood cool and calm, unperturbed by the event that had stirred us so deeply. Suddenly the mountain seemed to be a friend, a force for me to tie to, a symbol of stability and strength.

WARM-UP

The death of someone you love can be one of the most painful losses you experience in a lifetime. It is a loss, however, that is inevitable in all of our lives. For that reason, it is a recurring theme in literature. There are other losses, however, that most people experience from time to time, such as the loss of a friend who moves away, loss of youth, loss of health, loss of a job, loss of a pet, and so on. In your journal, record your feelings and thoughts about a loss you have experienced.

DISCOVERING NEW WORDS

Unless you live in certain mountainous areas of the country you probably do not know that basalt is a kind of volcanic rock. If there are any other words in the selection that are unfamiliar to you, consult a dictionary.

DISCOVERING THE MEANING

1. Douglas associates some lesser losses with the great loss of his father: no more pockets to search for candy and coins, and so on. What are some of the other specific losses he relates to convey his overwhelming loss of his father?

2. What effect do the words of the minister have on young Douglas?

3. How does the grief of his mother affect Douglas?

4. Douglas sees the mountain as "a friend, a force for me to tie to, a symbol of stability and strength." Have you ever had the experience of looking upon something in nature as a force, a friend, an enemy, a source of strength? Write about it in your journal.

DISCOVERING CONNECTIONS

1. To convey the sense of loss Douglas felt at the time of his father's death, he connects his great loss to lesser losses—no more pockets to search for candy and coins, and so on. These small effects make the overwhelming loss of his father real to the reader. If you have lost a pet, a friend, or someone else you love, what are some specific, concrete examples of effects of the loss? Record those examples in your journal or incorporate them in a paragraph or essay.

2. Write a journal entry, a paragraph, or an essay about the causes or the effects of an event in your life.

Life Without Fuel?

Isaac Asimov

Isaac Asimov is one of the best known science fiction writers of the century. He has written over 200 books, both fiction and nonfiction, and numerous articles. In "Life Without Fuel," which was first published in Time in 1977, Asimov uses the cause-and-effect mode to support his thesis.

So it's 1997, and it's raining, and you'll have to walk to work again. The subways are crowded, and any given train breaks down one morning out of five. The buses are gone, and on a day like today the bicycles slosh and slide. Besides, you have only a mile and a half to go, and you have boots, raincoat and rain hat. And it's not a very cold rain, so why not?

Lucky you have a job in demolition too. It's steady work. Slow and dirty, but steady. The fading structures of a decaying city are the great mineral mines and hardware shops of the nation. Break them down and re-use the parts. Coal is too difficult to dig up and transport to give us energy in the amounts we need, nuclear fission is judged to be too dangerous, the technical breakthrough toward nuclear fusion that we hoped for never took place, and solar batteries are too expensive to maintain on the earth's surface in sufficient quantity.

Anyone older than ten can remember automobiles. They dwindled. At first the price of gasoline climbed—way up. Finally only the well-to-do drove, and that was too clear an indication that they were filthy rich, so any automobile that dared show itself on a city street was overturned and burned. Rationing was introduced to "equalize sacrifice," but every three months the ration was reduced. The cars just vanished and became part of the metal resource.

There are many advantages, if you want to look for them. Our 1997 newspapers continually point them out. The air is cleaner and there seem to be fewer colds. Against most predictions, the crime rate has dropped. With the police car too expensive (and too easy a target), policemen are back on their beats. More important, the streets are full. Legs are king in the cities of 1997, and people walk everywhere far into the night. Even the parks are full, and there is mutual protection in crowds.

If the weather isn't too cold, people sit out front. If it is hot, the open air is the only air conditioning they get. And at least the street lights still burn. Indoors, electricity is scarce, and few people can afford to keep lights burning after supper.

As for the winter—well, it is inconvenient to be cold, with most of what furnace fuel is allowed hoarded for the dawn; but sweaters are popular indoor wear and showers are not an everyday luxury. Lukewarm sponge baths will do, and if the air is not always very fragrant in the human vicinity, the automobile fumes are gone.

There is some consolation in the city that it is worse in the suburbs. The suburbs were born with the auto, lived with the auto, and are dying with the auto. One way out for the suburbanites is to form associations that assign turns to the procurement and distribution of food. Pushcarts creak from house to house along the posh suburban roads, and every bad snowstorm is a disaster. It isn't easy to hoard enough food to last till the roads are open. There is not much in the way of refrigeration except for the snowbanks, and then the dogs must be fought off.

What energy is left cannot be directed into personal comfort. The nation must survive until new energy sources are found, so it is the railroads and subways that are receiving major attention. The railroads must move the coal that is the immediate hope, and the subways can best move the people.

And then, of course, energy must be conserved for agriculture. The great car factories make trucks and farm machinery almost exclusively. We can huddle together when there is a lack of warmth, fan ourselves should there be no cooling breezes, sleep or make love at such times as there is a lack of light—but nothing will for long ameliorate a lack of food. The American population isn't going up much any more, but the food supply must be kept high even though the prices and difficulty of distribution force each American to eat less. Food is needed for export so that we can pay for some trickle of oil and for other resources.

The rest of the world, of course, is not as lucky as we are. Some cynics say that it is the knowledge of this that helps keep America from despair. They're starving out there, because earth's population has continued to go up. The population on earth is 5.5 billion, and outside the United States and Europe, not more than one in five has enough to eat at any given time.

All the statistics point to a rapidly declining rate of population increase, but that is coming about chiefly through a high infant mortality; the first and most helpless victims of starvation are babies, after their mothers have gone dry. A strong current of American opinion, as reflected in the newspapers (some of which still produce their daily eight pages of bad news), holds that it is just as well. It serves to reduce the population, doesn't it?

Others point out that it's more than just starvation. There are those who manage to survive on barely enough to keep the body working, and that proves to be not enough for the brain. It is estimated that there are now nearly 2 billion people in the world who are alive but who are permanently brain-damaged by undernutrition, and the number is growing year by year. It has already occurred to some that it would be "realistic" to wipe them out quietly and rid the earth of an encumbering menace. The American newspapers of 1997 do not report that this is actually being done anywhere, but some travelers bring back horror tales.

At least the armies are gone—no one can afford to keep those expensive, energy-gobbling monstrosities. Some soldiers in uniform and with rifles are present in almost every still functioning nation, but only the United States and the Soviet Union can maintain a few tanks, planes and ships—which they dare not move for fear of biting into limited fuel reserves.

Energy continues to decline, and machines must be replaced by human muscle and beasts of burden. People are working longer hours and there is less leisure; but then, with electric lighting restricted, television for only three hours a night, movies three evenings a week, new books few and printed in small editions, what is there to do with leisure? Work, sleep and eating are the great trinity of 1997, and only the first two are guaranteed.

Where will it end? It must end in a return to the days before 1800, to the days before the fossil fuels powered a vast machine industry and technology. It must end in subsistence farming and in a world population reduced by starvation, disease and violence to less than a billion.

And what can we do to prevent all this now?

Now? Almost nothing.

If we had started twenty years ago, that might have been another matter. If we had only started fifty years ago, it would have been easy.

WARM-UP

List all the jobs that would be eliminated in your city or town if there were no cars, no buses, no trucks, no vehicular traffic of any kind.

DISCOVERING NEW WORDS (Choose the word or phrase that best defines the word in italics.)

1. *demolition*   (a) construction   (b) destruction, especially with explosives

   (c) transportation   (d) scrap collecting

2. *nuclear fission*   A nuclear reaction in which an atomic nucleus splits into parts. Consult your dictionary or a science textbook for a more complete definition.

3. *nuclear fusion*   A nuclear reaction in which nuclei combine to form more massive nuclei with the simultaneous release of energy. Consult your dictionary or a science textbook for a more complete definition.

4. *hoarded*   (a) burned   (b) saved   (c) sold   (d) given away

5. *procurement*   (a) growing   (b) sale   (c) obtaining   (d) waste

6. *posh*   (a) old-fashioned   (b) fashionable   (c) paved   (d) muddy

7. *ameliorate*   (a) pay for   (b) justify   (c) budget   (d) make better

8. *cynics*   People who believe   (a) any thing you tell them   (b) that the end justifies the means   (c) that all people are motivated by selfishness   (d) that they deserve the best

9. *mortality*   (a) birth rate   (b) death rate   (c) sickness rate   (d) polio rate

10. *encumbering*   (a) burdening   (b) freeing   (c) scary   (d) starvation

11. *subsistence farming*   Farming that produces   (a) enough to keep people alive   (b) a surplus   (c) enough to produce wealth   (d) year-round crops

DISCOVERING THE MEANING

1. How will lack of fuel affect suburbanites if Asimov's predictions are fulfilled?

2. What are some of the good effects of lack of fuel? Could a shortage of fuel improve the quality of life for Americans?

3. Do you think it is possible that in this century a fuel shortage could be as serious as Asimov predicts?

DISCOVERING CONNECTIONS

Some common concerns of thinking people include the following issues: pollution of our atmosphere, our lakes, rivers and oceans; hunting of animals that are threatened by extinction; drug-related crimes; homelessness. Write an essay about one of these problems or another problem that concerns you.

SUGGESTED TOPICS FOR CAUSE-AND-EFFECT
PARAGRAPHS AND ESSAYS

1. A happy or unhappy childhood

2. Success or failure in school

3. Popularity or unpopularity in school

4. A wide circle of friends or a lack of friends

5. A happy or unhappy marriage

6. Good or bad reading habits

7. Good or bad job experiences

8. Unemployment

9. A wise or poor decision about choosing a mate, buying a car, selling a home, leaving a job, or making other important choices

10. The increase of drug abuse

11. Tastelessness on talk shows or on bumperstickers

12. Illiteracy

13. Teen-age pregnancy

14. Illegal college recruiting practices

15. Anorexia or bulimia

16. Alcoholism

Part IV

Handbook

Discovering the Power
of Good Grammar

Chapter 22

Handbook

Golf is a frustrating game for many people because they do not know the basics. There are proper and improper ways to grip the club, address the ball, swing the club, play out of the rough, and putt the greens. If the club is gripped incorrectly, the ball on impact slices off to the right or hooks to the left. If the golfer moves his head or looks up while teeing off, the result is usually a topped drive or a complete miss.

Some people never learn the basics of golf, but every Sunday they play, usually very badly. The game of golf then becomes work rather than play. As a result, many give up the game. That's unfortunate. If they took some lessons, they could probably master the fundamentals they need to make golf challenging and fun.

The same applies to many people who write. Some enjoy it; others hate it. Those who hate it often try to avoid writing. Some actually get physically ill when they get an unexpected writing assignment. That's too bad. Things could be different if they took the time to master the fundamentals with a pro.

The pro in this case is your classroom instructor. The Handbook is a manual of instruction that is meant to reinforce what your instructor teaches in the classroom. Accordingly, the handbook section is brief.

OVERVIEW

The Handbook contains some basic principles of writing. We have purposely omitted many fine points of writing. We are not concerned here with style, diction, audience, and so on. *This does not mean that those points are unimportant.*

Let's return to the golf analogy. Instructors don't attempt to prepare people to compete at the Masters Tournament in Augusta, Georgia. They teach players the basics so that they can go to a public or private golf course and have fun. If, in the process, some students master the basics and get very serious about the game, the instructors can then begin to teach them the fine points of championship golf.

The same holds true of writing. We believe that you will learn to write and write well if, in the beginning, you do not have to learn a multitude of rules. For this reason, our Handbook covers only the basics. Your instructor will undoubtedly acquaint you with more sophisticated points of grammar to make your writing even more effective. Here is a summary of what the handbook covers:

I. BASIC THINGS TO KNOW ABOUT WORDS AND HOW THEY FUNCTION IN A SENTENCE

Nouns and pronouns
Avoiding faulty pronoun reference
Verbs
Adjectives
Adverbs
Conjunctions
Prepositions

II. BASIC THINGS TO KNOW ABOUT WRITING CORRECT AND EFFECTIVE SENTENCES

Definition of a sentence
Subject and verb
Subject and verb agreement
Consistent verb tense
Recognizing and avoiding fragments
Avoiding comma splices
Recognizing and avoiding fused (run-on) sentences
Simple sentences
Compound sentences
Complex sentences
Avoiding awkward construction
Combining sentences
Avoiding misplaced modifiers
Avoiding dangling modifiers
Parallelism
Recognizing and revising nonstandard English
Using numbers
Avoiding common mistakes
Avoiding cliches

III. BASIC THINGS TO KNOW ABOUT PUNCTUATION

End punctuation
Internal punctuation

Punctuation of quoted material and titles
Word punctuation

I. BASIC THINGS TO KNOW ABOUT WORDS AND HOW THEY CAN FUNCTION IN A SENTENCE

Nouns:

A noun is a word that names a person, place, thing, or concept. The following words are nouns:

man	openness	Russia
woman	familiarity	Washington
child	liberty	lifeguard
family	anger	John
friend	policy	Ramsey
car	bigotry	Maybelline

Nouns are often the subjects of sentences.

Jill has graduated from the eighth grade.

The *embarrassment* of the guest was obvious to all.

Wall Street is the financial district of New York.

The *prisoners* clamored for freedom.

Tennis is an excellent exercise.

Nouns are sometimes the objects of verbs and prepositions.

He held the *baby*. (Object of verb)

They thanked the *neighbors*. (Object of verb)

Please get the *book*. (Object of verb)

Come into the *room*. (Object of preposition)

The rain fell softly on the *lawn*. (Object of preposition)

PRACTICE EXERCISE 22.1
Nouns

DIRECTIONS: Underline the nouns in each of the following sentences.

1. It snowed so much that the snow plows could not clear the roads.

2. The family gathered to celebrate Thanksgiving.

3. The fire completely gutted the first floor of the home.

4. Security police captured the man who was vandalizing the buses.

5. Maureen likes herbal teas, but Fran prefers coffee.

6. Jim left the hospital four days after surgery.

7. Shonda resolved to destroy her credit cards.

8. Leatrice likes to read the newspaper in the morning.

9. The surprise party for her sixteenth birthday was well attended.

10. Apartment owners were warned to keep their dogs on leashes.

Pronouns:

A pronoun can be used in place of a noun. Pronouns are classified as:

Personal Pronouns

Examples: I, you, he, she, it; we, you, they

I value your criticism.

She decided not to vote.

We enjoyed the beauty of Glacier National Park.

Relative Pronouns

Examples: who, which, that

I am the writer *who* curses keyboards.

We saw a village *which* was deserted.

He wants to play for a team *that* wins.

Interrogative Pronouns

Examples: who, which, what

Who is the woman in the field?

Which is the car you intend to buy?

What is the correct way to express sympathy?

Indefinite Pronouns

Examples: one, any, each, anyone, somebody, nobody,

everybody, everyone, all.

If *one* is interested, he should call the manager.

Any of you could have sounded the alarm.

All were invited to the meeting.

Nobody should be asked to pay.

Note: In the course of your writing experience, you will become familiar with other types of pronouns such as the reflexive, demonstrative, intensive, reciprocal.

PRACTICE EXERCISE 22.2
Pronouns

DIRECTIONS: Underline the pronoun in each of the following sentences, and in the blank write what kind of pronoun it is (personal, relative, interrogative, indefinite).

_____ 1. Who shall defend this child?

_____ 2. Can't anyone play this game?

_____ 3. The police captured the suspect who was terrorizing the neighborhood.

_____ 4. What were the firemen doing to cause such laughter?

_____ 5. None of the books was sold at the auction.

_____ 6. We could not get near the rock concert.

_____ 7. Richard could not decide which hair style was more appealing.

_____ 8. The principal asked everyone to contribute to the hunger fund.

_____ 9. Was everyone on the jury in agreement with the verdict?

_____ 10. Who are the students taking the course?

Faulty Pronoun Reference

Pronouns are words that can be used in place of nouns. Since pronouns are stand-ins for nouns, they must agree in number, person, and gender with their *antecedents*. An antecedent is the noun that is replaced by the pronoun.

Vague pronoun reference
Frank told Pete that he had won the lottery. (It is not clear who won the lottery, Frank or Pete.)

Clear pronoun reference
Frank told Pete, "You have won the lottery."
or
Frank told Pete, "I've won the lottery."

Vague pronoun reference
Donna is an excellent tutor, and she uses this to pay her way through college.

Clear pronoun reference
Donna is an excellent tutor, and she uses this skill to help pay her way through college.

Faulty pronoun reference
Neither Jon nor James would state their position on amnesty for illegal aliens.

Clear pronoun reference
Neither Jon nor James would state his position on amnesty for illegal aliens.

Faulty pronoun reference
Steve became irate after they told him that they would not accept his passport.

Clear pronoun reference
Steve became irate after the immigration officials told him they would not accept his passport.

PRACTICE EXERCISE 22.3
Pronoun Reference

DIRECTIONS: Rewrite the following sentences so that the pronoun reference is clear and not ambiguous.

1. Georgeanne was annoyed when they did not have a copy of Laura Taylor's *Honor Bound* at the library.

   _____

   _____

   _____

2. At Ralph's Sunoco Station, they always give you high-quality service.

   _____

   _____

3. Deidre told Angela that she could not come to the party because Terry would be there.

   _____

   _____

4. Neither of the boys was happy with their presents.

   _____

   _____

5. Jesse went to the community college because he felt they could help him with his career plans.

   _____

   _____

6. Dr. Jasney told the student that he would be late for the first class.

_____

_____

7. Cara is basically a happy baby, but it does not always show.

_____

_____

8. The Sextons spent all morning hitting golf balls on the practice range, but did not improve.

_____

_____

9. Each word processor has their own special features.

_____

_____

10. Amzad went to the computer lab because he thought they could help him to learn COBOL.

_____

_____

PRACTICE EXERCISE 22.4
Faulty Pronoun Reference

DIRECTIONS: Correct the following examples of faulty pronoun reference. In some cases you may have to rewrite the sentence.

1. The coach said they played a very good game.

   _____

   _____

2. I wonder if they will ever fix the drawbridges over the Cuyahoga River.

   _____

   _____

3. Marie told Aimee she was going to be the homecoming queen.

   _____

   _____

4. At Rego's Stop n Shop, you don't have to wait very long in the check-out lines.

   _____

   _____

5. I wish they would ban smoking in all restaurants.

   _____

   _____

6. Edna wrote her sister Belle every day when she was in Ireland.

   _____

   _____

7. After the accident, Maria told Juanita she had to meet the insurance adjustor.

8. Every autumn in Munich, Germany, they have a celebration called *Oktoberfest.*

9. At school they are trying to get students to join *Students Against Drunk Driving (SADD).*

10. In the early part of this century, to start the Model T, you had to crank it.

PRACTICE EXERCISE 22.5
Correcting Faulty Pronoun Reference

DIRECTIONS: Correct the following examples of faulty pronoun reference. Draw a line through the incorrect pronoun and write the correct pronoun above it. If the pronoun has an antecedent, circle it. In some cases, changing the antecedent to make it agree with the pronoun will help you avoid the awkward phrase "his or her."

1. One of the men sitting at that table left their credit card.

2. I wish they would discover a cure for cancer.

3. A child under twelve should be accompanied by their parents.

4. Kathleen warned Mary that she would lose the election if supporters did not work harder.

5. Cardiologists routinely test every new patient to check their cholesterol level.

6. The military base requires you to go through a special clearance procedure before proceeding beyond the gate.

7. Each of the men and women aboard the *Challenger* will be remembered for their courage.

8. If a person smokes, their chances of developing lung cancer increases dramatically.

9. Neither Jesse nor Christopher brought their binoculars to the air races.

10. The neighborhood the author describes in her latest novel is Monterey, California, where they lived when she was a child.

Verbs:

Verbs are words that express action or state of being.

He *hit* the baseball into the bleachers.

The torpedo *struck* the ship on the port side.

I *am* worried about the rise of illiteracy.

Betty *became* ill after eating lobster.

Verbs are called *transitive* when they need an object to complete their meaning.

He *hit* (verb) the baseball (object) into the bleachers. (Without the object the sentence would be incomplete.)

The torpedo *struck* (verb) the *ship* (object) on the port side. (Without the object to complete the meaning of the transitive verb, the sentence would be meaningless.)

Verbs are called *intransitive* when they do not need an object to complete their meaning.

They *arrived* on time.

President Franklin D. Roosevelt *died* on April 12, 1944, in Warm Springs, Georgia.

Some verbs are called *linking* verbs because they link or connect a word in the sentence to the subject. Linking verbs do not show action but express a condition or a state of being. The most common linking verb is some form of the verb *be*.

The United States Senate *is* a group of one hundred elected officials. (The verb *is* links group to United States Senate.)

Steffi Graf *is* a professional tennis player. (The verb *is* links tennis player to Steffi Graf.)

The gift of a tractor *seemed* generous at the time. (The verb *seemed* expresses a condition or state of being.)

The baseball crowd *fell* silent in the last of the ninth. (The verb *fell* expresses a condition or state of being.)

PRACTICE EXERCISE 22.6
Verbs

DIRECTIONS: Underline the verbs in the following sentences.

1. The linebackers blitzed the quarterback.

2. The concert goers gave a standing ovation to the symphony orchestra.

3. After a month's delay, the gifts finally arrived.

4. The school children were taken on a field trip to the Natural History Museum.

5. Leris seemed puzzled by the letter from her fiance.

6. Isiah Thomas is a superb professional basketball player.

7. The hometown fans were very subdued after the opposing team's quick score.

8. The tourists were angry with their tour guide.

9. The pit bull dog seemed friendly enough.

10. The jurors appeared to be tired after the six-week trial.

Tense

Tense indicates time.

Present tense usually indicates actions that are ongoing, such as the verb *swim* in the sentence, "I swim often." Another form of the present tense, usually formed by adding -ing to the simple present, indicates that an action is in the process of occurring. Example: He's *swimming* at the Y.

Past tense shows that an action was completed in the past, such as the verb in the sentence, "I *ran* all the way to my second class."

Future tense indicates actions that will happen in the future, such as the verb in the sentence, "He *will enter* the contest."

All three tenses, however, can be expressed in several different ways. In this handbook, we deal only with one of the most common errors in using verb tenses, that is, the failure to be consistent.

In writing sentences, do not shift tenses unnecessarily. If the sentence contains a series of verbs, keep them all in the same tense unless there is a good reason for changing to another tense.

John *wrote* a letter, *studied* his chemistry notes, and *watched* the Superbowl game on television.

Notice that all the verbs in this example are in the past tense: *wrote*, *studied*, and *watched*. Now, look at the next example.

After John *writes* a letter and *studies* his chemistry notes, he *will watch* the Superbowl game on television.

The first two verbs are in the present tense: *writes* and *studies*. The third verb, however, is in the future tense. It is correct, because there is a reason for the shift in tense.

PRACTICE EXERCISE 22.7
Consistent Verb Tense

DIRECTIONS: In the following sentences, cross out the verbs that are not consistent, and write in the correct tense.

1. Pictures were taken, eyewitnesses were questioned, and the wrecked car is being towed.

2. Lisa opened the gift, uttered a cry of delight, and she kisses her husband John.

3. The minister observed his congregation, raised his eyes to heaven, and prays for peace.

4. The mailman walked the street, delivered the mail, and exchanges small talk with the school crossing guard.

5. The jury listened to the witnesses, weighed the evidence, and delivers the verdict.

6. The Campbell family gathers around the tree, exchanged gifts, and enjoyed the turkey dinner.

7. Arleen, Eileen, and Mary Kay went to the museum, shopped at the mall, and go to a Woody Allen movie.

8. The auctioneer looks over the crowd, starts the bidding, and sold all the auction items.

9. Sounding the fire alarm, Morris waits for the fireman, and told the office workers not to panic.

10. In the crucial game, the referee blows the whistle, drops the yellow flag, calls the other officials into a huddle, and asked for help on the play.

PRACTICE EXERCISE 22.8
Consistent Verb Tense

DIRECTIONS: In each of the following sentences, a verb tense is used incorrectly. Cross out the incorrect verb tense, and write in the correct form.

1. When the FAA officials found the plastic fragments, they announced that the plane is sabotaged by a bomb.

2. After the lake freighter unloaded its cargo of iron ore, the ship captain has a party for the crew.

3. Before David went home for the holidays, he cleans his room in the dorm.

4. The movie actor says in the interview that his childhood was a very happy one.

5. While Carmelita was doing her term paper on Shakespeare, she gets a call from a panic stricken classmate.

6. Shonda studied the campaign issues, asked questions of the candidates, and decides not to vote.

7. When a television cameraman was knocked unconscious after a play near the end zone, some obnoxious fans in the bleachers throw snowballs at him.

8. The highways were icy, the snow was falling hard, but Azam decides to drive to see his girlfriend in Lansing.

9. The storm on Lake Ontario came up quickly, threatens small boats, and frightened people on the shore.

10. Kim studied for days before the final test, reviewed previous tests, attended study sessions, and gets the highest grade.

Adjectives

An adjective is a word that modifies a noun or pronoun. The following examples illustrate the function of adjectives:

A *soft* rain fell on the fields. (*Soft* modifies the noun, rain.)

George Washington was the *first* president. (*First* modifies the noun, president.)

She was *happy* for the children. (*Happy* describes the state of the person represented as "she.")

They appeared *willing* to negotiate. (*Willing* describes the state of the persons represented as "They.")

PRACTICE EXERCISE 22.9
Adjectives

DIRECTIONS: Underline the adjectives in the following sentences.

1. Louis still believes in the importance of the family farm.

2. Luciano Pavarotti is a well-known tenor.

3. Buick believes it has the best American car on the road.

4. The Audubon Society has an annual bird-counting activity.

5. Many people care about the natural world of animals and flowers.

6. Some episodes in the television show *Midnight Caller* have provoked angry protests.

7. Brave young men have died in wars they did not understand.

8. Hair care is a billion-dollar industry.

9. The computer store offered a cash rebate on the purchase of a personal computer.

10. It makes good sense to wear a wool sweater on a cold day.

Adverbs

An adverb is a word that modifies a verb, an adjective, or another adverb.

The rain fell *softly* on the field. (The adverb *softly* modifies fell; it tells how the rain fell.)

Michael was *very* tall for his age. (The adverb modifies the adjective "tall"; it tells how tall Michael is.)

Lucinda whispered *very softly* to her child.

(*Softly* modifies the verb *whispered*; *very* modifies the adverb *softly*.)

PRACTICE EXERCISE 22.10
Adverbs

DIRECTIONS: Underline the adverbs in the following sentences.

1. The Hotel Chelsea is an extremely interesting hotel on W. 23rd Street in New York.

2. The hotel caters especially to musicians, who often play their instruments very loudly.

3. Opera singers can be heard diligently practicing their arias.

4. Long ago, Mark Twain lived in the Hotel Chelsea.

5. Surprisingly, none of the Hotel Chelsea's guests complains about the sounds and noises in the building.

6. Thomas Wolfe, a well-known American writer, worked quietly on some of his novels at the hotel.

7. Ballerinas can often be seen earnestly and diligently practicing their dance routines in the halls of the hotel.

8. Some fear that new owners of the Chelsea may someday demolish the hotel to make way for expensive apartments.

9. The hotel proprietor patiently tolerates the eccentricities of his guests.

10. Sometime when you are in New York, visit this historic landmark.

Conjunctions

A conjunction is a word that connects various elements of a sentence. Conjunctions are either *coordinating, correlative* or *subordinating.*

Coordinating conjunctions such as *and, but, or, nor, for, so, yet* connect words or phrases of equal rank in a sentence.

> Scott *and* Christopher are fraternal twins. (Scott and Christopher are both subjects, so they are of equal rank.)

> Marlene was tired, *but* she went to the party anyway. (The conjunction *but* connects two clauses of equal rank.)

He will not seek the nomination, *nor* will he accept a draft at the convention. (The conjunction *nor* connects two clauses of equal rank.)

Tania is a beautiful woman, *yet* she values her intelligence more than her beauty. (The conjunction *yet* joins two clauses of equal rank.)

Correlative conjunctions such as *both, and; either, or; neither, nor; not only, but also; whether, or* join elements of equal grammatical rank in a sentence.

Both the generals *and* the admirals agreed that the invasion should take place.

Neither the team owners were willing to compromise *nor* were the the players.

Not only the teachers *but also* the custodians will refuse to cross the picket line.

Subordinating conjunctions (such as *after, although, as if, because, if, since, when, where, while, until, unless*) connect subordinate clauses to main clauses.

Since Tom did not know how to play bridge, the group decided to play pinochle. (The conjunction *since* introduces the subordinate clause and connects it to the main clause.)

Whenever the Faists play bridge, they invariably win.

Unless the voters approve the levy, extracurricular activities will be curtailed.

PRACTICE EXERCISE 22.11
Conjunctions

DIRECTIONS: Underline the conjunctions in the following sentences. In the space provided, indicate what kind of conjunction is used: (coordinating (CRD), subordinating (SUB), correlative (CL).

_____ 1. Not only did Tom pass the test, but he also scored the highest number of points.

_____ 2. Both the principal of the school and the assistant principal deplored the teacher's lack of class preparation.

_____ 3. A trip to Europe is expensive, but staying at youth hostels can cut the cost considerably.

_____ 4. Neither the Russian rescue teams nor those from foreign lands were able to save all of the Armenians who were buried under the earthquake's rubble.

_____ 5. While the city police have closed down many crack operations, citizens feel that not enough is being done to stop the flow of drugs.

_____ 6. While some television movies based on plays or books are well done, students should not fail to read the books or plays.

_____ 7. Since the New York Giants lost to the New York Jets in the final game of the 1988 season, the Giants were not in the play-offs.

_____ 8. The United States withdrew from the Vietnam War because the American people no longer supported the conflict.

_____ 9. Neither government officials nor military leaders believed the war could be won.

_____ 10. Not only did the Vietnam War cause physical pain, but it also left psychological scars on many who served in Vietnam.

Prepositions

A preposition is a word that shows the relationship of a noun or pronoun to another part of the sentence. Some common prepositions are *on, under, to, with, over, before, about.*

A compound preposition is made up of more than one word.

ahead of

in front of

on account of

The preposition or compound preposition with its object and modifiers is known as a *prepositional phrase.*

The prepositions (including compound prepositions) are italicized in the following examples, and the prepositional phrases are enclosed in parentheses.

My parents frequently showed me examples (*of* good writing).

(*In front of* the house) were plants I had never before seen.

(*Before* the stock market crash) the Dow-Jones average soared (*beyond* our wildest dreams).

Prepositional phrases function as adjectives when they modify nouns or pronouns.

The house (*behind* the fire station) burned last night. (The prepositional phrase modifies the noun *house.*)

Prepositional phrases function as adverbs when they modify a verb, an adjective, or another adverb.

The house burned (*to* the ground) last night.

The prepositional phrase modifies the verb *burned.*

PRACTICE EXERCISE 22.12
Prepositions

DIRECTIONS: Underline the prepositional phrases in the sentences below.

1. The professor placed his lecture notes on the lectern.

2. The music of Sibelius, a Finnish composer, is frequently heard at concerts.

3. Dylan Thomas was a brilliant Welsh poet who sometimes spent too much time in New York bars.

4. The Book Merchant's window displayed a variety of beautifully illustrated children's books.

5. In some countries audiences stand while singing the Alleluia chorus of Handel's *Messiah.*

6. The Holy Sepulcher is a rock-hewn tomb found in a garden outside the walls of Jerusalem.

7. In Shakespeare's play *Othello,* Iago convinces Othello that Desdemona is unfaithful to him.

8. Charles Dickens' novels often depict a world of poverty in 19th century London.

9. Ernest Hemingway, whose *The Old Man and the Sea* won a Pulitzer Prize in 1954, ended his life with a bullet in 1961.

10. Willy Loman is the main character in an Arthur Miller play, *Death of a Salesman.*

II. BASIC THINGS TO KNOW ABOUT WRITING EFFECTIVE SENTENCES

A *sentence* is a group of words that contains three elements: a subject, a verb, and a complete thought. A group of words containing these three elements is also called an independent clause.

1. Everyone (subject) needs (verb) a good friend.
2. The flowers (subject) are dying (verb) for lack of rain.
3. The book sale (subject) was (verb) a great success.
4. Rebecca (subject) missed (verb) the family reunion.
5. Lightning (subject) struck (verb) the old oak tree.

Each of the sentences above contains a subject and a verb and a complete thought, the third element that is so important for a sentence. If that element is missing, even if the group of words contains a subject and a verb, it is not a sentence. Notice what happens when we change the beginning of the sentences above.

1. Since everyone needs a friend.
2. Although the flowers are dying for lack of rain.
3. Because the book sale was not a success.
4. When Rebecca missed the family reunion.
5. After lightning struck the old oak tree.

Although all of the above groups of words have a subject and a verb, they do not make a complete thought. They leave the mind suspended, wondering what is coming next. Word groups that have subjects and verbs but do not make a complete thought are called *dependent clauses*. When these dependent clauses try to masquerade as complete sentences, we call them *fragments*.

Subject

A subject of the sentence is a noun or pronoun that the sentence is about. To find the subject of any sentence, ask who or what the sentence is about.

Dark clouds are appearing on the horizon. (What are appearing?)

The drought is continuing. (What is continuing?)

He could not find the street. (Who could not find the street?)

They called the police immediately after the robbery. (Who called the police?)

The third game of the 1989 World Series was called because of an earthquake. (What was called?)

Verb

A verb is a word that tells what the subject is doing. To find the verb, ask what the subject is doing.

Kay and Sal phoned from the airport. (What did the subject *Kay and Sal* do?)

The barge rammed a pleasure boat on the Thames. (What did the subject *barge* do?)

The president fired the air traffic controllers. (What did the subject *president* do?)

The airlines raised fares. (What did the subject *airlines* do?)

PRACTICE EXERCISE 22.13
Subjects and Verbs

DIRECTIONS: Underline the subject in each statement below. Draw a circle around the verb.

1. Jack and Jill are two children in a Norse myth.

2. Jack and Jill were kidnapped by the moon while drawing water.

3. The children are still to be seen in the moon with the bucket hanging from a pole resting on their shoulders.

4. George Orwell wrote *Animal Farm* to mock the Russian revolution under Stalin.

5. Lewis Carroll wrote *Alice in Wonderland.*

6. Alice can become a giant or a pygmy by nibbling alternate sides of a mushroom.

7. Alice meets Humpty Dumpty, Tweedledum and Tweedledee, the White Knight, and many others.

8. Geoffrey Chaucer wrote *Canterbury Tales,* stories by pilgrims going to the tomb of Thomas á Becket.

9. In Dante's *Inferno,* traitors are frozen in the ice of the ninth circle.

10. Many of John Steinbeck's stories are about the miserable living conditions of migrant workers in California during the 1930s.

Subject/Verb Agreement

The subject and the verb in a sentence must always agree in person and number. If you use a singular subject, you must use a singular verb. If you use a plural subject, you must use a plural verb.

Subject-verb agreement usually requires that the verb form end in -s in the third person singular of the present tense.

WALK

Person	Singular	Plural
First	I walk	we walk
Second	you walk	you walk
Third	he, she, it walks	they walk

Notice that the verb form is exactly the same in every instance except the *third person singular*.

Agreement with the Verb *Be* and the Verb *Have*

The verb *be* has several irregular forms.

Present Tense

I am	we are
you are	you are
he, she, it is	they are

The verb *have* has an irregular form in the third person singular:

I have	we have
you have	you have
he, she, it has	they have

Some people use nonstandard forms of the verbs *be*, such as "I be," "they be," or "he have." These forms should not be used in writing except when quoting someone directly.

Agreement with a Compound Subject

Generally, a compound subject requires a plural verb form.

Gail and Paul rent a cabin at the lake every summer.

The subject (Gail and Paul) is plural; therefore, it takes a plural verb (rent).

Marcella and Dorma celebrate their birthdays together every year.

The subject (Marcella and Dorma) is plural; therefore, it takes a plural verb (celebrate).

Cooking and ice hockey are my hobbies.

The subject (cooking and ice hockey) is plural; therefore, it takes a plural verb (celebrate).

Agreement with Compound Subjects
Joined by *or* or *nor* and Other Conjunctions

When subjects are joined by certain words—*either, neither, nor, not only, but also,* the verb agrees with the subject closer to the verb.

> *Either* the hourly pay *or* the health benefits increase in the new contract.

> *Either* the health benefits *or* the hourly pay increases in the new contract.

In the first example, *benefits,* a plural subject, is closer to the verb, so it takes a plural verb, *increase.* In the second example, *pay,* a singular subject, is closer to the verb, so it takes a singular verb, *increases.*

Agreement with Indefinite Pronouns as Subjects

> Each of the game show contestants seems at ease.

The subject (each) is singular; therefore, it takes a singular verb (seems). Note that the subject is *each,* not *contestants.*

> Neither of the airlines has a direct flight to London from Pittsburgh.

The subject (neither) is singular; therefore, it takes a singular verb (has).

Agreement with Subjects That Follow Verbs

> High on the mountain top *were* sturdy little *evergreens.*

> Where *are* the *groceries* I just bought?

Agreement When Intervening Words
Are Between Subject and Verb

> A *collection* of short stories *was* the group's favorite book.

> *Each* of the students in the Spanish class *is* fluent in Spanish.

> *Cindy,* along with Tony, *was* looking to see if Paula got off the plane.

> *Salmon fishing,* along with trout fishing, *was* her favorite form of recreation.

The *computer,* especially personal computers, *has* changed the way many students do their assignments.

Agreement with Collective Nouns as Subjects

Words that describe a group of individuals who act together for a common purpose are called collective nouns. Collective nouns are *singular* nouns, and they require *singular* verbs.

The *crew* was happy that Kathy would be the coxswain.

The *group* of students was demonstrating outside the principal's door.

The *committee* was asked by the negotiator to stop its stalling tactics.

The *team* was very angry that the third base umpire had ejected the manager and two players from the game.

A *group* of wild geese was honking loudly as it flew south for the winter.

The *jury* was given instructions by the judge before retiring to reach a verdict.

PRACTICE EXERCISE 22.14
Subject/Verb Agreement

DIRECTIONS: Draw a circle around the correct verb in the parentheses in each of the following sentences.

1. Wolfgang Amadeus Mozart, along with Ludwig von Beethoven, (was, were) famous for composing great pieces of music.

2. There (is, are) many who don't know that Beethoven composed the *Ninth Symphony* when he was totally deaf.

3. Unlike Mozart, Beethoven (was, were) not a child prodigy.

4. Some people (thinks, think) that Beethoven is the greatest musical genius the world has ever known.

5. One of Mozart's most famous operas (is, are) *The Marriage of Figaro*.

6. Several of Mozart's string quartets (represents, represent) his musical genius.

7. The movie *Amadeus* (tells, tell) the story of this gifted genius.

8. In the movie, Mozart's father (takes, take) his seven-year-old son on concert tours of Europe.

9. In the film, concert audiences everywhere (acclaims, acclaim) the young genius, Mozart.

10. In one of the final scenes, Mozart, sick and penniless, (dies, die) at age thirty-five in Vienna.

PRACTICE EXERCISE 22.15
Subject/Verb Agreement

DIRECTIONS: Draw one line under the subject in each of the following sentences. Circle the verb form that agrees in number (singular or plural) with the subject.

1. Each of their children (has, have) a pet.

2. Neither the student nor her parents (like, likes) to watch black and white movies.

3. Where (is, are) all the young men?

4. At the very end of the line (was, were) an elderly woman.

5. Diners who (smoke, smokes) (is, are) seated in a separate room.

6. It really (doesn't, don't) matter.

7. Political science and art (was, were) her best subjects.

8. Frank, along with Mary, (was chosen, were chosen) for parts in the play.

9. In addition to the Smith family, the Joneses (is coming, are coming) to the concert.

10. Neither the vase nor the crystal glasses (was broken, were broken).

Recognizing and Avoiding Sentence Fragments

Groups of words that do not express a complete thought are called *sentence fragments*. One way to help eliminate sentence fragments from your writing is to *listen* to what you have written. The fragments are italicized in each of the following examples:

After I awoke. I dressed quickly and ran for the bus.

We went to the parking lot. *After the concert was over.*

We found the lost keys. *After we returned.*

When it was nine o'clock. The class decided the professor was not coming.

PRACTICE EXERCISE 22.16
Recognizing and Avoiding Sentence Fragments

DIRECTIONS: Underline the fragment in each of the following statements below; then rewrite the statement to make a complete sentence.

1. James Joyce is an Irish author. Who became one of the best known writers of literature.

2. One of Joyce's stories in "The Dubliners" is *The Dead.* A story about Gabriel Conroy and his wife Gretta.

3. After a party one night. Gretta tells Gabriel about Michael Furey, a young man, now dead, with whom she was in love.

4. Because of a song she heard at the party. Gretta remembers Furey.

5. On hearing of his wife's love for Furey. Conroy feels shut out of his wife's life.

6. Watching the snow, a symbol of death, fall outside. Conroy realizes the power of the dead over the living.

_____

_____

_____

7. Although Joyce never returned to Ireland after 1912. The subject matter of all his work is the city of Dublin.

_____

_____

_____

8. Joyce lived for many years with Nora Barnacle. Before he married her.

_____

_____

9. If you ever visit Dublin. Make sure you take a short trip to Sandy Cove, where there is a fine James Joyce museum.

_____

_____

_____

10. Joyce worked long hours. Taking seven years to complete his famous novel _Ulysses._

_____

_____

_____

PRACTICE EXERCISE 22.17
Recognizing and Avoiding Sentence Fragments

DIRECTIONS: Underline the sentence fragments in the following exercise; then repair the fragments by connecting them to related sentences or by changing the punctuation.

1. Gardening can be fun. Especially when your flowers begin to bloom and your vegetables ripen.

   _____

   _____

   _____

2. Sitting on the park bench was a man in his twenties. Wearing an army surplus jacket and jeans.

   _____

   _____

   _____

3. The Wildflower Center has grown rapidly and vigorously. With a permanent endowment of more than a million dollars.

   _____

   _____

   _____

4. The candidate's wife visited Boston to argue for art in subway stations. And lobbied for the project in Washington.

   _____

   _____

5. The musical version of *Les Miserables* has become a smash hit. Causing renewed interest in Victor Hugo, author of the novel.

_____

_____

_____

6. I would like to support my neighbor in her campaign for a seat on City Council. Although I cannot afford to contribute money.

_____

_____

_____

7. Whenever Luis sees his former teacher. He is reminded of the only F he got as a freshman.

_____

_____

_____

8. My father has stopped eating eggs for breakfast. Because they are high in cholesterol.

_____

_____

_____

9. Unless you return that book today. You will be assessed a fine.

_____

_____

10. I am taking a vacation this year. Even if I have to borrow the money to do it.

_____

_____

Recognizing and Avoiding Fused or Run-On Sentences

A run-on sentence (also called a fused sentence) contains two or more independent clauses that have not been properly separated. (Independent clauses can stand alone because they have a subject and a verb and express a complete thought.)

Writers combine independent clauses in one sentence when they want to convey to the reader a close relationship between the two clauses. When that happens, the writer must connect the clauses *with a semicolon* or *with a comma and a coordinating conjunction.*

Note: You cannot connect two independent clauses with just a comma. If you choose to use the comma to connect independent clauses, you *must* use a coordinating conjunction (such as *and, but, or, nor, for, so, yet*) with the comma. Without the coordinating conjunction you have a run-on (or fused) sentence such as the following:

> More than 300,000 people went to Edgewater Park to view the fireworks display, there was a tremendous traffic jam afterwards.

> The manager was ejected from the game, he cursed the umpire, picked up a handful of dirt and threw it on him.

> A husband and wife should not wallpaper a living room together, there are too many occasions for arguments.

Comma Splice

A comma splice happens when a writer separates two independent clauses by a comma instead of a comma and a coordinating conjunction. The result is a fused (run-on) sentence.

> Bruce didn't care for the movie, Ann liked it very much.

> The television was on all afternoon, Dennis hardly watched it.

> The coast guard officers searched all the yachts in the marina, they did not find a trace of illegal drugs.

Correcting Run-On Sentences

You can correct run-on or fused sentences in one of the following ways:

1. Make each independent clause into a separate sentence.
2. Use a semicolon between the independent clauses.
3. Use a comma and a coordinating conjunction (such as *and, but, or, nor, for, so, yet*) between the independent clauses.
4. Change the structure of the sentence.

My family moved from Indiana to Ohio, I had to leave all my friends.

Method 1:   My family moved from Indiana to Ohio. I had to leave all my friends.

Method 2:   My family moved from Indiana to Ohio; I had to leave all my friends.

Method 3:   My family moved from Indiana to Ohio, and I had to leave all my friends.

Method 4:   Because my family moved from Indiana to Ohio, I had to leave all my friends.

PRACTICE EXERCISE 22.18
Correcting Run-on or Fused Sentences

DIRECTIONS: Correct run-on or fused sentences in one of the following ways: 1) Use a period and start a new sentence; 2) use a comma and a coordinating conjunction; 3) use a semicolon; 4) change the structure of the sentence.

1. Eleanor Roosevelt, the wife of President Franklin D. Roosevelt, devoted herself to women's and children's issues, she became famous in her own right.

_____

_____

_____

_____

2. Lucy Mercer was her personal secretary, Eleanor found that Lucy was having an affair with her husband, who at the time was Undersecretary of the Navy.

_____

_____

_____

_____

3. Eleanor did not divorce Franklin, it would have ruined his political career.

_____

_____

4. Eleanor wrote "My Day," a newspaper column, many newspapers throughout the country carried it.

_____

_____

5. President Roosevelt died at Warm Springs, Georgia, on April 12, 1945, he did not live to see the end of World War II.

_____

_____

6. Eleanor later found that Lucy Mercer was at Warm Springs when the President died, she was furious with those who had invited Lucy.

_____

_____

7. Eleanor Roosevelt remained active in the Democratic party, office seekers eagerly sought her endorsement.

_____

_____

8. She worked hard to help create the United Nations, she thought the UN was the world's best hope for a lasting peace.

_____

_____

9. Eleanor was not a physically attractive woman, however, she had great intelligence and courage.

_____

_____

10. Eleanor Roosevelt was devastated by her husband's infidelity, she did not let the affair keep her from developing her talents.

_____

_____

PRACTICE EXERCISE 22.19
Correcting Run-On Sentences

DIRECTIONS: Correct the following run-on sentences. You will notice that not all methods of correcting run-on sentences work equally well with each example.

1. During the Great Depression of the 1930s millions of investors lost their savings, thousands of banks closed their doors.

_____

_____

2. Red Smith graduated from Notre Dame University in 1927, he had decided to become a journalist.

_____

_____

3. Georgia O'Keeffe lived in New Mexico, she painted the landscapes and architecture of the Southwest.

_____

_____

4. The airline offered a discount on flights to Europe, customers had to purchase their tickets before March 15.

_____

_____

5. I wanted desperately to get a job in the college bookstore, I knew two other applicants who had more experience.

_____

_____

6. Frank covered his cheeseburger with mustard, he ate the whole thing in two gulps.

_____

_____

7. The surgeon general of the United States claims that cigarette smoking kills 350,000 people a year, he recommends placing warning labels about addiction on packages of tobacco products.

_____

_____

_____

_____

8. My grandfather joined the Retired Senior Volunteer Program, he delivers mail to hospital patients.

_____

_____

9. Gail volunteered to arrange the flowers for her neighbor's party, she has worked in a flower shop for years.

_____

_____

_____

10. John decided to accept the promotion, he knew he would get better medical benefits.

_____

_____

Simple Sentences

A simple sentence is a group of words that has a subject and a verb and makes a complete thought.

> The United States Navy (subject) was patrolling (verb) the Persian Gulf.

> Medical researchers (subject) are working (verb) to find a cure for AIDS.

> Management and labor (compound subject) are negotiating (verb) behind closed doors.

> Labor negotiators (subject) are asking (verb) for more information and are threatening (verb) to leave the negotiating table.

> NOTE: The last two sentences are simple sentences even though one has a compound subject and the other has a compound verb.

Complex Sentences

A complex sentence is one that has an *independent clause and a dependent clause.* In other words, it has one word group that has a subject and a verb but cannot stand alone as a complete sentence, and it has another word group with a subject and verb that can stand alone.

> When the child picked up the gun (dependent clause), he did not know it was loaded (independent clause).

> The congregation sat down (independent clause) after the choir sang the opening hymn (dependent clause).

> Before the president vetoed the legislation (dependent clause), he conferred with the members of his party (independent clause).

Compound Sentences

A compound sentence is one that has two or more independent clauses. In other words, it has two or more word groups that have subjects and verbs and are capable of standing alone as simple sentences. But for reasons of variety or emphasis, the writer decides to join these independent clauses or simple sentences.

> The cavalry began the charge (independent clause), and the infantry followed (independent clause).

> Pontiac is doing well with its Pontiac 6000 LE (independent clause), but the company discontinued the Fiero in 1988 (independent clause).

PRACTICE EXERCISE 22.20
Identifying Simple, Complex, and Compound Sentences

DIRECTIONS: In the space provided, identify the kind of sentence that follows (S for Simple Sentence; CX for Complex Sentence; and CP for Compound Sentence).

_____ 1. A poll tax was often used to keep blacks and other minorities from voting.

_____ 2. Lou Gehrig was a first baseman for the New York Yankees.

_____ 3. George III was king of England when the thirteen American colonies revolted.

_____ 4. Robert Frost and Emily Dickinson are well-known American poets.

_____ 5. Elie Wiesel survived the Nazi concentration camps of Auschwitz and Buchenwald, but his parents and a sister did not.

_____ 6. Archie Bunker is a television character whose name has become identified with bigotry.

_____ 7. Samuel Clemens was a writer whose pen name was Mark Twain.

_____ 8. They visited the Louvre in Paris, and then they traveled to see the cathedral at Chartres.

_____ 9. John Dillinger was a famous gangster in the 1930s, and he became Public Enemy No. 1.

_____ 10. After Edward Everett spoke for two hours at the dedication ceremony, President Abraham Lincoln delivered his short and famous Gettysburg Address.

Avoiding Awkward Sentence Construction

Faulty sentence construction results when writers do not construct their sentences carefully. The writer must make sure that the subject and predicate fit together grammatically.

> _Faulty_: Although five hundred students passed the college entrance test does not mean that the college will accept all five hundred students.

Revised: The fact that five hundred students passed the college entrance test does not mean that the college will accept all five hundred.

Faulty: The reason Clare was late was because she was visiting her sister Ann. (*The reason that* means *because.*)

Revised: The reason Clare was late was that she was visiting her sister Ann. Or Clare was late because she was visiting her sister Ann.

Faulty: A designated hitter is using a player to bat in place of the pitcher.

Revised: A designated hitter is one who bats in place of the pitcher.

Faulty: Computers every day are coming down in price.

Revised: Every day, companies are reducing the prices of their computers.

Faulty: When they designed the road, you could tell where there was faulty engineering.

Revised: The engineering faults were obvious even when they were designing the road.

Faulty: A sentence is when you have a subject, a verb, and a complete thought.

Revised: A sentence contains a subject and a verb and makes a complete thought.

PRACTICE EXERCISE 22.21
Avoiding Awkward Construction

DIRECTIONS: Rewrite the following sentences in such a way that you eliminate awkward constructions that confuse the reader.

1. Jack Barton is a shrewd vice president is why he is in charge of hiring new people for his company.

   _____

   _____

2. When you braked on the icy road, the car was out of control.

   _____

   _____

3. The reason the team lost in the play-offs was when highly emotional players were penalized for unsportsmanlike behavior.

   _____

   _____

   _____

4. With every turn on the narrow Scottish road, a surprise awaited the rented car.

   _____

   _____

5. You have a short circuit happen when too many lighting fixtures are plugged into one socket.

   _____

   _____

6. Metal fatigue is what happens when a plane has too many takeoffs and landings.

   _____

   _____

7. With every answer the witness gave to Attorney Betty Reuben, it got him more angry and confused.

   _____

   _____

8. When you have too much snow and high winds, it often causes whiteouts on the freeways.

   _____

   _____

9. The fact that Feldman Mechanical is a first-rate company, they got many contracts for the downtown development project.

   _____

   _____

   _____

10. While singing the National Anthem, the antics of the ball players were not appreciated by the fans.

    _____

    _____

    _____

PRACTICE EXERCISE 22.22
Avoiding Awkward Sentence Construction

DIRECTIONS: Rewrite the following sentences in such a way that you avoid awkward constructions that can confuse readers.

1. A computer virus is when your floppy disks become infected from other faulty disks.

   _____

   _____

2. With every attempt the stroke victim made to speak, it got him more angry and frustrated.

   _____

   _____

3. The fact that Alonzo knew the computer he had many requests from students to teach them.

   _____

   _____

   _____

4. While ice fishing, the lake suddenly began to melt.

   _____

   _____

5. The reason she did not get the job was because she did not have a good resume.

   _____

   _____

6. While sitting on the patio, a huge groundhog was seen coming out of the lawn.

_____

_____

7. When you moved the monitor for the computer, the cable was probably damaged.

_____

_____

_____

8. The instructor demonstrates how to use the laser printer and replacing the cartridge on the dot matrix printer.

_____

_____

_____

9. Every week during summer vacation at least two children were struck by cars on bikes.

_____

_____

_____

10. Any country that can put a man on the moon, it should be able to find a cure for the AIDS virus.

_____

_____

_____

Combining Sentences

You can often make a series of simple sentences more effective if you combine them into one sentence. That sentence may be a simple sentence, a compound sentence, or a complex sentence. By doing this, you can avoid repetition and give emphasis to major ideas.

> John wanted a new car. (simple sentence)

> His father persuaded him to buy a used car. (simple sentence)

Although the two sentences are correct, they would be more effective if they were combined:

> Although John wanted a new car, his father persuaded him to buy a used one. (complex)

PRACTICE EXERCISE 22.23
Sentence Combining

DIRECTIONS: Combine each set of simple sentences into one sentence.

1. In the 1989 World Series, the Oakland Athletics defeated the San Francisco Giants in four straight games.
   They won because of their speed on the bases.
   They won because of an awesome display of batting power.
   They won because of their superior pitching.

   _____

   _____

   _____

   _____

   _____

2. The planes were delayed at the airport.
   There was a fierce blizzard.
   The passengers were not happy.

   _____

   _____

   _____

   _____

3. An earthquake destroyed many cities in Armenia.
   More than fifty thousand people were killed.
   Thousands of people were left homeless.

   _____

   _____

   _____

   _____

4. A Pan American airliner exploded over Locherbie, Scotland.
   It happened right before Christmas, 1988.
   Authorities said that the cause of the explosion was a plastic bomb.

   _____

   _____

   _____

   _____

   _____

   _____

5. Joyce Carol Oates wrote a short story called "The Lady with the Pet Dog."
   It is a modern version of Anton Chekhov's story of the same name.
   Oates tells the story from a woman's point of view.

   _____

   _____

   _____

   _____

   _____

6. President George Bush graduated from Yale University.
   He was a good student.
   He played first base for the college baseball team.

   _____

   _____

   _____

   _____

7. Will Rogers was a famous American humorist, actor, and columnist.
He poked fun at politicians of both parties.
He died in a plane crash in Alaska in 1935.

_____

_____

_____

_____

_____

8. The snow storm paralyzed the city.
There were many accidents on freeways.
Motorists abandoned their cars on city streets.

_____

_____

_____

_____

9. Registration for college courses in the winter quarter was down.
The unemployment rate in the city was high.
Many students did not have tuition money.

_____

_____

_____

_____

10. Ronald Reagan was once a Hollywood actor.
He never won an Academy Award.
One of his best acting performances was in the movie *King's Row*.

_____

_____

_____

_____

Misplaced Modifiers

When a writer does not put a word or a phrase close to the word it is meant to modify, a misplaced modifier results.

Faulty placement: The phone *almost* rang fifteen times before he answered it. (Implies that the phone was trying to decide whether to ring.)

Correct placement: The phone rang *almost* fifteen times before he answered.

Faulty placement: Juan admired the tall building *walking down the street*. (That would be some sight to see.)

Correct placement: *Walking down the street*, Juan admired the tall building.

Faulty placement: Sandra sent the child to the cafeteria *that was hungry*. (Implies that the cafeteria was hungry.)

Correct placement: Sandra sent the hungry child to the cafeteria.

Faulty placement: We could see the helicopter *sitting on our balcony*. (The sentence implies that the balcony must be unusually large.)

Correct placement: *Sitting on our balcony*, we could see the helicopter.

Faulty placement: Many entertainers have the same types of shows *such as comedians, jazz singers, and musicians*.

Correct placement: Many entertainers *such as comedians, jazz singers and musicians* have the same types of shows.

PRACTICE EXERCISE 22.24
Recognizing and Avoiding Misplaced Modifiers

DIRECTIONS: Underline the misplaced modifier in the following sentences, and then use an arrow to indicate where the modifier should be properly placed.

EXAMPLE: Christopher bought a racquet from the club pro that was moderately priced.

1. The pilot signaled the mechanic with a wave that the plane was ready for a takeoff.

2. The mechanic started the engine with a smile.

3. The plane taxied to the runway loaded with gasoline and supplies.

4. The young pilot looked at the crowd on the field with a nervous stomach.

5. The plane started down the runway that was lined with spectators carrying too heavy a load.

6. At a baseball game in New York, 40,000 fans stood and said a silent prayer for the pilot worried about the flight.

7. For thirty hours there was almost no news of the plane and its pilot.

8. Many Parisians drove to Le Bourget air field in cars sensing that history was being made.

9. The plane landed safely with 100,000 Parisians cheering wildly.

10. The pilot stepped out of the plane and told the crowd with a smile, "I am Charles Lindbergh."

PRACTICE EXERCISE 22.25
Avoiding Misplaced Modifiers

DIRECTIONS: Underline the misplaced modifier in each of the following sentences, and then draw a line and arrow showing where the modifier should be placed. In some cases, you may have to rewrite the sentence.

EXAMPLE: *Faulty:*   Eddie and Barbara found a shirt in the store that was just the right size.

         Correct: Eddie and Barbara found a shirt that was just the right size in the store.

1. The prisoner who tried to escape was found by a police dog hiding in the bushes.

_____

_____

2. The racquetball player was returning the serves with an arrogant sneer.

_____

_____

3. They returned from the airport after a month's vacation by taxi.

_____

_____

4. He bought a car in the salesroom that was slightly used.

_____

_____

5. The accident just occurred one mile north of the turnpike last week.

_____

_____

6. The foundering Indians needed some relief pitching badly.

_____

_____

7. The baseball scouts were looking for pitchers in the South with good, strong arms.

_____

_____

8. Tom borrowed a car from a friend that had four on the floor and cruise control.

_____

_____

9. Juanita wore a corsage on her wrist that was made up of beautiful orchids.

_____

_____

10. Adrienne looked forward to coming to New York for several days.

_____

_____

11. The movie was shot on location with a great number of stunts and sound effects.

_____

_____

12. Clare bought a dog from a neighbor with only one hind leg.

_____

_____

13. The swimmers who were drinking on the beach excessively began to shout and scream at passers-by.

_____

_____

14. Terry sold an old table to an art dealer that needed sanding.

_____

_____

15. The Mohars reported the theft to the police when they returned.

_____

_____

Dangling Modifiers

Modifiers are said to be dangling when they open a sentence but are not immediately followed by the word or words they are meant to modify.

> *Having checked the tires, oil, and the gas gauge,* the car was ready for the trip. (It would be nice if the car could do all those things by itself.)

> *While waiting for the television repairman,* the faucet in the kitchen sink sprang a leak. (Implies that the faucet was waiting.)

> *While teaching the class,* a roach suddenly scampered across the floor. (Perhaps looking for its paycheck?)

PRACTICE EXERCISE 22.26
Avoiding Dangling Modifiers

DIRECTIONS: Underline the dangling modifier in each sentence. Then rewrite the sentence so that the phrase clearly modifies a word or phrase in the sentence.

1. While walking down Main Street, some walnuts fell from the tree and hit Sue in the head.

   _____

   _____

2. Soaked to the skin, a taxi finally stopped and picked up the passengers.

   _____

   _____

3. Freefalling from the airplane, the parachute's ripcord was pulled easily.

   _____

   _____

4. Waiting for a gate at the airport, the flight attendants asked the passengers to remain seated.

   _____

   _____

5. Flossing her teeth, the dental assistant tried to look again at Carmen's cavity.

   _____

   _____

6. While backing out of the driveway, two squirrels started fighting over a walnut.

   _____

   _____

7. Removing the water from my bird bath, the robins flew to the one in the next yard.

   _____

   _____

8. Running to second base, the ball hit Scott in the ankle.

   _____

   _____

9. Jumping out of a bush, my grandmother was startled by the Great Dane.

   _____

   _____

10. While talking on the phone, the dog barked loudly.

    _____

    _____

11. Walking along the beach, the moon looked beautiful.

    _____

    _____

12. At the age of ten, my mother taught me the facts of life.

    _____

    _____

13. After washing the dishes, the phone rang.

    _____

    _____

14. Startled by the explosion, the train was slowed down by the engineer.

_____

_____

15. Having given money to the Red Cross, the United Way had trouble getting people to contribute to its fund-raising drive.

_____

_____

_____

PRACTICE EXERCISE 22.27
Avoiding Dangling Modifiers

DIRECTIONS: Underline the dangling modifier in each of the following statements and rewrite the sentence.

1. Arriving at European ports of embarkation, authorities checked to see if the emigrants had passports to come to America.

   _____

   _____

   _____

2. Having fumigated the baggage, ferry boats took the emigrants to the large ships in the Hamburg harbor.

   _____

   _____

   _____

3. Carrying wicker baskets, the ship captain could easily pick out the peasants going to America.

   _____

   _____

   _____

4. Having tied up all their belongings in a sheet, the ship's deck was soon overcrowded with the poor from nearly every country.

   _____

   _____

   _____

5. Thinking about leaving their homelands forever, clergymen comforted and reassured the homesick.

_____

_____

6. Being suspicious of foreigners, food from other countries was not shared by the passengers.

_____

_____

7. While crossing the Atlantic, card games for the men and sewing for the women helped the passengers pass the time.

_____

_____

_____

8. Feeling depressed, songs from their homeland made some passengers cry.

_____

_____

9. Having contracted contagious diseases on ship, the captain ordered some passengers to be deported.

_____

_____

10. While sailing past the Statue of Liberty, cheers and shouts went up among the immigrants.

_____

_____

Parallelism

Parallelism requires that you coordinate or balance equal elements in a sentence. Nouns should be balanced with nouns, verbs with verbs, phrases with phrases, and clauses with clauses.

When driving an eighteen-wheeler, a truck driver must be *competent* and *alert*. (Parallel adjectives)

She *heard* the apartment buzzer, *picked up* the phone, and *asked* the person in the lobby to identify himself. (Parallel verbs)

If you are in an accident, remember to do the following: *attend* to the injured, *get* the name and address of the other driver, *file* a police report, and *notify* your insurance agent as soon as possible. (Parallel verbs)

The judge ruled that the defendant acted *maliciously* and *deliberately*. (Parallel adverbs)

Our military forces showed their strength *on land, on sea,* and *in the air*. (Parallel prepositional phrases)

PRACTICE EXERCISE 22.28
Parallelism

DIRECTIONS: Rewrite the italicized group of words in each of the following sentences so that the sentence has parallel construction throughout.

EXAMPLE: Faulty: Mr. Pfaff told his sons Mike and Joe to cut the grass, to trim the hedges, *and the garage should be painted.*

Correct: and to paint the garage.

1. H. L. Mencken was an American journalist, literary critic, and *he wrote essays.*

_____

2. Sarah likes novels by Alice Walker, poems by Robert Frost, *and she enjoys short stories by John Cheever.*

_____

3. Gracie May read about the Battle of Gettysburg, the Battle of Shiloh, and *about a bloody fight at a place called Bull Run.*

_____

4. Louise read the morning newspaper, made her bed, telephoned her mother, and *was enjoying the music on WDOK-FM.*

_____

5. Yesterday, little Jacquelyn played with her stuffed panda, tried to build a house from Lego blocks, and *was singing Mother Goose nursery rhymes.*

_____

6. A loving family, a sense of humor, and *friends who are honest* can often make the difference between a happy life and an unhappy one.

_____

7. She has crossed the Mississippi, has camped in Yellowstone Park, and *Mt. Ranier was even climbed by her.*

_____

8. When he is alone in his study late at night, the father of eight lights up his pipe, plays a Mozart recording, and *is wishing that the solitude could last for a week.*

_____

9. Last month my father retired, helped his brother move, and *was considering joining a volunteer group at his church.*

_____

10. After their married children left with their families, the Di Nardos cleaned the house, put away the toys, and *were rearranging the furniture.*

_____

Using Numbers in Sentences

Spell out numbers when they are one or two words.

> Jack told his daughter Julia there were twenty policemen on the SWAT team.

> There were seventy-six trombones in the band.

When the numbers are more than two words, use figures.

> A chorus of 150 voices joined the symphony orchestra.

> The room measured 1,600 square feet.

Journalists use figures for numbers over ten and numbers in a series.

Avoiding Common Mistakes

Incorrect	*Correct*
just between you and I	just between you and me
just between he and she	just between him and her

(The preposition *between* always takes the objective case.)

Incorrect	*Correct*
she don't	she doesn't

Incorrect	*Correct*
he feels badly	he feels bad

(*Bad* is an adjective; *badly* is an adverb. You can say, "Tom swung badly at the curve ball." Badly is an adverb that modifies the verb and tells us how Tom swung.)

Incorrect	*Correct*
The car runs good.	The car runs well.

(*Good* is an adjective; *well* is an adverb that modifies the verb *runs.*)

Incorrect	*Correct*
very, very tired	very tired or extremely tired

(It is incorrect to use the same adverb to modify another adverb. Don't say, "It's too, too bad." Say, "It's too bad.")

Do not confuse the verbs *lie* and *lay. To lie* means *to recline.* It is an intransitive verb and does not take a direct object. *To lay* means *to place* or *to put down.* It is a transitive verb and requires a direct object.

When I watch football on TV, I usually *lie* on the floor.
(*Lie* is in the present tense.)

When I watched football last night, I *lay* on the floor.
(*Lay* is the past tense of the verb *lie.*)

After I had *lain* on the floor for two hours, my back ached.
(*Lain* is the past participle of the verb *lie.*)

Each day after I study, I *lay* my computer manual on the table.
(*Lay* is the present tense.)

I'm positive that I *laid* my computer manual on the table yesterday.
(The past tense of the verb *lay* is *laid.*)

I have *laid* the manual there ever since I bought the computer.
(The past participle of the verb *lay* is *laid.*)

Remember the distinctions between *its* and *it's*.

>*It's always* means *it is.* (*It's* too calm for surfing.)
>*Its always* denotes possession. (The dog chased *its* tail.)

Remember the distinctions between the adverb *too* and the preposition *to*.

>You are standing *too* close *to* the edge.

Remember the distinctions between *there, they're,* and *their*.

>*There* usually indicates *place.* (The missing child was found right *there.*)

>*They're* is a contraction for *they are.* (*They're* swimming in the lake.)

>*Their* is a possessive pronoun. (The children played quietly with *their* dolls.)

Avoid using nonstandard English in formal writing. For a more complete discussion of standard and nonstandard English, see Chapter 4, The World of Words.

PRACTICE EXERCISE 22.29
Recognizing and Revising Nonstandard English

DIRECTIONS: Replace the nonstandard English with standard English.

1. They just mad cause the Down the Street gang running things.

   _____

2. They be fighting with each other.

   _____

3. He don't really want to meet his girlfriend.

   _____

4. You know why he like to jog?

   _____

5. They scarf down Chicken McNuggets.

   _____

6. Larry don't care about nothing but winning.

   _____

7. Sometime he act normal.

   _____

8. Then all a sudden he talk like he out of control.

   _____

9. The counselor, he rapping with the gang.

   _____

10. We don't know whether Momma mad or joking.

_____

11. Ain't youse had enough beer?

_____

12. After watching the news on the tube, he went to the fridge for a snack.

_____

13. Tonya's goal this year is to save for a new set of wheels.

_____

14. I didn't hear nothing about the meeting.

_____

15. Morris thought the company was not getting enough bread for the deal.

_____

Avoiding Cliches

Cliches are words or expressions that were probably fresh and attractive when they were first written or spoken but have been so overused and overworked that they have become tiresome or trite. Can you think of some cliches that are not listed here?

in the nick of time	without a shadow of a doubt
out of the blue	face the music
tried and true	chip off the old block
true blue	laid to rest
birds of a feather	dyed-in-the-wool
burned the midnight oil	deader than a doornail
Father Time	the old college try
man of the world	back to the wall
spitting image	by the same token
by hook or by crook	

III. BASIC THINGS TO KNOW ABOUT PUNCTUATION

Punctuation at the End of a Sentence

Use a period (.), question mark (?), or an exclamation mark (!) at the end of a sentence.

Period

> The sailboats are lining up for the regatta.
> Fast-food restaurants are great for families that are traveling.

Question Mark

> Is the Senate still in session?
> Will the president sign the legislation?

Exclamation Mark

> Stop that!
> Quick, turn to the right!

PRACTICE EXERCISE 22.30
Recognizing and Punctuating Sentences

DIRECTIONS: Punctuate the following piece of writing. Reading it aloud may help you decide where sentences begin and end.

after the rain stopped we resumed our softball game with the faculty they were winning five to four in the first half of the ninth inning but we knew we had a good chance to win the game our English instructor was coming up to bat we knew that was a sure out two of our best hitters would be coming up to bat in the last half of the inning surprisingly our English instructor hit a home run unfortunately she hit our only softball into the river now we'll never know whether we would have won in the last half of the ninth inning

Punctuation Within a Sentence

A comma, semicolon, colon, dash, and parentheses are used to punctuate sentences internally.

Use a comma to separate adjectives that modify the same noun.

> A large, yellow balloon came floating down the road.

> The tired, hungry stranger was ill.

Use a comma to separate items in a series.

> You will need keys for the car, money for the parking garage, and a sign for the car window.

> Joel worked at a gas station, a pizzeria, and a car wash to earn his college tuition.

Use a comma between two independent clauses that are connected by a coordinating conjunction such as *and* or *but*.

> The owner fired the manager after the game, but he should have fired some of the players.

> The Southwest is a nice place to live, but a shortage of water is making it less attractive.

Use a comma after a dependent clause that introduces a sentence.

> After the employees left the plant, the manager began checking their offices.

When her car ran out of gas on the deserted road, Betty wondered what she would do.

Use a comma or commas to set off words that are really not essential to the sentence.

Manners, then, are essential to society.

There are, to be sure, several reasons why he should be invited.

Nevertheless, I will not invite him.

If the date is used within a sentence, use a comma after the year.

The third game of the 1989 World Series was to be played on October 14, 1989, at Candlestick Park in San Francisco; but an earthquake intervened.

PRACTICE EXERCISE 22.31
Commas

DIRECTIONS: Place commas where they are needed in the following sentences.

1. Michelangelo was an Italian sculptor painter architect and poet of the Renaissance.

2. One of the best known artists in the world Michelangelo studied in Florence Italy.

3. Three men who influenced him were Giotto Dante and Savanorola.

4. In 1496 on his first trip to Rome he produced the *Bacchus* statue.

5. In 1498 he produced the famous *Pieta* one of his best known statues.

6. In 1504 he completed his *Holy Family* one of his best known paintings.

7. Although Michelangelo is a sculptor and a painter he is also a famous architect.

8. Michelangelo the architect erected the Dome of St. Peter's Basilica one of the most famous landmarks in the world.

9. If you ever get to Rome you will not want to miss his painting of *Creation* and the *Last Judgment* which he painted on the ceiling of the Sistine Chapel.

10. In addition to his work as a painter sculptor and architect Michelangelo also excelled as a poet.

PRACTICE EXERCISE 22.32
Commas

DIRECTIONS: Punctuate the following sentences by placing commas where they are needed.

1. John and Norma were watching a horror movie so they didn't hear the neighbors calling to tell them their car was on fire.

2. Pattie told Bill to make sure that he brought home a hammer nails screw driver and pliers.

3. Jamie looked for her wedding ring in the bedroom in the kitchen and in the bathroom.

4. The ring however was not in any of those places. Mark her loving husband had secretly taken it to the jeweler for another diamond setting.

5. After the colorful balloon descended crowds of people milled about it.

6. When Gene was young his friends and he often went to Euclid Beach Park to ride the Flying Turns the Cyclone and the Dodgem.

7. Harry was failing in history political science and economics but he was passing English and math.

8. Frankly the movie was a big bore a complete waste of time and money.

9. There are some advantages to be sure in leasing a car rather than buying one.

10. Oh well next baseball season our team will win the pennant in its division.

11. On May 27 1927 Charles Lindberg became the first person to fly solo across the Atlantic Ocean.

12. On October 14 1989 the stock market plunged more than one hundred ninety points causing investors to be concerned worried even panic-stricken.

13. Most small investors lost a lot of money but some were lucky enough to get out in time.

14. Maria was interested in track volley ball and field hockey.

15. Michael and Margaret along with their son Brian were visiting their friends Colm and Pat who live near Denison University in Granville Ohio.

Semicolon

Use a semicolon to connect two independent clauses that are not connected by coordinating conjunctions such as *and* or *but.*

> The husband wanted to keep the house; his aging wife wanted to sell it.
> One man was arrested; more will be arrested tomorrow.
> The general manager thought his speech was funny; the audience thought it insulting.

Colon

Use a colon to show that a list or a series of items is to follow.

> No Fourth of July picnic would be a success without the following: beverages, hot dogs, mustard, pickles, and fireworks.
> My opponent should be defeated because he did these outrageous things: deceived the elderly, had some relatives on a phantom payroll, and accepted kickbacks on contracts.

The Dash

Use a dash when you want to make a side comment or when you want to emphasize something in the sentence.

> He came to visit us without—I found this amusing—even a change of clothes.
> One of the members of the class—a lovely person—could not attend the reunion.

Parentheses

Use parentheses when you want to break up the continuity of a sentence, minimize some information in the sentence, or include some illustrative or supplementary material.

Sexagenarians (the word has a nice sound to it) are allowed to exaggerate their past.

John Henry Newman said that the purpose of a liberal education is to produce a gentleman (and, we should add, a gentlewoman).

A growing group of people who lobby for human concerns is Mothers Against Drunk Driving (MADD).

Punctuation of Quoted Material

Use quotation marks to enclose the exact words of a speaker.

Barry said, "I will not tolerate bigots."

Use single quotation marks to enclose a quotation within a quotation.

Tom asked, "Are you the person who wrote the word 'exceptional' on my term paper?"

Note: Place periods and commas inside the quotation marks. Place colons and semicolons outside the quotation marks.

"I knew then in childhood," writes Wallace Fowlie, "as I know now in my seventieth year, that the Bible is the great educator."

He memorized Frost's "Stopping by a Woods on a Snowy Evening"; it was easy to commit the poet's words to memory.

Punctuation of Titles

Place in quotation marks the titles of short poems, articles, essays, short stories, and episodes of radio and television programs.

Poem
"To an Athlete Dying Young" by A.E. Housman
"Mothers" by Nikki Giovanni

Essay
"Pity the Serfs at Our Medieval Universities" (*N.Y.Times*)
"Touching All Bases" (*BYTE* Magazine)

Short Story
"The Girls in Their Summer Dresses" by Irving Shaw
"The Lesson" by Toni Cade Bambara

Episodes of television programs
"The World in Darkness" (an episode of *CBS News Sunday Morning*)

PRACTICE EXERCISE 22.33
Quotations

DIRECTIONS: In the following statements, enclose the words of the speaker in quotation marks. Place quotation marks around the titles of short stories, poems, or short works. Set off a quotation within a quotation with single quotation marks.

1. Anita said, I should have started on this project much earlier.

2. In his inaugural address, President Kennedy said, Ask not what your country can do for you. Ask what you can do for your country.

3. The instructor told the class to read Alice Munro's short story How I Met My Husband.

4. He could not remember who said Cross that bridge when you come to it.

5. Brenda said, I just know that the statistics exam will contain questions from material I didn't review.

6. The Dead is a short story in James Joyce's *Dubliners*.

7. The paper was not delivered again this morning, Carrie said, and I am angry.

8. In the movie *Casablanca*, Humphrey Bogart says to Ingrid Bergman, Here's looking at you, Kid.

9. Roger said, In the movie *Casablanca* Bogart did not say, Play it again, Sam, but Play it, Sam.

10. Are you telling me that this library does not have a computer? Mark asked the librarian.

Punctuation of Words

Capitals

Capitalize the first word of a sentence and the first word of a line of poetry.

First word of a sentence:
We cannot change the world, but we can change ourselves.

First word of a line of poetry:
Stone walls do not a prison make,
    Nor iron bars a cage;
(From "To Althea, From Prison," by Richard Lovelace)

Capitalize *names* of persons, places, companies, works of art, events.

John Cunin, chairman of Bearings, Inc.

Margaret McCarthy, executive director of the Retired Senior Volunteer Program (RSVP)

The Statue of Liberty

The Gettysburg Address

Lake Michigan

The Alamo

Capitalize titles when they precede a proper noun.

The first lady accompanied President Bush.

The citizens of the country welcomed Secretary General Mikhail Gorbachev.

It was Chief Justice William Rehnquist who wrote the majority opinion.

PRACTICE EXERCISE 22.34
Capital Letters

DIRECTIONS: Draw a circle around the words that should be capitalized in the following statements.

1. Walt frazier played professional basketball for the New york knickerbockers in the sixties and seventies.

2. he tells his story in his autobiography, *walt frazier: one magic season and a basketball life.*

3. in 1970 the knicks beat the los angeles lakers in the seventh game of the championship series.

4. The game was played at madison square garden in new york.

5. frazier believes it was easier to play against wilt chamberlin than bill russell.

6. because defense is not applied in today's game, frazier thinks that players like magic johnson, isiah thomas, and larry bird look better than they really are.

7. frazier says, "the knicks won because we were the most intelligent team."

8. frazier wrote the book with neil Offen.

9. the autobiography was published by times Books and has illustrations.

10. at $17.95, it makes a nice gift for someone who closely follows the national basketball Association.

PRACTICE EXERCISE 22.35
Capitalization

DIRECTIONS: Correct the following sentences by capitalizing the words that should be capitalized and drawing a line through unnecessary capitals.

1. In the Summer, they planned to backpack in the black hills of south dakota.

2. While walking through lakeview cemetery they discovered the grave of john d. rockefeller, the founder of standard oil company.

3. If you turn and walk South when you reach elm street, you will come to st. james church.

4. In july, 1988, the democrats held their national convention in atlanta, georgia.

5. The site of the republican convention that same year was new orleans, louisiana.

6. When the musical south pacific first played on broadway, the name of joshua logan, one of the authors, was omitted from the Program.

7. John glenn had been one of the seven original astronauts before he became a senator from the state of Ohio.

8. The reverend Jesse Jackson was in memphis, tennessee when the reverend Martin Luther King, jr., was assassinated in 1968.

9. In july 1988, George Bush, vice president of the United States, went before the general assembly of the united nations, and defended the downing of an iranian airliner by an american naval vessel in the persian gulf.

10. All the Engineering Majors were asked to assemble in the auditorium for an address by the President of the College.

Apostrophe

To show possession for a singular noun, add an 's.

the friend's coat	James's teacher
the flag's stars	Thomas's doctor
the boy's book	the bank's interest rates
the tiger's tail	the college's policy

To show possession for a plural noun that ends in -s, add only the apostrophe.

friends' children	stores' hours
relatives' reunion	mothers' pleadings
colleges' schedules	rabbis' letters

To show possession for a plural noun that does not end in -s, add 's.

men's clothes
women's fashions
children's programs

To show individual ownership, add the apostrophe and -s to both names.

Bob's and Sue's cars
Terry's and Larry's offices

To show joint ownership, add the apostrophe and -s to the last name only.

The daughter and the son's bank account
Frank and Mimi's home

To show the omission of a letter in a word, use the apostrophe.

It's raining.	We're finished.
It doesn't matter.	I've told him three times.
Aren't you going?	He'll be there.
Class of '93	nine o'clock

NOTE: Do not use it's to show possession. *It's* means *it is.* *Its* denotes possession.

PRACTICE EXERCISE 22.36
Apostrophe

DIRECTIONS: In each of the following sentences, an apostrophe is either missing or used incorrectly. Cross out the incorrect word, and write the correct word in the space provided to the left of each sentence.

_____ 1. Hed never heard of the seven deadly sins.

_____ 2. The legislator had forgotten to bring the chairmans copy of *Roberts' Rules of Order.*

_____ 3. Leslie borrowed Janes copy of *Gone with the Wind.*

_____ 4. The "New Deal" was a term used in President Franklin D. Roosevelts first term.

_____ 5. The children were highly amused by the cartoon show, but their parents were'nt.

_____ 6. Miamis Orange Bowl parade is a spectacular event before the game.

_____ 7. Many of the Rhine Rivers castles are centuries old.

_____ 8. Jackie Robinsons acceptance into the National League was slow and painful for him.

_____ 9. The bank on the corner closes it's doors every day at three o'clock.

_____ 10. For many years, Norman Rockwells drawings were featured on the cover of the *Saturday Evening Post.*

Italics

Use italics for titles of books, movies, plays. (In handwritten or typewritten works, underline the word or words.)

Gone with the Wind (Book)

Casablanca (Movie)

Death of a Salesman (Play)

General Hospital (Daytime soap opera)

The Cosby Show (Television comedy series)

Use italics for emphasis.

The paper was *not* delivered.

You do *not* have my permission to sign my name.

Use italics for foreign words that are not commonly used in English.

guten Morgen (good morning)

entre nous (just between us)

merci beaucoup (thank you very much)

Words like ad nauseam, siesta, and kindergarten are foreign words that are now so commonly used in the English language that they are no longer underlined or italicized.

Vocabulary Self-Test Answers

Chapter 14

"Sportswriters Come To Unexpected Ends," Ira Berkow
1. d   2. c   3. a   4. c

"Sam, Be A Man," Robert Caro
1. d   2. a   3. b

"An Awakening," Helen Keller
1. a   2. b   3. c   4. a

"Salvation," Langston Hughes
1. b   2. a   3. b   4. d   5. d   6. a   7. c

Chapter 15

"Death of a Star," Lance Morrow
1. a   2. c   3. b

"Sleek as a Beaver," Tom Wolfe
1. c   2. a   3. a   4. c   5. d

"Cotton Picking Time," Maya Angelou
1. c   2. d   3. a   4. d   5. d   6. b   7. a   8. b   9. d   10. c   11. b   12. a   13. c

Chapter 16

"Tell Me About Me," William Sloane
1. c   2. b

"The Company Man," Ellen Goodman
1. a   2. a   3. a

"I Want a Wife," Judy Syfers
If you cannot find the word *nurturant* in a dictionary, try to define it through the context in which it is used.

St. Paul, 1 Cor. 13
1. b   2. c

Chapter 17

"Fear Is Like Fire"
1. b   2. a

"Roses for Some Mothers on Father's Day"
1. d   2. b

"If They Really Had a Nice Day," Richard Cohen
1. b   2. c   3. c   4. a

"What If Peace Stormed the Earth?" George Eppley
1. c   2. a   3. a   4. a   5. d   6. b   7. b   8. a   9. b   10. d   11. c

Chapter 18

"Requiem for an Elephant," Cynthia Moss
1. d   2. a

"How to Write with Style," Kurt Vonnegut
1. a   2. b   3. d   4. a

Chapter 19

"How to Press Flesh," Glen Waggoner
1. c   2. a   3. c   4. a

"The Three New Yorks," E. B. White
1. b   2. a   3. c   4. b   5. a   6. a   7. c   8. d

Chapter 20

"Elderly, Not Old," Dorothea Greenbaum
1. c   2. a

"That Lean and Hungry Look," Suzanne Britt
1. c   2. definition provided   3. c   4. b   5. c   6. a   7. c   8. d

"A Grateful Society Will Celebrate," George Eppley
1. b   2. a   3. d   4. a   5. c   6. c

Chapter 21

"Life Without Fuel?" Isaac Asimov
1. b   2. definition given   3. definition given   4. b   5. c   6. b   7. d   8. c
9. b   10. a   11. a

Glossary

ABSTRACT/CONCRETE   Abstract words refer to ideas that cannot be perceived through the senses. Words that refer to ideas that can be perceived through the senses are **concrete**.

ALLUSION   A reference to a real or fictional person, place, object, or event. Effective writers use only those allusions that they assume will be understand by the audience they are addressing. Example: In Langston Hughes' autobiography, he writes about a special meeting for children at a church revival "to bring the young lambs to the fold." The phrase is a Biblical **allusion**. Hughes assumes his readers are familiar with the New Testament story of the shepherd who leaves his ninety-nine sheep to search for the one lost sheep and return it to the fold.

ANALOGY   An extended comparison in which the writer clarifies a concept by comparing it to something familiar to the audience he or she is addressing. Example: In Martin Luther King's published version of his famous "I Have a Dream" speech, he used an **analogy** when he compared the Constitution and the Declaration of Independence to a check and promissory note that all people have a right to cash.

ARGUMENT   **A mode of development** used by writers to persuade others to adopt a particular point of view. (*Discovery* does not include a chapter on Argument.)

BRAINSTORM   An unstructured **prewriting** exercise to help stimulate ideas. It involves jotting down thoughts as they occur, no matter how unrelated they seem.

CAUSE AND EFFECT   A mode of development writers use to explain why something happened (causes) and the consequences of what happened (effects).

CLASSIFICATION AND DIVISION   Modes of development used by writers to explain concepts. Writers use **classification** to put things into categories; they use **division** to analyze the component parts of a subject.

CLAUSE   A group of words that has a subject and a predicate. An **independent clause** can stand alone; it is a complete sentence. **A dependent clause** cannot stand alone.

CLICHE   A word or phrase that has been used so often that it has lost its power. Examples: happy as a lark; a raving beauty; the apple of his eye.

CLUSTER   A **prewriting** technique writers use to organize ideas generated through **brainstorming**.

COHERENCE   A quality of good writing achieved primarily by arranging ideas in some logical order or sequence and using transitional words and phrases to help the reader move from one idea to another.

COMPARISON AND CONTRAST   **Modes of development** used by writers to clarify concepts. **Comparing** means looking at similarities; **contrasting** means looking at differences.

CONTRAST   See **Comparison and Contrast**.

CONNOTATION/DENOTATION   Connotation is the implied meaning of a word; denotation is the dictionary meaning of a word.

DEFINITION   A **mode of development** used by writers to explain concepts by clarifying words, ideas, and issues.

DENOTATION   See **Connotation/Denotation**.

DESCRIPTION   A **mode of development** writers use to present their perception of something through concrete details.

DICTION   A writer's choice of words. Ordinarily, only formal diction should be used in writing. Nonstandard diction (street language, slang, informal expressions) can be used to achieve a particular effect.

DIVISION   See **Classification/Division**.

EFFECT   See **Cause and Effect**.

EXAMPLE   A mode of development writers use to explain concepts by presenting illustrations (examples) that support a thesis.

FALLACY   A failure to use logical reasoning. A common logical fallacy, "post hoc ergo propter hoc," is explained in Chapter 21, "How Writers Analyze Causes and Effects."

FRAGMENT   An incomplete sentence punctuated as if it were a complete sentence.

GENERAL/SPECIFIC   (See **Specific/General**)

IRONY   A deliberate attempt to convey a meaning different from the literal meaning of a statement.

LINKING VERB   A verb that expresses a state of being and requires a subject complement.

MAIN IDEA   The **main idea** of a paragraph is usually expressed in a **topic sentence**. The other sentences of the paragraph support that idea.

MODES OF DEVELOPMENT   Strategies that writers use to develop the main idea of a paragraph or essay. The modes that *inform* are **narration** and **description**. The modes that *explain* are **definition**, **example**, **process**, **comparison/ contrast**, **classification/division**, **cause and effect**. The modes that *persuade* are **persuasion** and **argument**.

NARRATION   One of the modes of development. **Narration** is telling what happened in fact or in fiction. See Chapter 14, "Guidelines for Writing **Narrative** Essays."

PARAGRAPH   A group of unified sentences. The main idea is usually expressed in a topic sentence and supported by the other sentences. See Chapter 9 for an extended explanation.

PARALLELISM   Refers to consistency in structure within a sentence or other segments of writing. Example: The president took the oath of office, embraced his family, and gave a moving speech. The verbs *took, embraced,* and *gave* are in the same tense because they refer to actions that occurred at the same time and are governed by the same subject. It would be incorrect to write: The president took the oath of office, embraces his family, and gives a moving speech.

PERSON   In essays, person refers to the point of view writers use. First person (I or we), indicates that the author or authors are speaking from their own identity or an assumed one. Second person (you) is appropriate for letters, sermons, and other forms of writing that address the reader directly. Writers use third person (he, she, it, they) more than the other two persons in both fiction and non-fiction. It reflects more objectivity than first person and less intimacy than second person.

PREWRITING   All the unstructured activities that precede writing a rough draft. **Prewriting** includes **brainstorming**, **clustering**, **freewriting**, considering tentative **theses**, and writing **scratch outlines**.

PROCESS   A **mode of development** writers use to explain how to do something or what steps occurred in an event or situation.

ROUGH DRAFT   The first attempt at writing a paragraph or essay, usually following the **prewriting** activities and **outlining**.

SENTENCE   A group of words that contains a complete thought. **Sentences** begin with a capital letter and usually end with a period or exclamation mark.

SPECIFIC/GENERAL   **Specific** words refer to individual persons, places, things, qualities, actions. **General** words refer to groups of persons, things, qualities, actions. Oatmeal, for example, is a **specific** word that refers to an individual kind of cereal; cereal is a **general** word that refers to a group of breakfast foods.

THESIS   The controlling or main idea of an essay. Sometimes it is a comment on a fact; frequently it is a position that a writer takes on an arguable or controversial issue.

TONE   A reflection of the writer's attitude such as humorous, sarcastic, pious, serious.

TOPIC SENTENCE   The main idea of a paragraph.

TRANSITION   A word or phrase, such as *next, thus, in addition, however,* used to show the logical flow from one idea to another.

TRANSITIVE VERB/INTRANSITIVE VERB   A **transitive verb** expresses action and requires an object. An **intransitive verb** expresses action but has no object.

Index